Operational Assessment of IT

Internal Audit and IT Audit
Series Editor: Dan Swanson

PUBLISHED

Leading the Internal Audit Function
by Lynn Fountain
ISBN: 978-1-4987-3042-6

Securing an IT Organization through Governance, Risk Management, and Audit
by Kenneth Sigler and James L. Rainey, III
ISBN: 978-1-4987-3731-9

CyberSecurity: A Guide to the National Initiative for Cybersecurity Education (NICE) Framework (2.0)
by Dan Shoemaker, Anne Kohnke, Ken Sigler
ISBN: 978-1-4987-3996-2

Operational Assessment of IT
by Steve Katzman
ISBN: 978-1-4987-3768-5

FORTHCOMING

Practical Techniques for Effective Risk-Based Process Auditing
by Ann Butera
ISBN: 978-1-4987-3849-1

The Complete Guide to CyberSecurity Risks and Controls
by Anne Kohnke, Daniel Shoemaker, and Ken E. Sigler
ISBN: 978-1-4987-4054-8

Software Quality Assurance: Integrating Testing, Security, and Audit
by Abu Sayed Mahfuz
ISBN: 978-1-4987-3553-7

Internal Audit Practice from A to Z
by Patrick Onwura Nzechukwu
ISBN: 978-1-4987-4205-4

Operational Assessment of IT

Steve Katzman

CRC Press
Taylor & Francis Group
Boca Raton   London   New York

CRC Press is an imprint of the
Taylor & Francis Group, an **informa** business
AN AUERBACH BOOK

CRC Press
Taylor & Francis Group
6000 Broken Sound Parkway NW, Suite 300
Boca Raton, FL 33487-2742

© 2016 by Taylor & Francis Group, LLC
CRC Press is an imprint of Taylor & Francis Group, an Informa business

No claim to original U.S. Government works

Printed on acid-free paper
Version Date: 20160202

International Standard Book Number-13: 978-1-4987-3768-5 (Hardback)

Library of Congress Cataloging-in-Publication Data

Names: Katzman, Steve (IT auditor)
Title: Operational assessment of IT / Steve Katzman.
Description: Boca Raton, FL : CRC Press, 2016. | Series: Internal audit and IT audit ; 4 | Includes bibliographical references and index.
Identifiers: LCCN 2015037136 | ISBN 9781498737685
Subjects: LCSH: Information technology--Management. | Information technology--Auditing. | Auditing, Internal.
Classification: LCC HD30.2 .K3857 2016 | DDC 004.068--dc23
LC record available at http://lccn.loc.gov/2015037136

**Visit the Taylor & Francis Web site at
http://www.taylorandfrancis.com**

**and the CRC Press Web site at
http://www.crcpress.com**

To my dear wife, Diana,
with love and admiration. Diana, thanks for consenting
to put up with a computer nerd like me for this lifetime.

Contents

PREFACE   xi

ACKNOWLEDGMENTS   xv

ABOUT THE AUTHOR   xvii

PART I PRELUDE

CHAPTER 1 INTRODUCTION   3
           Overview   5
           Rationale   8

PART II GOALS

CHAPTER 2 THE ORGANIZATION   13
           Organizational Goals   13
           Measuring the Success of an Organization   14
           Voice of the Customer   18
           Process   21
           Productivity   22
           Measuring the Success of the Processes   25
           Summary   27

PART III OPERATIONAL ASSESSMENTS

CHAPTER 3 OPERATIONAL AUDITING   31
           Background   31
           Auditing   32

Operational Assessment	35
IIA Operational Auditing Definition	36
COSO Enterprise Risk Management	36
Sarbanes–Oxley Act	37
Barron's Accounting Dictionary Definition of	
Operational Auditing	38
Operational Assessment Drivers/Impetus	38
Operational Objectives	40
Operational Factors: The Three Es	40
Process	42
Operational Performance Goals	42
Value Add	43
Keep the End in Mind	44
CHAPTER 4 **OPERATIONAL ASSESSMENT PLANNING**	49
Customer Relationships	51
Risk Assessment	52
Business Acumen	52
RACI Matrix (or RASCI)	54
RACI Workload Analysis	56
Planning Memo	58
Project Charter	59
Critical Success Factors	60
Project Charter (Engagement Plan)	61
Adding Value	63
Key Performance Indicator	63
Operational Process	66
Process Review (As Is)	67
SIPOC Table (Answers the Question "What?")	68
Value Stream Map (VSM) (When)	72
Spaghetti Diagram: As-Is (Where)	80
Procurement Process Narrative	81
Activity: Procurement Audit Planning	87
The Customer	89
Customer Requirements	89
SIPOC Chart: Procurement Process	91
The Planning Data	95
The RACI Matrix	96
The SIPOC Matrix	97
The Spaghetti Diagram	97
The VSM	98
IT Support of the Business Unit	99
User Perception	99
IT's Business	100
Background	101
IT Support Goal	103
CIA and IT	103

Metrics: Business Dependency on IT 105
The OSI Model 107
Network Speed 109
Latency Delays 109
Serialization 111
Packetizing 113
Transmission Lines 115
Routing across a WAN 117
Business Continuity Planning 117
Planning Summation 120

CHAPTER 5   OPERATIONAL ASSESSMENT FIELDWORK 123
Failure Mode and Effect Analysis 123
Root Cause Analysis (RCA) 125
The Five Whys 127
Fishbone Diagram (Cause and Effect) 128
Pareto Principle (80–20 Rule) 131
Don't Jump to Conclusions 133
Brainstorming 134
Metrics 135
Continuous 136
Discrete 137
Standardization or Anarchy 141
Control Charts 142
Western Electric Rules 147
IT Control Charts 151
IT and the Business Process 152
Queuing 156
Available Data 158
Business Support VSM 163
Data Entry Screens 167
Organizational Network Transmissions 170
Utilization Assessment 172
WAN Environment 174
OSI Model 175
Data Collection 179
Control Chart Analysis 179
Control Chart Assessment 1 183
Observations/Perspective of Assessment 1 183
Control Chart Assessment 2 184
Observations/Perspective of Assessment 2 186
Other Graphical Charts 187
Bell Chart 187
Scatter Control Chart 188
Simple Network Management Protocol 190
IT Security 191
Physical Layer 193

Network Layer	193
Application Level	194
Database Level	195
Data Layer	195
Overview	195
The Fraud Red Flag	199
The Process	199
Process Analysis	201
Resource Reallocation	205
Bottlenecks	206
Fraud Red Flag Testing	207
Procurement Process Analysis	208
Process Observations	208
Opportunities	211
Process Considerations	213
The OSI Model	216
Business Continuity Management	218
Fieldwork Analysis	223
Purchasing Process	224
IT Considerations	228
IT Bottlenecks and Slowdowns	233

PART IV PUTTING IT ALL TOGETHER

CHAPTER 6	ASSESSMENT REPORTING	241
	Share the Picture	242
	Report Distribution	243
	Focus on the Issue/Concern	244
	Draft Report	249
	A Picture Can Say Volumes	252
	Presenting the Report	258
	Vet the Draft Report with Management	259
CHAPTER 7	IT AND COBIT	261
	COBIT Management Environment	265
CHAPTER 8	EPILOGUE	289
APPENDIX A:	RISK ASSESSMENT/MANAGEMENT	291
APPENDIX B:	WASHINGTON STATE AUDIT REPORT	295
APPENDIX C:	TYPICAL SWIM LANE DIAGRAM	323
BIBLIOGRAPHY		325
INDEX		327

Preface

Shortly after I retired from full-time employment, I received an e-mail from Dan Swanson, an interesting consultant and author from Canada, asking me if I would be interested in writing a book about auditing. I was intrigued about the prospect of sharing what I have learned over the years with other people.

Everything I know, I learned from other people who have written books, published articles, and provided online training (web based), as well as in-person seminars and briefings. My only contribution to the process is my assimilation of the data they so kindly shared.

You could consider this book as my way to say thank you and pass it forward.

Throughout my military career and civilian life, I have had the rare opportunity to meet some very interesting and informative people and to work in totally different environments with different computer systems throughout my information technology (IT) and audit career.

In fact, during my military career, I had only one assignment where I worked with a computer system that I had worked with during a prior assignment. In addition, while working as a military pay clerk, I had a special team assignment with a chemical, biological, and radiological response team to detect and identify chemical, biological, and radiation incidents or warfare. I also have an electronic background that started around the age of 12 when Herbie Levine and I built a superheterodyne radio receiver out of scrap parts in his bedroom and continued through my time at Brooklyn Technical High School in New York City and even while I worked at PACAF headquarters, the Air Force Weapons Lab and through today.

I decided to write this book and present the ideas in such a way as to allow the business person, the IT professional, and the auditor an equal understanding of the concepts shared in this book.

The only downside is probably my inability to write. While stationed at the Strategic Air Command headquarters, Colonel Wilkowske said that I write like I talk and vowed to make me into a reasonable administrative writer. Unfortunately, she was reassigned prior to fulfilling that goal. She did make a great dent, but you will find that I still write as if we were having a conversation.

The focus of this book is to present ideas and concepts of optimization and what an operational assessment looks like. After you understand what an operational assessment is supposed to be, we look at how the IT teams support the business units and the organization's objectives.

Throughout this book, I present issues, concerns, and environments that I have encountered throughout my career to demonstrate the issues and how I or we used the tools that I present in this book.

For a doctor to prescribe a cure, he or she must first diagnose the root cause of the malady or pain.

For you to assess the operational readiness and capability to support the business and the customers, you must gain a thorough understanding of the process.

This book introduces you to or reminds you of tools that should assist you in gaining a 360-degree view of the process.

- Without a process, nothing is accomplished.
- A process is one or more steps that take input, use resources, and create output.

To accomplish an assessment, we first use some tools to answer the following questions: Who? What? Where? When? And how?

Seek first to understand and then to be understood.

Stephen Covey

I also hope that the tools presented in this book make the job easier and more efficient and effective.

My father used to tell me, if a tool saves you an hour or more for a task you do multiple times, it is probably worth buying.

I hope this book provides you with ideas and concepts that you can use in your business as well as in your personal life.

Acknowledgments

Thanks also to the multitude of people who have provided books, articles, and training classes and those organizations such as the Institute of Internal Auditors and the ISACA for providing ideas, training, and frameworks to guide people in the right directions.

I would like to submit a special thanks to Dan Swanson for suggesting that I get involved in writing as well as recommending IT operational assessment as a focus area, and Rich O'Hanley at CRC Press for facilitating the process.

Everything I know I have learned from other people. I thank each of them for influencing my outlook, skills, and knowledge and for the information contained in this book.

About the Author

Steve Katzman is a retired master sergeant who spent four years in accounting and finance with a part-time (three-year) assignment with the chemical, biological, and radiological response team, and the rest of his 21-plus-year Air Force career in information technology (IT) and data communication before moving into civilian life.

After retiring from the U.S. Air Force, Katzman worked for an international manufacturer in Connecticut as a systems programmer, systems and network administrator, second- and third-level IT support, and project manager of networks.

When Katzman moved from Connecticut to North Carolina, he worked as an IT technical resource and contingency planner in banking and senior technology consultant in healthcare before joining KPMG as a senior consultant. After leaving KPMG, he joined the Bank of America as a vice president, internal IT audit, then as an independent consultant and subsequently for TIAA-CREF, a not-for-profit organization established by Andrew Carnegie in 1918 to help educators create retirement plans. He initially started with the IT Audit Team and subsequently was asked to move to the new Professional Practices Team, where he retired from full-time employment in April 2014.

Katzman is a past president and board member of the Charlotte chapter of the Institute of Internal Auditors (IIA). He was a volunteer instructor for the Charlotte ISACA chapter "Certified Information Systems Auditor" (CISA) candidate review program and has been a learning facilitator for the IIA since 2010.

As a volunteer IIA facilitator, Katzman has provided many virtual and on-site seminars covering tools and techniques for beginning auditors and audit leads, risk-based auditing, operational auditing, and Lean Six Sigma tools for auditors.

Katzman has over 35 years of computer and technology experience and 14 years in auditing (internal and external).

Katzman earned a BS degree in management information systems with a focus on business from Central Connecticut State University. He maintains Certified Internal Auditor, CISA, Certified Information Systems Security Professional (CISSP), Certification in Risk Management Assurance (CRMA), Certified in Risk and Information Systems Control (CRISC), and Information Technology Infrastructure Library (ITIL) foundation certifications. During his military career, he held a top-secret/Special Background Investigation (SBI) security clearance.

PART I
PRELUDE

1

INTRODUCTION

Although this book is designed to help auditors, and especially information technology (IT) auditors, accomplish an operational assessment, I tried to write it in such a way to also help the business unit manager as well as the IT gurus in an effort to improve their operations.

The real focus of this book is to help you improve your organization's business processes, which should help the business unit meet the goals of the organization more effectively. The focus is not on any specific technology, computing environment, enterprise risk, or resource program, infrastructure, etc.; it is on the organizational processes. Although the writing may introduce the reader to some Lean and Six Sigma (6σ) tools, techniques, and concepts, it is not meant to prepare the reader for green or black belt certification. If you are interested in Lean Six Sigma certification or implementation, there are other books and a number of training organizations that are quite focused on those areas of interest. This book is focused on helping you determine better and more economical ways to meet your customer's requirements. Your customer may be someone internal or external to your organization. It doesn't really matter who or where your customer is. The goal of any process is to service or supply a customer with what they covet.

A word to the wise: Lean Six Sigma is not a get-rich-quick checklist. Lean 6σ merely provides you with the tools and concepts that help you visualize your processes using different and varied perspectives to help you determine process wastes and bottlenecks along with determining the value and nonvalue steps in the process.

The plan behind this book is to provide you with tools and techniques to help you review a process and help the business unit improve the delivery of a quality product or service to the customer. The assessment process will review the economics as well as the effectiveness and the efficiency of that process. Whether your organization is profit based, not-for-profit, or even governmental, you cannot provide services or products at a continuous loss.

I recognize that the federal government coined the phrase deficit spending and maintains that debt is good for the nation; however, no normal organization can continue to exist spending more than its income.

Another focus area of this book is on adding value. For an operational assessment to be of value, the ultimate goal must be to provide either of the following:

- Assurance that the business unit process is effective and efficient and employs the financial assets and resources appropriately
- Assessment recommendation(s) that helps the business unit make adjustments to improve the operation and use resources more efficiently and/or economically

Even if you think you are adding value, your business unit partner or assessment customer must be the one to recognize that value.

When I was a teenager I thought I was handsome and debonair. Unfortunately I was one of the few people who recognized that fact. In fact, I may have been the only one to recognize those qualities.

The organization's leadership must recognize your value to the organization. If the business unit manager is the only person besides you who recognizes your qualities and value, he or she will miss you when they rightsize your area, division, or job. To help you visually show your value to the organization, I recommend using some of the graphical tools mentioned in this book to show the business manager and the senior leadership the current process steps and your proposed improvements, if improvements are economically worth it.

Tie any recommended changes to the organizational strategy, vision, and goals.

I have hopefully learned a number of things over my 4 years in accounting and finance, 35 years in IT, and 14 years in audit, plus a number of other part-time positions as a TV repairman, a garageman in New York, a good-humored ice cream vendor, bartender, etc., etc., etc.

Overview

Since most organizations have a mission, vision, and strategy,

- Chapter 2 focuses on the goals of the organization and the strategy that the organization employs to satisfy the needs of their customers. Chapter 2 also provides a perspective to gain insight into the needs, wants, thoughts, and ideas of the business or process customers.
    - In most cases, there is a stream of activity that focuses on providing a quality product or service to the external customer; however, there are normally even more business processes in support of that main artery of activity to satisfy the external customer. This secondary stream is focused on satisfying the internal customers.
    - We need to recognize and agree that every process in the organization must support the organizational goals and strategies either directly or indirectly.
    - If a process does not support the organizational strategies, then the question to answer is, why waste time and resources for that process?
    - Chapter 2 should provide some background into process improvement, measuring success, and productivity.
- Chapter 3 introduces operational auditing from The Institute of Internal Auditors' (IIA) perspective as well as its Barron's

financial dictionary definition. This chapter includes a focus on the following:

- The three Es (economic, effectiveness, and efficiency)
  - Triangle of process-independent and -interdependent entities
  - Value-added benefits balancing the three Es
  - Performance goals as opposed to market or financial goals
- Chapter 4 covers the operational assessment phases of planning.
  - The first phases of any assessment: Fieldwork and reporting will be covered later.
  - Here we introduce some Lean and Six Sigma tools and techniques to gain an understanding of the process and the lay of the land. By this, I mean that you do your reconnaissance of the territory.
    - Develop the project plan.
    - Develop a RACI (responsible, accountable, consulted, informed) matrix to accomplish a workload analysis and gain insight into the process and people—answer the question *who*.
    - Build an *as–is* SIPOC (source, inputs, process, outputs, customers) matrix to answer the questions *what*, *from where*, and *to where*.
    - Develop a value stream mapping to answer the questions *why* and *how long*.
    - Build an (*as–is*) spaghetti diagram to answer the question *where geographically*.
  - If you understand the business process before you show up on site, you will be more efficient and the business customer may accept the fact that you understand their business environment.

Some audit teams have gained a less-than-desired reputation by walking into a business unit, asking the business unit to teach them the business processes, and then weeks later the business unit reads the audit report about what the business unit is doing wrong.

Isn't this a Credibility gap?

- The more you know about the organization, business unit, and business process goals, the more confidence the business unit will have in your ability to help them improve.
- Chapter 4 also has an activity to provide insight into the business process in an effort to employ some of the concepts and ideas provided for the tools covered in this chapter.
  - The planning phase also includes a look into the technologies that will help or influence the business processes within an organization and a view of the latency delays caused by the various technologies.
  - We will also cover some insights into message traffic influenced by distance, speed, message size, appliances, and the Open Systems Integration (OSI) model.
- Chapter 5 moves us from the planning stage to the fieldwork stage.
  - Using the *as-is* information developed in the planning stage to answer the questions about bottlenecks, redundancies, business value that is no longer of value, waste, fraud, efficiency, and economy helps develop ideas for improvement.
  - Learn and employ other tools to recognize the *root cause* and establish the metrics needed to help with the process analysis.
    - Failure mode and effect analysis (FMEA)
    - The five whys
    - Control charts to analyze process capability, accomplish a trend analysis, determine anomalies, and find outliers (possible glitches or fraud)
    - IT metric collection (simple network management protocol [SNMP], etc.)
    - Metric analysis
    - Development of the *to-be* diagrams start during the analysis stage
- Chapter 6 moves the reader into the reporting stage of the assessment.
  - The use of value stream mapping and other tools to show the as-is and to-be environment as an illustration to your

business partner and any reader in support of your proposed recommendations
- The report distribution and my recommendations
- The issue and the impact, which are the key to any recommendations
- The five elements of an IIA finding
- A state auditor's report—great report—great effort—great issues/findings—no management action—was it worth it?
- Draft and final report
- Chapter 7 reminds you about the IT business process as it is expected to run according to an ISACA framework called Control Objectives for Information and Related Technology (COBIT). Most Certified Information Systems Auditor (CISA)–certified auditors use COBIT 5 to assess the IT functions.
  - In an effort to deal well with your external and internal audit teams, you should gain an awareness of COBIT.
  - COBIT is the framework that IT auditors expect the IT division to follow.
  - In this chapter we will look at the management steps that the audit teams will invariably check.
  - For the IT business manager, this should help you understand the auditor as well as performing a self-inspection in advance of an audit visit.
  - This chapter should help the IT auditor as well as the IT business manager.

Rationale

This book is written based on what I have learned over the length of my career and life. As I was growing up, my father used to tell us that "when we became adults, we would wake up each morning and go to work. If you learned something that day, then it was worth getting out of bed."

The information that I am sharing is based on various books and white papers that have influenced my thoughts along with a multitude of training classes provided by many different leaders, facilitators, teachers, and organizations.

Three really great influences pertaining to optimization and Six Sigma are *The 7 Habits of Highly Effective People*, the training presented by Stephen Covey, and the books called *The Goal* (Goldratt & Cox, 1986) and *Rath & Strong's Six Sigma Pocket Guide* (Rath & Strong Management Consultants, 2002).

Stephen Covey and *The 7 Habits of Highly Effective People* focus on communicating and building an understanding between you and the people in your life, whether it be business or personal relationships as well as career building.

Eliyahu Goldratt's book *The Goal* changed the way many manufacturers approached productivity. In the book, Goldratt presented the idea that productivity is not based on cost per unit production; what productivity is and the goal of the organization is to deliver the product or service to the customer and get paid. Goldratt's focus is on throughput as the process value, while resources and inventory are costs. Producing large or even huge lots of a product uses resources and builds inventory. Resources and inventory (raw material, work in process, and finished goods) are costs.

Some years ago a vendor provided me with *Rath & Strong's Six Sigma*. I don't even recall the vendor or whether I received the book at a technology show or from whom, but I use it quite frequently as a reference to gain ideas of tools and possible uses.

Throughout this book, I will be sharing information that I gleaned from people through demonstrations, newspapers, periodicals, books, webinars, conferences, etc.

In fact, *I firmly believe that everything I know, I have learned from other people.*

My only contribution to this book is how I assimilated the facts provided by others and put what I have learned over the years in this book.

I believe that it was Socrates who said something to the effect of "I cannot teach anybody anything; I can only help you think."

This book is intended to provide you with information to help you improve your operations or at least help you think about your processes and how you can help to ensure that they are effective, efficient, and economically sound.

When I was stationed at the Strategic Air Command headquarters in Offutt Air Force Base, Nebraska, Colonel Kathleen Wilkowske said that I write like I speak and vowed to make me into a reasonable administrative writer. As you review this book, you will realize that the good colonel was reassigned before she completed that quest.

Considering that I was born in Brooklyn, New York, where English was considered a foreign language, I sincerely hope that you will gain what I am trying to share.

As you read through the information presented in this book, you may find that I repeat various statements throughout the book. I don't believe that this is a sign of Alzheimer's, but I did want to express to you that I believe these points are important enough to repeat.

PART II
GOALS

2
THE ORGANIZATION

Before we can consider committing resources and impeding any business productivity to accomplish any assessment, we must understand the organization. Without this understanding, you will not be recognized as adding value to the organization. You will be considered a cost center, similar to the overhead expense of the building, equipment, etc.

If any business process is to be considered a value-added activity, the business process must be viewed as a partner and contributor to the productivity of the organization either directly or indirectly. Since the IT unit was formed to help make the business processes more efficient, we should look at some business processes and then determine how the technologies can help the business and organization be successful.

Based on the strategy and goals set down in the organization's strategic plan, each business unit and process should support the strategy either directly or indirectly. If you try to assess any process or business unit that does not help the organization meet its goals and strategic plan, then you are not providing real value.

Organizational Goals

Organizational goals are based on the mission and the strategy of the organization.

- *Profit-oriented organizations* are primarily focused on making money. No matter how many statements about helping humanity by providing a product or service are included in the mission statement, the organization is designed to provide a product or service to a customer in an effort to gain a profit over costs.

- *Not-for-profit organizations* are focused on providing a product or service that someone is willing to pay for.
  - Not-for-profit organizations cannot survive without income.
  - To obtain income, they must provide the service or product that meets or exceeds the contributor's expectations.
  - The contributor may be the recipient of the product or service or some benevolent person or group of people who will sponsor the delivery of that product or service.
- *Government organizations* are similar to not-for-profit organizations; however, the reputational risks to the political party in power sometimes overcome the effective use of resources, including monetary resources. (Deficit spending and the constantly growing national debt may be an example of the unbalanced checkbook.)

As a data center manager in the military, I requested a staff of 10 computer operators for our data center in an effort to maintain 2 members on duty at all times in accordance with the Occupational Safety and Health Administration (OSHA) guidance.

When Congress provided 75% of the U.S. Air Force budget request, my supervisor informed me that according to Congress, I could provide the OSHA required staffing for a 7-day-by-24-hour operation with 7.5 people.

Measuring the Success of an Organization

For a profit-oriented organization, the measures of success that they probably consider are the following:

- *Increasing net profit*—The revenue received from the customer less the organizational costs to providing the product or service
- *Increasing cash flow*—Having the cash flow to cover the costs for resources and inventory and/or providing for expanding the market and product research without borrowing against future sales

- *Increasing return on investment (ROI)*—Increasing the percentage of dollars returned to the organization for dollars spent on resources, buildings, equipment, people, etc.

For a not-for-profit organization, to measure their success they may look at the following:

- *Increasing donations*—Increasing donations so that the organization can service or provide for a larger number of users
- *Increasing cash flow*—Having the cash to pay for resources and inventory without going into debt to provide for the participants
- *Increasing ROI*—Increasing the number of people serviced for the donated dollars

For an organization, the above goals and measures may fit the need to measure the success of the organization; however, most processes and business units within the organization cannot be directly measured against the three organizational measures of success. Of course, each business unit, each process, and each step in the process very likely adds to the cost and influences the success of doing business; however, it may or may not have a direct quantifiable influence or impact on the revenue stream, cash flow, or ROI.

Most organizations are governed based on the strategy and goals of that organization. Those strategies have a direct influence on the way the external customer or recipient of the product or service is treated and how the organization will respond to their needs.

As you can see by the triangle in Figure 2.1, an organization can be depicted by three tiers:

- Tier 1—The pinnacle of the triangle is the strategy and goals of the organization. This tier is also considered the organizational governance tier.
- Tier 2—The area under the strategy and goals in the triangle is the external customer value stream. These business processes must support the organization's strategies and provide for the sales, production, and delivery of the goods or services to the external customer.

  The reason for depicting this structure as a triangle is to denote the importance of the customer-focused business processes as a foundation to successfully achieve the goals of the

Figure 2.1 Organizational focus areas.

organization. Those goals are built based on the organization's strategy with considerations of the organization's strengths, weaknesses, and opportunities.

We need to understand that if the external customer tier fails to provide for the external customer while maintaining an alignment with the strategy and goals tier, then the goals will not be met.

- Tier 3—There are an abundant number of business processes that are required for tier 2 to be successful. These underlying business processes provide the appropriate resources, equipment, and financial assets to provide the customer-facing business unit with the facilities to support and supply the external customer with the quality product or service.
  - The tier 3 business units include accounting (including accounts payable and accounts receivable), IT, human resources (HR), purchasing or procurement, and legal, just to name a few business processes.
  - Tier 3 business processes support both tiers 1 and 2 business processes. Without tier 3, both of the above tiers would falter and very likely not achieve their goals and the organizational strategy.

You may realize now that whether you name the tiers 2 and 3 business processes as *profit centers* and *cost centers*, respectively, if tier 3 *does not* support tiers 2 and 1, the organization may not have the capability to provide a quality product or service to the external customer and the chances of the organization meeting its goals and strategies are questionable. Also note that the tier 2 business processes have a direct impact on the relationship between the organization and the external customer; therefore, failure of those business units to achieve success would mean failure of the organization to fulfill its mission as it pertains to the outside customer. Once again, the strategy and goals will not be met if tier 2 or 3 is not successful.

The strategy and goals of the organization should be in the forefront of each of the business units within the organization. Those business processes producing the product or service for the customer that are external to the organization must support the strategy and the external customer, whereas the rest of the business processes must support the organizational strategy and the internal customer. Each of the business units must provide a quality product or service to their customer base (external or internal) for the organization to be successful.

Please note that many people differ in their description of quality. For the purpose of this book we will use the definition provided by Peter F. Drucker as shown in the following:

Quality in a product or service is not what the supplier puts in. It is what the customer gets out and is willing to pay for. A product is not quality because it is hard to make and costs a lot of money, as manufacturers typically believe. This is incompetence. Customers pay only for what is of use to them and gives them value. Nothing else constitutes quality.

Peter Drucker
American (Austrian-born) management writer (1909–2005)

As you will note, both quality and adding value are based on the customer. In Lean Six Sigma (6σ) they refer to the required quality as critical to quality (CTQ) and CTQ is based on the voice of the customer (VOC).

Voice of the Customer

Since we are focusing on the VOC to determine quality, we should consider the Kano model. Noriaki Kano was a renowned Japanese expert in total quality management and he developed the Kano model to depict customer desires and wants into three categories:

1. *Must be there*—These needs are expected by the customer. If unfulfilled, the customer will be dissatisfied, but even if that need is completely fulfilled, the customer may not be satisfied. (The car has brakes that work and a seat that fits the driver's body.) A higher braking power than other vehicles doesn't gain any more satisfaction if the buyer cannot see that as a need. If you don't know torque ratio and how it helps or hurts the vehicle, it really doesn't matter to the customer.

2. *More is better*—These needs have a linear effect on customer satisfaction from total dissatisfaction (expensive travel during unwanted hours) to customer expectation (reasonable prices and on-time flights) to exceeding expectations (cheap airline tickets without a reduction in service or comfort while fitting the customer's travel timeframe exactly).

3. *Delighter*—These needs do not cause dissatisfaction when not present but satisfy the customer when they are (added value: the airline that serves hot chocolate chip cookies during the flight with comfortable seating and headrests or the hotel that provides those cookies, free snack, and drinks plus breakfasts).

The Kano model is depicted in Figure 2.2. As you can see, the more is better graph is a linear graph starting at dissatisfaction to customer satisfaction and then to elation. The delighters start off as a standard expectation; however, the normal expectation can be exceeded and reach elation. But the must-haves are things that are expected, but there is little to no chance of customer elation. Providing a service or feature that has no recognized value to the customer would be a feature that the customer does feel they need. Multiple central processing units, disks, and memory that are added to a laptop that is used solely to play solitaire may be features and/or functions that are meaningless to that customer.

Once we understand what the customer wants and need, we can then look at the process that creates the product or service and the

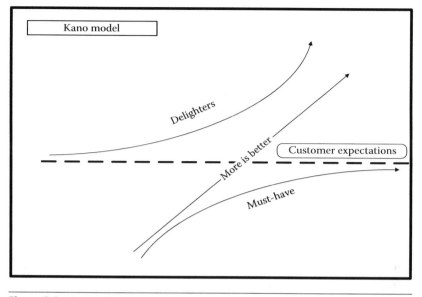

Figure 2.2   Kano model.

processes that support that customer value stream. The customer value stream consists of those processes and associated steps that create the features and functionality for the external customer (the buyer of the service or product). We need to classify those steps in a process to help determine if the step adds value to the customer, adds value to the business or organization, or adds any value whatsoever. To do this, I have added an annotation at the end of each step.

The annotation is as follows: *VA* denotes a value-add to the customer and *BV* denotes a business value and not a customer value, whereas *NV* denotes no visible value. Needless to say, when you see *NV*, you should question why that step is needed.

For example, if you went to a restaurant and ordered a hamburger and diet soda, the process value stream might consist of the following:

- A waiter asked how you wanted your hamburger (VA).
- The order was submitted to the kitchen (NVA).
- The chef cooked your hamburger to your specifications (rare, medium, etc.) (VA).
- While the chef cooked the burger, the waiter might bring you the diet soda (VA).

- When the burger was ready, the meal was put on a plate for pickup and the waiter picked it up to transport it to the customer's table (NV).
- The meal was served by the waiter (VA and BV).
- The customer ate the meal (VA).
- The waiter refilled the customer's glass with soda (VA), but this process is optional.
- The waiter asked about dessert (BV).
- The waiter boxed the leftover (optional VA).
- The waiter provided the customer with the bill (BV).
- The customer paid the waiter (BV).

As we will mention later in this book, transportation doesn't normally add value, but may be necessary to complete the process and deliver the product or service. Transportation has a cost; it is a time and resource consumer; it is one of the seven wastes listed by the Lean framework.

The primary value stream shown does not include any back-office processes such as the payroll department paying the chef and waiter, the dishwasher who provided the clean plates and utensils, the chef's trip to the market in the morning to get the trimmings for the burger, the bus person who cleared the table, the cashier, the meat or grocery delivery person, etc.

Behind most operational processes of delivering value to an external customer, you will have a multitude of other processes that do not directly add to the quality and functionality required by that customer. As you consider the value stream, you might also consider the Kano model and how the restaurant decided between serving the meal on a paper plate or a dinner plate, using plastic utensils or silver, the ambiance of the dining area, the waiters' charm and willingness to help, the cost of the meal, etc. These needs and wants add or subtract from the quality of the hamburger and the dining experience. Most chefs will tell you that the culinary success is enhanced or detracted by the food taste, presentation, aroma, and textures. The ambiance or environment also adds to the dining experience.

Marketing 101 teaches that people make buying decisions based on the triangle of product, price, and service. As we start on our operational assessment, we need to consider these three, for they could determine whether the external customer is willing to pay for the product or service.

For an operational assessment of a process supporting the internal customer, will the process provide that internal customer with the quality, features, and functionality that they need or will that customer consider outsourcing the service or product?

As you consider the Kano model for the customer, you must also consider Peter Drucker's definition of quality:

- What is the customer willing to pay for?
- Some customers envision a great ROI.
- Some customers have a taste for champagne but have a domestic beer wallet.

If you ever watch HGTV and follow some of the renovation shows such as *Property Brothers* and *Love It or List It*, you will note that the move-in–ready house with all the facilities and desires (gourmet kitchen, den, playroom, no-maintenance backyard, etc.) that the perspective home buyer wants in that prestigious neighborhood actually costs twice the buyer's budget or even more.

Once we understand the VOC and the customer's budget, we can review the value stream process for the product or service based on what the internal or external customer can afford.

Process

All accomplishments require a *process*:

- A *process is one or more steps* that use input and employ some resources to change the input into something more valuable.
  - The process customer can be an internal or external entity.
  - The value of the output is based on the customer's perspective.
- A *process can spawn* other processes and those processes can flow back into the originating process or continue with a life of its own and/or spawn other processes.

Let us look at the hamburger example.

The customer orders a hamburger and diet soda, which activates the process. The waiter asks the customer how they want the meat cooked and the flavor of diet soda they want. Once the information (customer order) is completed, the waiter spawns the kitchen process to build the hamburger and a bar order to fulfill the diet soda portion of the order. Including the wait staff, we have three separate business units to provide for customer satisfaction. The bar fulfillment time is shorter than the kitchen time, so the server provides the beverage while the customer is waiting for the order completion. If the restaurant provides free refills, then the cost to the customer is well received. If the diner ordered something that isn't scheduled for free refill, this early delivery may help the customer endure the wait for the hamburger and the customer may also order an additional beverage, which may increase the restaurant revenue. The kitchen has its own process to prepare and deliver the meal on a presentable plate, with any trimming to enhance the meal visually as well as tastefully.

Three business units that combine forces to provide a customer experience denote the value stream. Each of the business units has its own process to provide the drink, the meal, or the service. Hopefully in the eyes of the customer there is synergy. The customer's perceived value (taste, service, and ambiance) must be equal or better than the cost for the meal to satisfy and/or elate the customer. The restaurant gains revenue that provides a profit over costs as well as maintaining a customer base for future dining. The bottom line is that a win–win scenario will help ensure that the customer will return.

As Dr. Stephen Covey specified in his renowned book and training *The 7 Habits of Highly Effective People*, the only sane way to deal with a customer is to establish a win–win scenario. If the provider sets up a win–lose (the customer pays through the nose and the business makes oodles of money) environment, the customer won't come back. If the provider sets up a lose–win scenario (give the customer the store; provide the service or product at a financial loss, etc.), then the provider can't come back. The only sane and long lasting business approach is a win–win scenario.

Productivity

Productivity is defined as those steps which move you toward your goals and objectives. Whether the process is advertising to increase the market share in an effort to meet the organizational goal of increasing or maintaining market share or it is the steps to provide the customer with a positive experience in a restaurant or washing and polishing the car before delivering the car to the buyer, it may be in support of the organization's goals.

That being said, you may have to question any step or process that does not directly or indirectly move you toward your goal.

As you look at each of the processes within the organization, they each have costs; they each have customers; and they each must be productive to deliver the product or service to their customers. That is to say, each of the business processes first supports the organization's strategy and goal and then the process must provide the quality product or service to either the internal or the external customer for the organization to be successful.

Therefore, if we are to establish metrics to denote the *success of a process*, then we must focus on the inventory costs (raw material, work in progress, and finished goods) and resource costs as well as the productivity as the measures of a process success or failure.

Going back to the customer who ordered a hamburger and soda, let's look at the soda portion of the process shown in Figure 2.3.

As you will note, there are two areas involved in providing the customer with the diet soda of their choice, the waiter and the bartender, yet only the waiter is directly involved with the customer. Each of the team members is necessary to satisfy the paying customer. If we did the same thing with the hamburger, you may find that the dishwasher, the chef, the sous-chef, the bus person, and the waiter are equally responsible for the product and service rendered to the external customer. You may realize that there are only two or maybe three steps that add customer value to the process. The order and delivery of the drink order should be considered customer value if they are handled well. In addition, you might consider the ICE addition to be of value since the amount of ice might affect the taste of the drink. Those appear to be the only steps in the process that provide value to the customer's want or need. The rest of the steps may or may not be necessary, but those two steps are of value to the customer. They are the value stream to satisfy the customer needs. We will be looking at other value stream maps later in this book.

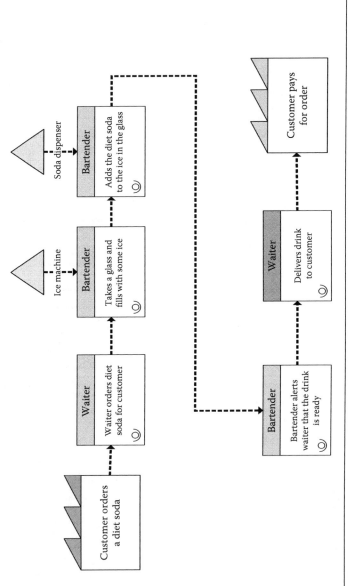

Figure 2.3 Process flow.

Measuring the Success of the Processes

As we mentioned earlier in this chapter, the measure of the success of an organization cannot be directly applied against each and every process supporting the successful attainment of the organization's goals and strategies.

Even as you look at the value stream process providing the customer with the end product or service, you will have only the revenue from the customer less the direct cost of the customer facing processes. You will not have a measurement of the supporting processes such as purchasing or building the inventory that goes into the final processes, HR that provided the people to accomplish the customer-facing process, IT automation that provided the information about the customer and the customer order, and marketing.

As we can see, to provide the organizational measures of success (net profit, ROI, cash flow), we need to incorporate the costs of all processes, resources, inventory, and revenues. Therefore, if you are to measure the success of any specific process or group of processes, you need to look at the resources, the inventories, and the productivity of the processes being assessed.

Each process has an output that should be considered as the productivity of the process. The speed at which the output is ready to be presented to the customer is called *throughput*. In all cases, throughput is measured as how many pieces or services can be produced or performed over a period (per minute, per hour, per workday, per month, etc.).

As shown in Figure 2.4, a process consists of input (raw material inventory), the process using some resources (building, more inventory, data, people, machines, etc.) to create an output of finished goods or services.

Since the goal of the process is to produce the customer output, then when the output is produced, it is ready for the customer. You can and I believe that you should measure the output over time as soon as a process is developed and approved. That way you set a baseline and that baseline can be used in the future to determine if the process is still in control. If there are major differences in throughput, then very likely something has changed.

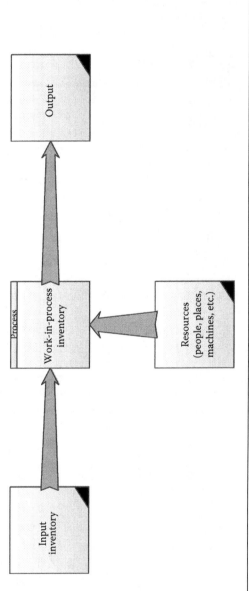

Figure 2.4 Process.

If things have changed significantly, then it may be necessary to accomplish an operational assessment or audit.

Summary

- What we must understand is that an operational assessment focuses on the process.
- The process must directly or indirectly support the goals and strategy of the organization.
- All processes take input (material, information, process instructions, forms, etc.); use resources (labor, equipment, work environments, etc.); and produce a product or server based on the customer's needs and/or wants.
- Quality is not what you put into a product or service.
  - Quality is what the customer is willing to pay for.
- Operational improvement is to develop a balance between the effectiveness (VOC), the efficiencies (asset utilization to meet the customer's needs), and the economics (the cost of meeting the customer's needs against what the customer is willing to pay).

"Doing the *right* things the *right* way is the key to a successful process."

PART III
OPERATIONAL ASSESSMENTS

3
OPERATIONAL AUDITING

Background

It has been said that auditing is one of the world's oldest professions. It had its beginning even before the first documented book on accounting and auditing was written. The first known book was written by a Franciscan friar named Luca Pacioli (1445–1517) in 1494. He was an Italian Franciscan friar and mathematician who was dubbed "the Father of Accounting" because of outlining the double-entry bookkeeping process and reconciliation in a book called *Summa de Arithmetica, Geometria, Proportioni et Proportionalita* (*Everything about Arithmetic, Geometry and Proportions*). Fra Luca Pacioli and Leonardo da Vinci became great friends and mentors for each other while they were supported by the same patron. da Vinci provided the figures for the text in Fra Luca's book *Divine Proportion*.

Although the concepts were not Fra Luca's innovations, he was the first to organize and document what businesspeople had been doing throughout the ages. Believe it or not, most of the concepts described in his book (double-entry bookkeeping, trial balance, etc.) are still in use by today's accountants and certified public accountants. I could only hope that some of the concepts that will be shared in this book last one third as long as Fra Luca's concepts.

Luca Pacioli, an Italian Franciscan monk, wrote *Summa de Arithmetica, Geometria, Proportioni et Proportionalita* in 1494, and it was the first full description of this method of accounting. He is referred to as the Father of Accounting and Bookkeeping (Wikipedia).

Auditing

Auditing was initially used to assess the accuracy and correctness of the financial activities of an organization, empire, government, etc. Greek and Roman writings mention accounting and auditing rooms.

Over the years, auditing had achieved a rather unhealthy reputation when the feudal tax collector would levy a tax for the lord and additional taxation for the tax collector.

During the time of Jesus in first-century Israel, there were publicans and tax collectors who could walk up to a man and tax him for what he was carrying, and much more. These tax collectors were hated and despised because they were usually fellow Jews who worked for Rome. There were many taxes needed from the provinces to administrate the Roman Empire. These taxes paid for a good system of roads, law and order, security, religious freedom, a certain amount of self-government and other benefits.

The publican is from the Latin word "publicanus," and from the Greek word "telones" which mean a tax gatherer. The publican is mentioned quite often throughout the life of Christ.

Luke 15:1—"Then drew near unto him all the publicans and sinners for to hear him."

Even today, if you mention that you are an auditor; many people equate you with an Internal Revenue Service (IRS) tax auditor. Some people even hold up a cross in their defense when you mention that you are an auditor. I thought the cross was reserved for vampires, but I guess I don't know everything.

My first connection with auditors happened when I was in the U.S. Air Force. Each major command had an inspector general (IG) as well as the General Accounting Office (GAO) for the Department of Defense. The IG did operational audits, while the GAO was known for financial audit and audit of misuse of government funds. During my first assignment as a pay clerk and member of the Second Combat Support Group during the 1960s, the Strategic Air Command IG flew in for an operational readiness inspection. My sergeant told me that if I knew the answer to the inspector's question, answer it honestly; however, *do not* provide any other information over and above the direct answer. If fact, answer yes or no if at all possible. If you add more info, it would get them to delve deeper and disrupt our service even more than the IG had originally planned (the IG audit program).

We used to joke about the IG visits and their relationship to the two biggest lies in our universe. When the IG landed, some colonel or above would meet the wing or base commander and say, "I am Colonel such and such, the IG team leader, and we are here to help you." (That was the second biggest lie.) Then the wing or base commander would say, "I am Colonel/General such and such" and "We are glad to have you here" (the biggest lie).

We sometimes referred to the IG as "the Gotcha Guys," a group of noncommissioned officers and officers who got their jollies from finding fault with other people. We often imagined that they relished in finding where you didn't dot your i's or cross your t's. That would somehow advance their position within the universe.

Please note that this perspective was due to the fact that the auditors had no skin in the game. They would show up giving you a list of things that you had to do to alleviate the things that they didn't like and then leave the area. Many of the controls that they listed for us to do were new steps that were not integrated into the process. In addition, the rationales for those additional steps (controls) were not understood by the people trying to maintain productivity while Congress was trying to reduce the defense budget (doing more with less resources).

Even early in my auditing career, I found that many people associated the auditor with the IRS tax auditors and some auditors still maintained a gotcha personality.

Over the years, the audit profession has adjusted with the environment and auditors have changed their image and become the organization's business partner (consultant and assessor). Part of that change is attributed to a prior chief executive officer (CEO) of the Institute of Internal Auditors (IIA) by the name of Bill Bishop. His focus was on the organization and not the controls. He and the IIA leadership that followed recognized that risks and controls were part of the business and that the auditors are there to help the business succeed.

Financial auditing has been around since ancient times. As governments and industries started to regulate their domains, auditors have added compliance auditing to their focus areas. In addition, each time there has been a downturn in the economy, auditors were asked to assess the operational environment to help ensure that the processes are efficient, effective, and economically sound.

Internal auditing is defined by the IIA as an independent, objective assurance and consulting activity designed to *add value* and *improve an organization's operations*. It helps an organization accomplish its objectives by bringing a systematic, disciplined approach to evaluate and *improve the effectiveness of risk management, control, and governance processes.*

The above definition is also included in the Committee of Sponsoring Organizations of the Treadway Commission (COSO) enterprise risk management (ERM) framework. I would like to point out some key phrases that I underlined in the definition to help us stay on the same page throughout the upcoming chapters.

Since I became an auditor at the turn of the century, I have seen and I applauded the many great changes from the gotcha mentality of an audit to the "helping the organization to succeed" mentality.

For years auditors have been telling the organizations what they did wrong in the *past*, but now auditors are looking toward the future and recommending ways to improve the organizational operations. The auditor has become a proactive partner to the business units.

Don't get me wrong; there are still auditors that follow those old checklists—those best practices that some external audit firm published—that one-size-fits-them-all checklist of probable issues, etc. Let's face it; even some audit committee members expect to see issues coming from the audit staff, not performance improvement recommendations.

Operational Assessment

As for the Air Force IG, they would monitor how fast our alert facilities could react and have planes airborne or how fast and efficient our fire, security, and chemical, biological and radiological (CBR) teams could get to the contingency command posts. Operational assessment and operational auditing are by no means new to the business world. Each time there has been a downturn in the economy, organizations as well as governments have focused their energies on trying to do more with less, rightsizing and focusing on what is needed as opposed to what was wanted.

Since auditors are trained in developing systematic disciplined approaches to an assessment, they have been and will be called upon to assist the business units in their efforts to reduce costs while providing quality results for the customers (internal or external). Lean Six Sigma uses the critical to quality (CTQ) based on the voice of the customer (VOC) as its focus for all the activities deemed necessary within any process.

As you may know, Lean and the Six Sigma frameworks are based on assessing process activities or steps to determine waste and reduce the number of errors. We will take a deeper look into some of the tools and techniques of these frameworks and how they can be helpful to our operational assessment as we progress in future chapters, especially as we look at the planning and fieldwork phases of an assessment.

With each downturn, recession, and/or even a dip in the purchasing trends of a nation, organizations are asking their members to do more with less and asking audit teams to use their systematic approach to help management find ways to become more efficient and save money.

IIA Operational Auditing Definition

Defining, measuring, evaluating, and improving the economy, efficiency, and performance effectiveness of the organization's operations and constituent activities irrespective of function, purpose, or level within the organizational structure.

The key to the IIA definition are the three factors of a process (economy, efficiency, and performance effectiveness), and as with the current COSO ERM framework, the focus is on all entities within the organization irrespective of function, purpose, and level within the organization. This definition opens the internal auditor to those processes that don't impact the financial reporting or adherence to the laws and regulation. Although both financial and compliance auditing are extremely important to the organization, helping the business unit processes become more effective, efficient, or economically viable helps the organization stay financially sound. Efficient uses of resources as well as risk mitigation/treatment are ways to help the organization succeed in meeting their objectives, goals, and strategies.

COSO Enterprise Risk Management

The expansion to all business units and entities does support the COSO ERM frameworks established by the COSO, a forum created by the Treadway Commission.

During the late 1980s the Treadway Commission, in response to the downfall of many savings and loan banks across America, formed COSO, a group of five private sector organizations with focus on providing leadership to an organization's executive management and government entities on critical aspects of organizational governance, business ethics, internal control, ERM, fraud, and financial reporting. COSO established a common framework and model to be used by all.

Admittedly, COSO was not really embraced by most industries until years later. The original COSO framework focused on true and accurate financial reporting. In Canada, a similar variation of COSO framework was established by the Criteria of Control Board (CoCo). The Board of Governors of the Canadian Institute of Chartered Accountants was charged with issuing guidance on designing, assessing, and reporting on the control systems of organizations. Neither COSO nor CoCo was embraced by most industries. They saw the frameworks as a cost and did not see a dollar benefit or return on investment (ROI). Even after the COSO framework was revised to establish the ERM viewpoint, the framework didn't gain a great following. It wasn't until the Enron fraudulent accounting, followed closely by the WorldCom debacle, where investors lost billions of dollars in stock that was ultimately considered worthless, after which the United States established the Sarbanes–Oxley Act (SOX), that COSO was once again moved to the forefront of thought and action.

Sarbanes–Oxley Act

In actuality, the SOX did not say anything about COSO, CoCo, or any other framework, but the Securities and Exchange Commission maintained that all publicly traded organizations must use an established framework to control fraud and help ensure that the financial controls would be in place to help ensure that the financial reporting is *true* and *accurate*.

Because SOX focused only on the financial controls for reporting, I have always thought that it did not go far enough to stop a major organization from closing its doors. The major initiative that I thoroughly applauded was that the SOX held the CEO and the chief financial officer (CFO) accountable for any financial misstatements or lack of controls. This was definitely a step in the right direction. Up to that point, the CEO and the other C-suite executives had to show due diligence when it came to risk, controls, and security. Now they had to put money where their mouth was.

In the past, the CEO or the CFO could assign someone to accomplish the task and when asked for funding, they could tell the person to include the funding in the next budget request. Now that the CEO and the CFO are responsible, the funding will probably be supplied.

Barron's Accounting Dictionary *Definition of Operational Auditing*

Evaluation made of management's performance and conformity with policies and budget. The organization and its operations are analyzed, including appraisal of structure, controls, procedures, and processes. *The objective is to appraise the effectiveness and efficiency of a division, activity, or operation of the entity in meeting organizational goals.*

Recommendations to improve performance are also made. The primary user of an operational audit is management.

As you will note in the Barron's definition, this assessment is the property of the organizational management. It is and should be accomplished in an effort to improve the organization and to help ensure the proper use of resources by all entities within the organization. It is not just for financial or regulatory reporting or compliance. It is for the organization by the organization to improve effectiveness and efficiencies so that the economics will meet the needs of the customer and the profitability of the organization. For not-for-profit organizations, it will mean continued existence based on the best use of contributions and funding. In both environments, it is income minus costs ([revenue] – [all operational expenses]).

Operational Assessment Drivers/Impetus

As mentioned previously, the rationale for an operational assessment normally comes from management or the industry with the results being provided to business management for their acceptance and action plans to improve or maintain a viable and efficiently effective operation to help the organization succeed in meeting its goals and prosper.

In many cases, the impetus or drivers of focusing organizational resources in an operational assessment are the following:

- Management believes that the costs are higher or delivery time is longer than necessary. The factors for their concern may be as follows:
  - Competitive organizations appear to be delivering the same quality product or service faster and/or at a lesser price.
  - Industry metrics show faster or more economical delivery of the product or service.
  - A previous baseline metric is no longer being met.
  - Process variance appears to be out of control.
- A process of high importance to the organization needs to be periodically adjusted to meet the business changes, risks, and customer desires (VOC).
- High-value operation or process bottlenecks need to be periodically reviewed to maintain or improve customer delivery. (Bottlenecks are discussed in a later chapter.)
- Organizations are redeveloping their strategy, product line, service, or customer base.
- Over the years, internal controls have been added to but not integrated into a process that was once efficient, effective, and economically sound.
  - If these controls inhibit the delivery performance to the customer, the process may need to be revised or redesigned.
  - Most application programs were initially designed to be efficient and effective; however, over the years, new customer requests or application problems arose to warrant program patches and program adjustments.
    - Over the years, these add-on and ad hoc changes have reduced the efficiencies of the process.
    - Reengineering the program may be required.
    - The estimated cost of the rework must be considered against the increased efficiency and updated capacity of the updated process.
    - If the savings is 5 milliseconds per transaction and you have 200 people doing that transaction 20 times per day, the time savings is 20 minutes per day or 5.200 minutes per year (86⅔ hours).

Operational Objectives

Operational objectives relate to the effectiveness and performance efficiencies of any organizational entities and the safeguarding of organizational resources against waste or loss. Operational assessment is concerned with the way processes meet the goals employing resources so that the process output adds customer and/or business value above the process cost. If the expected ROI of your organization is 10% above the investment, then the revenue must be greater than 110% of the operating expenses.

Operational Factors: The Three Es

The triangle is said to be one of the strongest structures in architecture. Look at the pyramids, suspension bridges, etc. The power of three has emerged in many other areas of literature and our professions, such as the holy trinity in religion and the holy trinity of cooking, which, according to Chef Emeril Lagasse, is celery, green pepper, and onions. The financial audit trilogy is to help ensure that

1. Everything in the general ledger (G/L) account belongs there.
2. Everything that belongs in the G/L account is in there.
3. When you produce a financial report, the G/L account is depicted accurately.

An operational assessment is based on three independent factors:

1. Effectiveness—To be effective, the business process must accomplish its mission and provide the customer (internal or external) with the appropriate quality product or service based on the VOC and what the customer considers CTQ.
2. Efficiencies—These focus on providing quality product in a cost-effective manner to meet the CTQ requirements as expected by the customer while protecting the financial assets of the organization.
3. Economy—The cost of producing the product or service should not exceed the value that the customer places on that product or service.

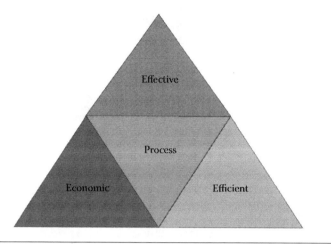

Figure 3.1   Process triangle.

Although these three factors, shown in Figure 3.1, are considered and can be independent factors, they are interdependent as well. As you increase the *effectiveness* owing to a change in customer requirements, the cost will likely increase as well. If the business decides to reduce the effectiveness by reducing the functionality or features of the product or service, then the *cost* will likely be reduced as well. You could surmise that the effectiveness of a product or service is directly proportionate to the cost of the process to produce that product or service.

John: Honey, I got a great deal on a new dog fence.

Jill: Maybe we can trade our two Pekinese for two St. Bernards.

Too much economy and not enough effectiveness

If you find a more *efficient* method or process to provide the customer the quality, features, or functionality that they are willing to pay for, the *costs* to provide it will likely reduce. After the implementation of a process (manual or automated), changes to the customer requirements (*effectiveness*) will likely cause a decrease in *efficiencies* until the process is adjusted to integrate and optimize the new requirement.

Some economic decisions do affect the efficiency as well as the effectiveness of a process. The cause and effect should be weighed during the decision-making process and if an adverse impact to the efficiency or effectiveness is warranted at this time, then later the decision should be reviewed with regard to the more current environment. The business needs of an organization as well as the technology costs to the organization are dynamic; therefore, the processes used to satisfy the customers must be revisited periodically to help ensure that they are still viable, feasible, effective, efficient, and economical.

Process

Nothing is ever accomplished without a process. A process is one or more steps that take input and use resources to create or develop something better (of more value).

Since all accomplishments in the world require a process, operational assessments are based on process review for effectiveness, efficiency, and economy.

Operational Performance Goals

Operational performance goals and associated measures of success could be as follows:

- Customer satisfaction (internal or external customer)
- Resource optimization
- Productivity
- Capability
- Capacity
- Cycle time
- Quality (may be included in customer satisfaction or separate)
- Problems, concerns, or process failure trends

Needless to say, based on your organizational environment and strategy, there could be other goals and criteria. Since the operational assessment may be the result of a management concern about a business entity and the operational performance of that entity, you may be asked to find the source or root cause of an adverse trend or increasing cost-to-value ratio.

The key factors that you must keep in the forefront of your mind while doing an operational assessment are the goals of the organization and the customer needs.

Value Add

Most organizations are governed and staffed based on the viewpoint of value versus costs. If you are to be perceived as a value to the organization, the management and the senior leadership must recognize your value and contributions.

Many auditors, risk managers, workers, and leaders truly believe in their minds that they add value to an organization. They provide their talents, abilities, and skills to that organization; however, the organization may not recognize the value of an assessment and/or recommendation that they provide. They may act on an audit assessment recommendation while not totally understanding the rationale for doing so. I believe that this is the reason some internal audit functions as well as IT and other functions are ultimately outsourced.

Does your organization recognize your value?

I am not focusing on your job responsibilities or all the steps and toil that you go through to accomplish your tasks, but your value to the organization. If you believe that you and your team are adding value to the organization, you must consider the following questions:

1. Who determines your value to the organization?
2. What would the business unit consider valuable?
3. Are your communications with the business entities that you service done in their language based on their key performance goals or is the communication based on your business language?

When considering the value to the organization, a vice president (VP), a senior VP, or someone with the ear of the CEO or other C-suite executives (chief information officer, CFO, chief operating officer, etc.) must be aware of your value. Don't keep your team's value a guarded secret and don't believe for a minute that outlining your process steps or responsibilities to a senior leader equate to adding value.

For you to be considered of value to the organization, leadership needs to be aware of how you add value; how you influence new ideas, cost savings, increased ROI, increased net profit, and an understanding of the business. Otherwise, you may add value to a business line manager, but not be recognized at the organizational level.

To add value to the business process, you must understand those processes and the key performance indicators or key success factors of the organization, the business unit that you are servicing, and the processes to be assessed.

Keep the End in Mind

Throughout any engagement we need to ensure that everyone is on the same page. This is especially true if the assessment is being done by multiple personnel, each looking at different facets of the process or multiple processes to service the customer or end user.

Each person that you deal with, whether it is a team member, business unit manager, or process worker, has a different perspective based on his or her experiences and viewpoints.

Are we all correct?

Of course, we are. We may just have different ways of assimilating data based on our experience perceptions. When house hunting, my wife can look at a room and determine how she can arrange our furniture and alternatives to the initial arrangement when she needs to have a change. I, on the other hand, look to determine where the electrical outlets and TV cable outlets are situated and if our home computer network will work. My wife has an artistic eye and can look at things or rooms and see what it could be, while I just look at the technical stuff that is in place.

The perspectives of different people will help them see things in a different light.

As I held a picture out in front of me at arm's length toward my grandson, I asked him to describe in detail what he saw.

As he described what he was seeing, I realized that *I must be experiencing the generation gap* or he was taking artistic license.

Based on his description, he was seeing something similar to the picture shown below:

However, based on my point of view or perspective, I know it looked like this:

Based on our differing perspectives, we have a tendency to see and communicate based on our background, training, and points of view.

"There is my way, your way, and reality."

We need to see the business process through the eyes of the process owner or process workers to be able to understand their concerns, needs, and points of view. We need to gain an understanding of their perspectives as well as your own concerns. We have to learn to look at things with a 360-degree perspective. A doctor may order a magnetic resonance imaging or computerized tomography scan to obtain more information and a more global view of the problem area before diagnosing the root cause of the symptoms. Look at the process as if you were looking at a global view of the Earth. Then review each area of the globe from a lower altitude to gain a more precise view of the steps necessary to build or operate that business process—a segment of the whole organization.

In this book, I will provide some tools to help you gain a more diverse perspective of the process in an effort to help you understand the inventory flow, a spatial viewpoint of the data and/or product flow, work flow timing, workload, etc.

Please note that an assessment cannot be accomplished in a vacuum. I am a firm believer that all process improvement and any assessment should be done as a collaborative process including the business unit personnel as well as any stakeholders. Anyone who can add value to the assessment should be included. We have no special insight or talent and no one person knows everything about the process. We all have our perceptions based on experiences, training, and perspectives. In some cases personal gain influences how some people look at a process, so make sure that they know you are there to help them succeed.

Keep the end in mind (Covey, 1990). The business managers must understand you and agree with your findings or they will not apply any of your recommendations. The worst statement that I have ever heard during an operational audit was when I asked a person why they spent time doing a few of the steps and the answer they provided was "the auditor said to do those steps."

Clearly, the rationale for the extra steps was not understood by the personnel whose task it was to accomplish those steps. If people understand what they are doing and why they are doing it, they will find ways to make it better. Years ago, there was a management theory called management by objective and that spurred many organizations to build teams to accomplish the whole product or service so that the team provided for a happy customer and that team and each member had their name and reputation on that outcome. The theory was about ownership of the finished product. If a person doesn't know why they are doing something, they won't take pride or ownership about the outcome.

For the business unit to understand you, you and the business managers must have a common core of knowledge and language. You should use their business language and not audit language (inherent and residual risks, mitigating risks, etc.) or any other acronym-based language.

Gain insight into how senior leadership rates that business unit's productivity or their value and then relate your assessment, findings, and recommendations with respect to their goals and aspirations.

In his highly acclaimed book *The 7 Habits of Highly Effective People*, Stephen Covey wrote, "*Seek first to understand and then to be understood*" (Covey, 1990).

4
OPERATIONAL
ASSESSMENT PLANNING

The first step in building any project, including an operational assessment, is the data gathering or planning stage.

From what I have seen over the years, some audit teams and organizations undervalue the planning process. In the military you never deployed teams into an area until you did your reconnaissance. Reconnaissance always precedes action whenever possible. Get to know the landscape, the rivers, the valleys, the terrain, the environment. D-day waited for the reconnaissance photos as well as the weather reports to let them know when the weather conditions were more favorable to cross the English Channel and embark on a major offensive.

It is my fervent belief that the two most important phases of any assessment are the planning stage and the reporting stage.

The planning phase, if done correctly, sets the stage for an efficient and thorough fieldwork operation, whereas the reporting stage must convey your concerns to the business unit owner and the staff. The report needs to be understood, accepted, and valued by the business owner if they are to do anything to implement your recommendations and improve their operation.

- If you enter into the fieldwork stage and cannot communicate your understanding of the business unit's goals and issues, how can the business manager rely on your findings?
- If you don't speak the business language, how can you discuss their process and how your planned assessment will focus on their real business needs?

49

- If you don't understand the business unit and your assessment customer (business unit partner), you may be looking in the wrong place and measuring things that don't really impact that business unit's goals or their use of the financial assets and resources. (See Appendix B for a thorough audit that had issues, recommendations, and no impact on the auditee, except for a thoughtful thank you to the professional audit team and their opinion—more about that audit later.)

If the business unit management doesn't have confidence that you know what they are trying to accomplish, management may not value your input. If they don't honestly believe that you understand their goals, key performance indicators (KPIs), guidelines from senior leadership, and regulatory requirements, they will not support your recommendations. If they disagree with your issue impact or likelihood, will they have a reason to implement what you recommend?

Over the past years I have seen a few auditors and consultants who walk into an office and ask to be trained on what the business unit does and how they do it. Then about a month or so later, those auditors or consultants provide a report telling their business unit management and the C-suite executives (chief information officer, CEO, CFO, etc.) about the issues and the need for them to change the way they do things—from a trainee to a guru in less than a month.

While doing a Statement on Auditing Standards No. 70 (SAS 70) assessment of a Federal Credit Union, the auditors told me that their CEO kicked a National Credit Union Administration (NCUA) auditor off the campus during an audit out-brief. The auditor brought up a few issues that would have been addressed by the organization and then the young auditor went on to tell the CEO that according to current regulations the credit union could charge more for the services to their customers and thereby increase profits. At that point the CEO stood up and told the auditor that since he knew nothing about why a credit union exists, he needs to leave the property immediately and don't bother ever coming back. The CEO then wrote a letter to the NCUA letting them know that if they ever send another representative who didn't know that the credit union customers are the owners, he would lose faith in their ability to govern and he would no longer allow them access to the credit union.

If you don't show the assessment customer that you know who they are and what they do, why should they accept any of your recommendations?

If you plan to provide any reasonable and feasible recommendations to the business unit, they need to have confidence in you and, therefore, your recommendations. That means that the team or person accomplishing the assessment must be credible. Also, the report must convey the information so that the assessment team and the business unit see the exact same picture and understand the business reasons for any and all of the recommendations.

Customer Relationships

Before I retired from full-time employment, the organization that I was with had a customer relationship program where each audit team lead, manager, director, etc., had a business partner with whom they would meet at least each quarter of the year. During my first meeting with one of my business partners in IT, he told me that, although the SOX auditor told him that he had to write a series of e-mails to himself to cover the request, the approval, and the loading of a utility program on his new employee's personal computers (PCs) so that the request and the authorization for that software load would be documented, he just couldn't find the time to do it. He also told me that he didn't have the time to send the e-mails and then document each e-mail into the log that the auditor recommended.

I asked which auditor advised him to write himself a series of e-mails and log each e-mail as it arrived to track the request, the authorization, and the implementation of the PC software load so that his employee could do the work the employee was hired to accomplish. I was so glad to find out that the auditor was not one of our internal auditors, but someone from an external firm.

Admittedly, the application in question was protocol analyzer software that could bypass security protocol and view data across a network. It was commonly used by the IT member to help diagnose whether a computer problem was caused by faulty data, hardware overload, or the application program.

Risk Assessment

If you are an auditor and subscribe to the IIA standard framework, you should normally accomplish a risk assessment to help ensure that the project that you are planning will help to alleviate some risk or issue that is important to the organization. Most internal and external audit teams subscribe to the IIA approach to risk-based assessments, which require a risk assessment to determine the precedence and/or priority of the risks facing the organization. Then with each project or engagement, the IIA framework focuses on the individual process risks.

For more information about risk assessments, please review Appendix A. Admittedly, I do include my own approach to the risk assessment process. It is in alignment with the IIA approach, but I add some of the quantifications that I and my organizations have employed.

Business Acumen

By gaining an understanding of the business unit goals, the unit's customers, the customer expectations or quality requirements, you will be more efficient during the fieldwork stage and the business unit will realize that you are aware of their domain and tasks.

The ultimate result of any assessment is the business unit's acceptance of the findings and any action on the recommendations that you provided. The ultimate result is common understanding of the facts presented to help the business unit meet its goals or enhance its opportunities.

All business processes can be improved.

For an assessment to be successful, the planning should allow the fieldwork to be effective and efficient and the report should either provide the business unit with the confidence that they are doing the right things and doing them right or provide appropriate recommendations to the business unit on how they can do things even better.

Please remember that an internal audit team is assigned to provide an assurance or consulting service. If you look up the definition of assurance, you will find the following:

1. A positive declaration to give confidence; a promise
2. Confidence or certainty in one's own abilities

In the military, before you move anyone into an area, you would do a reconnaissance to learn about the terrain, the environment, etc. Before you drive to a faraway place, you would probably look at maps or go online to ascertain the best, fastest, or most scenic routes to your destination. You might look at lodging, weather, cost of gas, etc. The more that you know in advance, the more you can prepare for the trip and the more successful the trip will be.

Prior to starting any assessment, the team should gain as much information about the business process and management concerns or fears (delivery performance, lack of quality, etc.).

To understand the business concerns, we should try to answer the following questions: Who? What? Where? How? Why?

Or use the questions provided by Courtney Thompson's presentation (Thompson, 2014) at the IIA 2014 All Star Conference:

- What is going on?
- How do we know?
- Whose job is it?
- How do we do that?
- How do we know if it is working?
- How would we know if it wasn't working?

This book will provide insights into some Lean Six Sigma, project management, and statistical tools which should help us understand the process as it is today (as is). During the fieldwork and the reporting phase of the assessment, we will use some more tools to develop and report the recommendations as the to-be environment. Each tool should provide a different perspective or viewpoint for the environment and the process. Not all tools may fit all assessments, but use the tools that make sense and try to gain a 360-degree view of the process as well as the perspectives of the stakeholders in the process (customer, business unit manager, organization, worker, etc.).

"Seek first to understand, then to be understood."

When I was a senior associate with KPMG, the partner or managers would work with the client to set up and sell the audit engagement. Then they would find an auditor who was available to do the assessment (Health Insurance Portability and Accountability Act of 1996, Federal Deposit Insurance Corporation review, SAS 70,

Gramm–Leach–Bliley Act gap analysis, etc.). For many of the engagements I would show up knowing the name of the main business contact and probably the computer system and applications they were employing for their main business processes. Through those key business contacts I would ascertain the names of the people I needed to talk to about the processes. For some organizations, that contact would make the meeting arrangements and attend all meetings. Others were more open and allowed us to meet with the workers in private. As part of the fieldwork visit, we would also have to take the time to review the current documentation, policies, and procedures prior to doing a walk-through, interview, or any testing. In essence, we did a major portion of the planning during our on-site fieldwork. For many of the KPMG clients, I would be called upon to help those organizations with other assessments or consulting services later. Needless to say, during the second and future audits, and consulting engagements, I was able to use my on-site (chargeable) time more efficiently due to my familiarity with the processes and the people.

Each time I was introduced to a new organization, I wish that I had received a responsible, accountable, consulted, informed (RACI) matrix of the organization or business unit showing who was responsible for what and how they did the job. That would have helped tremendously. As I returned to those clients later in my tenure, I was more aware of the people, process, and politics; therefore, I was able to be more efficient which, of course, provided more value to the client. The original RACI matrix has been adjusted by some organizations to expand the C annotation into separate meanings. The C was divided so that the C *was consulted* prior to the process step, where the new S was used to show a subject matter expert (SME) who *could be consulted* prior to or during a process step (responsible, accountable, support, consulted, informed [RASCI]).

RACI Matrix (or RASCI)

A RACI matrix is a tool primarily used by many in project management. The original RACI matrix has been revised to include an S to denote a support person (SME); therefore, if you have a business process that refers to the RACI as RASCI, don't be alarmed.

RACI and RASCI are acronyms for "responsible," "accountable," "consulted," "informed," and, last but not least, "support":

- *Responsible*—The person or position responsible for accomplishing the task or step; the doer.
- *Accountable*—The person or position accountable for ensuring that the task or step is completed on time and correctly. Normally the accountable person is the responsible person's manager or supervisor. The accountable person has the responsibility to train, fund, and manage the responsible person's available time. For minor impact or noncomplex steps the person responsible to do the step can also be accountable for that step.
- *Consulted*—A person or position that is consulted prior to any action on the task or Step. This position may be necessary if the task is extremely complex or important or if there are forces outside the responsible person's purview that has to work in coordination with the task. This could also be a sign of micromanagement or lack of training of the responsible person.
- *Informed*—A person who should be made aware after the task is completed. Many times this is a project manager or someone tracking the status that has no insight or influence into the task itself.
- *Support*—A person who has specific knowledge or ability and may be consulted (SME) should there be any questions or concerns on the part of the responsible or accountable person.

The matrices are normally set so that the person or the position name is along the top of the matrices and the tasks or steps go down the left side of the matrices (Table 4.1). The body of the matrices would contain the letters (R, A, S, C, and I).

There are some rules which should assist you with your analysis of the RACI or RASCI matrices.

Table 4.1   RACI

STEP	WAITER	HOST	CHEF	BUS PERSON	DISHWASHER	MANAGER
Seat customer		R				A
		R				
						A
Provide a menu	A	R				A
Ask about drinks	R					A
Cook dinner	A		R			
Deliver dinner	R	R				A
Eat dinner	A					
Clear dishes	R			R		A
Wash dishes				R	R	A
Provide bill	R	A				
Pay bill	R					A

RACI Workload Analysis

Here are some thoughts that you can use to accomplish a workload analysis:

- If the business unit cannot ascertain who is responsible for the task, who is accountable for the task, or how each step is tracked, the management may then need some organization and training. (Unless there is a process, there is no way to improve the process.)
- Since too many cooks are said to spoil the broth, a horizontal review of the matrix should have only one R.
  - If you have multiple Rs for one task, duplication of the effort could occur as two or more people may take the same action for the same customer request or maybe no one would accomplish the task, thinking that the other would do it.
  - To ensure that the task is done by someone and not duplicated, an additional task may be required to schedule the execution of the task and/or notify the other responsible person to help ensure no duplication of efforts for each task; this would increase the number of process steps.
  - If the task or step is very generic (clear the dishes in a restaurant), a second person could do it and the primary

person would be made aware that the task has been accomplished.

- A horizontal review should also ensure that each line has one person responsible to accomplish the task; otherwise, the task may not be done.
- Each horizontal line (step) should have one R and one A.
  - Since the accountable person must have the wherewithal to ensure that the responsible person has the training, the abilities, and the raw material to accomplish the task, the accountable person is normally the responsible person's manager (work or administrative manager).
  - If a task or step is not complex and it does not interface with other teams, then one person or role could be both responsible (R) and accountable (A).
  - Even though the CEO, the owner, and others in the hierarchy above the responsible person may be held accountable by others, the closest accountable person to the responsible person should be shown on the RACI matrices as the accountable person A.
  - If there are multiple As not in alignment with the organizational chart toward the C-suite, then there may be some confusion dealing with management of the responsible agent. In this case, no one may be truly accountable.
- C, I, and S are not mandatory and, therefore, should be shown when they are used for a specific step.
- If a review of the steps shows many Cs, the process may have an issue with micromanagement or some "go-for" management style.
  - If people need to get permission for each step, efficiency will be impacted and you may experience a large wait time between steps.
  - Micromanagement will also inhibit a responsible person from any thoughts of innovation, adding value, or recommending any process improvements.
- If the horizontal and vertical reviews of the step show many Is, then for the sake of efficiency, we need to question the need for each of the Is.

- If you are recording the process steps, there should be one system of record and not many different records.
- A vertical review of each person or position title should provide you with a view of that person's activities and workload.
  - A person responsible for too many tasks may be overworked, which could adversely affect their efficiency and/or effectiveness.
  - Those overworked personnel might take shortcuts and make errors, causing a reduction in effectiveness and an increase in wasted time, assets, effort, and rework.
- A vertical review of each person or position may denote a segregation of duties (SOD) issue.
  - If a person is responsible for both the physical and logical movements of an asset having value, that person could remove the asset and provide a business transaction to remove the asset from the organization's inventory.
  - The loss of the asset could be due to a misunderstanding or as part of a fraudulent act.
- If a review of a person or position throughout the process steps has no empty spaces, you need to ascertain if this person adds value to each step or is a micromanager.
- If no one is involved in a step (no R, A, C, and I), then is this step necessary and is this step being accomplished?
- If a person has too many Cs, is this person a bottleneck?

Planning Memo

The planning memo can contain more details than the project charter or plan. The project charter is an interoffice or interbusiness document denoting the goals and rationale for the assessment, whereas the planning memo is directed at the assessment team to outline the details needed to be successful.

The plan should provide an outline for the assessment team. A planning memo is normally developed to be used by the assessment team to coordinate their team efforts and as a guide to keep on track and inhibit scope creep. This could include a RACI matrix of the assessment team as well as a Gantt chart to denote timelines, etc.

The planning memo could include the following:

- Names of key contacts
- Sampling techniques to be used
- Population size
- Assigned team members for the assessment
- Tentative plan for the assessment work
- Tentative objective and scope
- Estimated time budget
- Planned start and stop dates
- List of prior audit concerns, problems, and senior leadership concerns
- List of assessment team concerns, thoughts, and ideas
- List of key contacts in the business unit (could be part of the business RACI)

The planning memo can be used as the source to develop the project charter and should parallel the charter with more details to keep the team in alignment.

Project Charter

To help ensure that the assessment team members as well as the business leaders are in sync with the assessment efforts and resources used for the engagement, a business plan or project plan should be established as a first step in the assessment.

If I had an hour to save the world, I would spend 55 minutes defining the problem, and 5 minutes solving it.

Albert Einstein
Theoretical physicist (1879–1955)

The project plan should outline the business reason or rationale behind the assessment effort as well as the expected value to be derived from the effort.

The plan should not be too limited in scope as to provide a negligible value; therefore, you need to have a senior leadership as a sponsor for the effort. This leader should be a person who can make changes for the better and hopefully hold some accountability and authority over the business processes involved in the assessment.

The project plan should provide an expected outcome, but to accomplish this, we first need to understand the concerns of the organization as well as the business unit or process being reviewed. This must be established during the planning stage. We should have the following:

- Enough business knowledge about the activities in review
  - If the knowledge or skill is not among the assessment team, then maybe a SME should be added to the team before you take one more step forward.
- A well-written engagement plan or project charter
- An understanding of the drivers for the process or business unit (KPIs, key success factors [KSFs], organizational scorecard, etc.)
- A clear assessment objective
- A request from a senior person outlining the concern for the organization's stability; to maintain a place in the industry would be a driving factor for the assessment
  - That senior leader or board member's concerns must be a key outcome of the endeavor. Either put the member's mind at ease or recommend how to improve the situation or trend.
- Credibility and trust between the assessment team and the business unit, which is a key to success

Critical Success Factors

As with most everything that you do in developing or improving a process, you need to consider your success factors:

- Delivery of process effectiveness
- Delivery of process efficiencies
- Reduction of costs associated with service provisioning
- Alignment of ITs with business objectives
- Business objectives and goals

Project Charter (Engagement Plan)

The business plan or project charter should have a name depicting the process improvement goals of the project. Try to employ some sort of action verb or goal-oriented name for the assessment project.

The project charter is used to document the following:

- Reason for the assessment project
- Objectives and any constraints of the assessment
- A communication plan
- A projected timeline and milestones
- Estimated deliverables and anticipated benefits
- Budget for the project
- Resources and business unit assistance required
- Introduction of the team members and their roles, including business unit resources
- Stakeholders and sponsors

At a minimum, the project charter should include the following:

- *The problem statement* to show why the assessment is being performed. Similar to a risk statement, the problem should be written as a business problem including the adverse effect the problem might have on the business unit and organization.
  - Link the problem to the organization's goals and strategy.
  - The statement should denote the frequency and/or impact to the process and the organization.
  - If the problem is chronic or periodic, then that should be stated.
  - The problem statement *should not* include possible solutions.
    - If you can state the solution, then the assessment is not necessary.
    - If you know a solution, the project goal of the assessment should be to validate or refute the possible solution as well as to find the correct solution to the problem.
- *The project goals* should outline what the expectations are when the assessment has been completed and any recommendations

have been implemented. The potential improvements (Table 4.2) could be the following:

- *Authorization* should denote who or which leader is concerned about the problem. This should be someone who is not only a stakeholder in the success of the process, but someone senior in the hierarchy of the business unit being assessed.

- The *project leader* would be the assessment team leader and main communicator for senior leadership questions and concerns.

- The *business unit leader* should include the business leader for the process being assessed and the main process owner.

- The *key stakeholders* should list those business managers directly or indirectly affected by the outcome of the process review.

- The *project priorities* should prioritize the order of tasks to be performed in the order of necessity or greater impact on the organization, the process effectiveness, economy, and efficient customer delivery.

- The *scope statement* should identify what processes and business units to be included in the assessment, and if possible, it should include a list of any resources from the business unit required for the completion of the assessment.

- The *time frame* should outline the start and estimated completion dates of the fieldwork along with an expected draft or final report. The *team must show a commitment* to the project and delivery of the outcome.
  - If any unforeseen events should preclude the anticipated dates, updated information should be provided

Table 4.2 Process Improvements

POTENTIAL IMPROVEMENT	POTENTIAL IMPACT
• Reduction of inventory levels	• Reduce capital investment in inventory
• Reduce equipment downtime	• Increase capacity
• Speed up delivery time	• Increase revenue
• Reduce time-to-market	• Increase revenue through increased sales
• Reduce rejects, returns, and rework	• Decrease material costs and increase ROI

as soon as possible and new commitment dates should be established.

- *Metrics* should be established to provide an estimate of the economic or process savings that could be attributed to the assessment project.

(While working on Six Sigma projects at the Bank of America, all green belt projects were required to have an estimated $1.5 million dollar savings to be approved. Also, to maintain your green or black belt, you had to save your organization over $1 million per year.)

Adding Value

If the organization is structured correctly, each business process should support the goals of the organization. If a process is encountered that does not directly or indirectly support the organizational goals, the assessment team should question why the operation is using resources and organizational assets.

Many business processes support the organization in some fashion but don't directly touch the customer's product or service. Human resources (HR), payroll, and many of the IT processes don't directly affect the quality or customer delivery.

Before we can effectively develop an assessment, we must understand the business goals and KPIs. Some organizations use KSFs in lieu of KPIs. Prior to any fieldwork, you should understand the metrics that the business unit believes makes them successful. These measurements may be developed by the business unit or the senior leader (C-suite) folks. If the business unit managers believe that the KPI or KSF measures their success in meeting the organization's goals, then the assessment should tie that metric into the assessment or the business manager may not see any of your recommendations as an improvement to their process.

Key Performance Indicator

As you look at a business unit's KPI, we need to realize that in some instances the business process KPI is different from the IT business process KPI. It is with great hope that senior leadership helped to ensure that the customer-focused KPI and the indirect business process KPIs complemented each other, or better yet, they formed a synergized affect to each other. Some KPIs may be simplified or complex.

For example, IT KPIs may be as follows:

- Availability (excluding planned downtime)
  - Percentage of actual uptime (in hours) of equipment relative to the total number of planned uptime (in hours).
  - Planned uptime = service hours minus planned downtime.
  - Planned downtime is downtime as scheduled for maintenance.
    - Could be named as preventive maintenance or it could be known as service outage duration
  - Percentage of outages due to incidents (unplanned unavailability)
    - Percentage of outages (unavailability) due to incidents in the IT environment relative to the service hours
  - Percentage of outages due to changes (planned unavailability)
    - Percentage of outages (unavailability) due to implementation of planned changes relative to the service hours
  - Percentage of unplanned outages/unavailability due to changes
    - Percentage of unplanned outages (unavailability due to the implementation of changes into the infrastructure. Unplanned means that the outage (or part of the outage) was not included in the plan for the implementation of the change.
  - Percentage of availability service-level agreements (SLAs) met
  - Business-related KPI that considers IT may be as follows:
    - Percentage of business projects that consider IT risks
    - Number of IT-related events with business impact due to a failure to escalate an IT issue
    - Number of IT-related events that induced a business impact in which a failure to escalate the event was a factor in event occurrence and/or the loss magnitude

(e.g., the risk manager did not know or there was an impaired ability to escalate the issue prior to the business impact)
- Percentage of downtime due to information security incidents
- Security incident resolution time by severity
  - Percentage of security incidents resolved within the agreed SLA by severity
  - Average time (e.g., in hours) between the occurrence of an incident and its resolution

Needless to say that these KPIs are but a few ideas in considering the IT service-level requirements for an organization to be both effective and efficient.

As I consider the business of IT, I am reminded of what I read in my first book regarding IT and computer security. It stated something to the effect that IT quality for their customers was driven by the acronym CIA:

- C stands for confidentiality, which mandates the need to protect the data entrusted to the IT team from sharing with anyone other than the business units that require the data to enhance the organization and make decisions for the organization and the customer.
- I stands for integrity and focuses on maintaining the integrity of the data throughout any automated process. Whether the application program was adding interest to the principle or calculating paychecks, the task will be accomplished correctly and the security will inhibit any unauthorized adjustments to any data maintained within their purview and control.
- A stands for availability. The focus of availability is to provide the data entrusted to the IT team to the appropriate organization's businessperson when the person requires the information that they derive from the data to make decisions or service their approved customers.
  - Please note that even though the acronym IT intimates that we handle information, the data entrusted to the IT team become information only when presented to the

person who can interpret the data as information to help provide a service or product to their customer.

- To IT the data are merely a bunch of digits.

Operational Process

Now that you understand the KPI, you can understand how the KPI may influence the process. Your assessment of the process should have been designed to provide the customer with the quality product or service while focusing on the KPI and/or the corporate scorecard rating. As mentioned earlier in this book, operational assessments are based on three Es:

- Effectiveness
  - Effectiveness is a measure of how well the process provides the quality that the customer wants or is expecting.
  - The VOC denotes the expectations to be met.
  - Effectiveness is what the customer is prepared to fund.
- Efficiency
  - The process efficiencies focus on throughput providing the product or service to the customer.
  - It is the best use of organizational assets.
  - And it is the cost of inventory and resources to provide that product or service.
- Economy
  - The economics of the process include resources and inventory.
  - The resources are the people, the equipment, the building, transportation, etc.
  - The inventory includes the following:
    - Raw material inventory used for the process, which includes any resource or input that is needed to produce the product or service, such as the following:
      - The customer request forms
      - The information and data to provide the results (cookbook, procedures, etc.)
      - Storage requirements prior to the process start

- Work-in-progress (WIP) inventory includes all partially completed products or services.
- Finished goods inventory if the product or service is ready to be delivered to the customer. However, it has yet to be delivered.

• Resources include the buildings used to house the process, the machinery, tools, desks, computers, and, of course, the people to accomplish the mission.

Since effectiveness focuses on what is critical to the customer, we can use the Lean Six Sigma acronym CTQ.

Please note that the CTQ is based on the customer requirements. Also, note that not all processes focus on ultimately providing quality to the external customer. Those processes or business units in the value stream that provide external customer quality are sometimes referred to as profit centers, whereas the many supporting processes and business units within an organization are looked upon as cost centers since they focus their product or service on the internal customer. The focus or division between cost center and profit center can actually have a negative connotation. If times are hard, many people look to reduce the size and funding of the cost centers in lieu of the profit centers. The quickest reduction in cost is unfortunately a reduction in staff size. Reducing the staff of a cost center alleviates the indirect support for the product or service; however, the reduction may have an adverse effect on the profit center by delaying the service that the cost center provides to the profit center. The effect may not be immediate, but may impact the profit center from achieving their objectives later. Taking too long to replace a value stream worker due to a reduction in staff or HR may have a direct adverse impact on the future capability of that value stream process to meet the customer requirements.

Process Review (As Is)

As I mentioned earlier, you must seek first to understand the process prior to developing ideas to improve the operation. If a physician provides a cure before he or she completes the examination, would you have confidence in his or her diagnosis? Better yet, will the patient survive and prosper?

During my military career, I reported to sick call while on a temporary duty assignment. I had injured my toe at the base swimming pool the day prior, and when I awoke, my toe was black and blue and it hurt like the devil. After talking to the triage nurse, I waited over an hour before I was sent in to the doctor's office. As I was entering his office, I had a tickle in my throat and coughed. Just as I sat down, the doctor gave me some Cepacol, all-purpose capsules, and some GI gin (cough syrup), then told me that if the cough didn't subside by tomorrow, I should return to sick call. I said, "Thanks, but how do I apply these to my toe?" He said, "Your toe? What are you talking about?" So I showed him my toe and he decided to prescribe something else.

You must diagnose before you prescribe.

Let us first look at a simple restaurant order process (Figure 4.1) and later we can review the business process with IT integration.

Now that we have outlined the process, we can start to gain a familiarity with the process. Since a productive process is defined as one or more steps that take input and create output of more value than the input, let us review the restaurant process employing a source, inputs, process, outputs, customers (SIPOC) table.

SIPOC Table (Answers the Question "What?")

As you consider the process, look at Table 4.3, a SIPOC table denoting the source, the input, the process, the output, and the customer of that process. If we ever consider reducing or removing any process step, we should understand what the step uses as input as well as what the output from the step is and where the output goes.

The SIPOC table shows each major step and includes the key process input variable (KPIV) (a.k.a. raw material inventory) and the source of the KPIV as well as the key process output variable (KPOV) and the disposition of the output for each step. The SIPOC matrix should show each major step, each required raw material, the WIP inventories, and the finished goods for each of those major steps. It is helpful to show the steps leading to the finished product or service (ready for use by the ultimate customer).

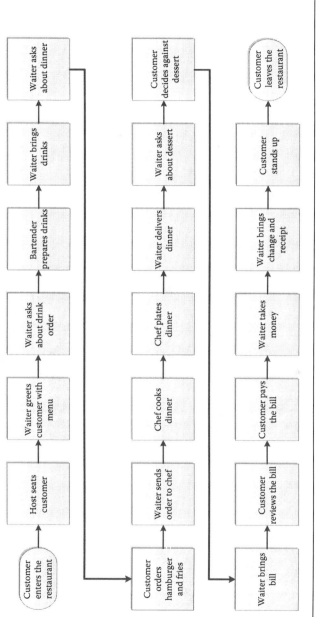

Figure 4.1   Restaurant visit.

Table 4.3   SIPOC: Restaurant Visit

STEP	SOURCE	INPUT	PROCESS	OUTPUT	CUSTOMER
1	Restaurant Supply, Inc. (RS, Inc.)	Table with four chairs Plates Utensils	Host seats the customer at a table	Comfortable customer	Customer
2	Staples	Order pad	Waiter takes drink and food order	Restaurant application	ABC Systems restaurant POS PC application
3	POS system	Drink order	Bartender makes the drink	Drink Billing tab	Customer Restaurant POS
	Ice machine Drink dispenser	Ice in glass Drink			
4	POS System Butcher shop Bakery Produce	Food order Ground beef Bun Lettuce leaf Two slices of tomato	Chef prepares hamburger and fixings to perfection	A perfectly cooked burger	Waiter
5	Waiter RS, Inc.	A perfect hamburger Plate and utensils	Delivery of meal to the customer	A satisfied customer Billing tab	Customer Restaurant POS
6	POS station	Customer request	Deliver bill to the customer	Bill	Customer
7	Customer's wallet	Cash	Customer pays bill	Till and revenue account	Restaurant POS
8	Customer's wallet	Cash	Add tip	Cash	Waiter
9	Waiter	Cash	Waiter shares tip	Cash	Chef and bartender

Note: POS: point of sale.

If you are going to assess any process and especially if you are planning to make changes to the process as an improvement, you must
first understand the process and the steps within the process, including the inventory, the source, and the destination. This way, you will
know what goes into the process and what the output is and where or
who it services.

You may note by action 9 in the SIPOC table that I am a believer of a waiter sharing tips with the bartender and/or chef/cook. Since I worked as a bartender in noncommissioned officers clubs and some hotels while serving in the military I am a believer that the size of the tip to the wait staff is based on the food, beverage, and service.

Process improvements can be like a double-edged sword. An improvement in one area may have an adverse effect in another area. We must understand the impact of any recommendation; therefore, it is imperative that we know the inputs, the outputs, and who depends on the outputs from the process steps. This way, we should gain a better understanding of the flow for the WIP inventory.

Who knows, we may decide to get our plates or other things from other more competitive companies, thereby reducing our costs. The reduction in cost would increase our profit; however, we need to ensure that the new plates or utensils do not take away from the customer experience. A customer doesn't expect paper plates and plastic utensils in a fine dining restaurant; nor does a customer expect bone china and tablecloths at a fast food restaurant. *It is about the customer and the organization.*

Using a similar SIPOC concept, you can present the IT environment servicing the customer as shown in Table 4.4.

Table 4.4   Baseline Speed Test (Customer Home Network)

ITEM	SOURCE	INPUT	PROCESS	OUTPUT	CUSTOMER REMARKS
1	ABC Cable Co.	Cable modem	Wi-Fi home network	Cable-ready data	ABC Cable Co.
	Motorola	Wi-Fi router			
	HP, IBM, etc.	Wi-Fi–ready laptops/PCs			
2	Home network	Message data ICMP ping	Internet access	Average ping speed 33 ms	ISP
		Download data		Average download speed 5.57 Mbps	
		Upload data		Average upload speed 31.75 Mbps	
3	WWW ISP	Customer request via	Corporate web server	Customer order	Customer application and database server
	AT&T	Dedicated T1			

Note: HP: Hewlett-Packard; ICMP: Internet control message protocol; ISP: Internet service provider; Mbps: megabits per second; WWW: World Wide Web.

As you can imagine, you could use the SIPOC diagram to isolate and track individual business processes from the customer to the customer and through billing, accounting, and customer payment.

For the network environment you could also include the source or the routers, modems, data service unit/channel service unit, hubs, etc. One thing that I would recommend when you get to the fieldwork portion of the study is to reflect back on the SIPOC matrix or the network functional diagram to help ensure that you compute the average or normal delays caused by the equipment. I would also recommend that even if you are dealing with a *hub* to amplify the local area network (LAN) signal, I normally add 1 ms per appliance as a minimum. As I mention during a case study, I also consider 5 ms for each microwave transfer and 300 ms for each satellite transfer. Also, please realize that the latency delays are for the message going in each direction.

Please also recall that the message load has a direct variance with the length of the message; that is why an echo check of the message is not used by data automation. The echo check reflects the exact message; however, the current message acceptance is based on a short *AK* for an acknowledgment and a *NAK* for a nonacknowledgment to show that the receiving system did not get the entire message.

Value Stream Map (VSM) (When)

After looking at some tools to answer the questions who and what, now we can look at *when*. For this we will employ VSM. Within value stream mapping, we will look at the following:

- The value of each step
- The time it takes to accomplish the step
- The time required between each step (lead and/or lag time)

For those of you who have studied the Lean framework, you will remember that the seven wastes in the Lean framework are the following:

- *Transportation*—Unnecessary transportation causes delays in production, which increase your WIP inventory as well as the risks of damage and loss of the product or documentation. Transportation other than to the customer adds no real value; therefore, if at all possible, only necessary transportation should be tolerated. Travel time is tolerated and accepted, but not loved.

- *Inventory*—Whether it is raw material, WIP, or finished goods, inventory represents a capital investment that is sitting there doing no one any good. Whether the finished good is a report, a product, or a service, the production cycle is not completed and, therefore, the product has no value to the customer until the customer receives it. If the process has not been provided to the customer, there is no revenue, just cost (inventory and resources).
  - If it adds no value to the customer and cost to the business unit, it should be kept to a minimum.
  - For thoughts and ideas about inventory reduction, you might review some information focused on just-in-time and supply chain management concepts.
- *Motion*—Motion is similar to unnecessary transportation. If a work center is designed with some standards and the placement of raw material or tools to be used for a process is such that the most used items are close at hand or easily accessible, the worker can get to them quickly with the least movement.
  - For a restaurant or bar, the cook or bartender should not have to continually go to a storeroom/walk-in freezer or search for the right ingredient to service a customer's request. In a bar, all service wells should have the most used liquors in the same space at each workstation (serving well) so that the customer will receive the correct drink with a minimum delay.
  - Although you can store the necessary raw material in abundance somewhere else, there should be a stash readily available near the cook or bartender for the day or shift use. If you can reduce the movement to a minimum, you will increase the efficiency and throughput or productive capability.
  - The same is true in a workshop where tools are kept in a standard space at each workstation or an office where the office supplies and reference materials are available to those who require these for their tasks.

- The standardization of the work space will help to ensure that if one person had to substitute for another or use their workstation for some reason, they would find what they need to satisfy the customer with limited motion and waste of time.
- *Waiting*—When goods or services are not being worked on or transported to a destination for delivery or further processes, or they are waiting for something, this situation is considered waiting. The time that a good or service is dormant, waiting for something (equipment, information, files, reports, people, etc.), is like putting dollars in a zero-interest account and paying someone to store it. Waiting serves no real purpose, yet it is prevalent in most industries, including internal audit.
  - How many times have you ordered something that went on back order?
  - In manufacturing unless you have achieved perfect job scheduling, you will always have a bottleneck. More about this as we move into fieldwork analysis.
  - How many times are you ready to work on something and have to wait for reports or information before you can do any analysis?
  - How many hours has the audit or assessment report been ready before you can provide it to your business partner (customer)?
- *Overproduction*—Overproduction occurs when more resources are employed to produce more than the customer wants delivered at the time.
  - This creates additional finished goods inventory that cannot be delivered; therefore, you must store it.
  - Similar to creating a backlog, overproduction uses capital that may or may not ever provide revenue.
  - Please realize that having inventory ready for the customer is warranted in many industries, but it is directly reliant on the marketing research to help ensure that the finished goods would be purchased by the customer.
  - Supermarkets have inventory on their shelves and in their storerooms ready for distribution to the customers.
  - Toy manufacturers could not feasibly produce the number of toys purchased for Christmas within the few months

prior to Christmas; therefore, just after Christmas they design and start production for next year's gifts. Then they market the new toys and games so that there is the demand for the following Christmas gift giving.

- The same is true for diamond wedding rings for the June bride and roses for Valentine's Day.
- Production to finished goods is not a bad thing unless the finished goods never get to the customer. Then it is a total waste of raw material and production costs.

- *Overprocessing*—Overprocessing occurs whenever resources are expended to produce a product or service that the customer doesn't care about.
  - If you spend thousands of extra dollars to build car brakes that stop a vehicle 1 foot faster than normal disk brakes, would the customer be willing to spend those extra dollars for a 12-inch stopping distance advantage?
  - Based on the organization's risk appetite, what is the expense of establishing controls that would bring the risks to zero? It would require total redundancy and duplication of process and people at double the costs as opposed to a risk with an impact that was within the organization's tolerance level (5% or so error rate).
  - Overcontrolling is just as detrimental as undercontrolling.
- *Defects*—Whenever defects occur, extra costs are incurred. From the cost of returning a defective item, reworking the item, rescheduling workforce, or trashing the item, it is a cost to the organization as well as a detriment to the reputation of the organization.

When building a VSM, most people start with a normal flow chart of the business process. For our purposes, let's use a process that portrays money movement from a bank account through the Federal clearinghouse to Automated Clearing House (ACH) network, a secure transfer system connecting all U.S. financial institutions. The Electronic Funds Transfers (EFT) is monitored by the U.S. Government and Federal Reserve for compliance to the Electronic Funds Transfer Act (EFTA), Regulation E. The funds transfer is referred to as ACH or EFT depending on who is communicating the process. Ultimately the money movement takes dollars from one financial institution's account and moves it to another account and/ or financial institution. In today's economic processes, many banking customers use this process a normal bill pay convenience.

The flow chart for a common EFT transaction is shown in Figure 4.2.

To build a VSM from a normal flow chart (Figure 4.3), you

- Include the average time it takes to complete each step.
- Include the average time between steps (transportation, data transfer, e-mail, movement, etc.).
- Consider the following abbreviations:
  - VA stands for value add and should be kept. The only question one might ask is "Can it be done more efficiently?"

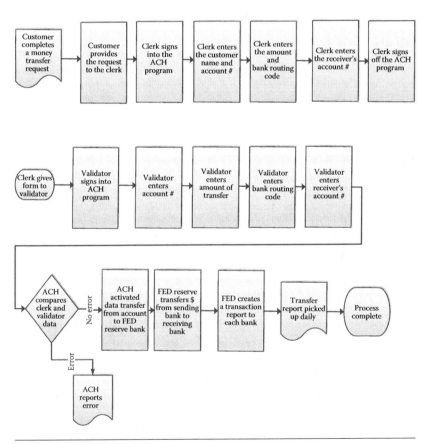

Figure 4.2 Automated cash handling.

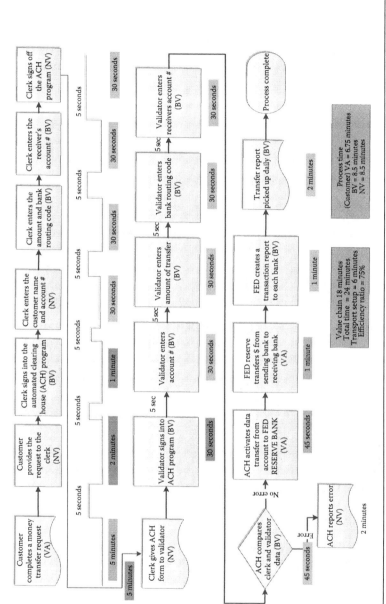

Figure 4.3 VSM EFT.

- BV stands for business value add. The questions about this step might be "Does it still add value" and "Can it be accomplished more effectively?"
- NV or NVA stands for no value or no value add. Needless to say, you should probably delete this step; however, you might review the SIPOC and RACI diagrams prior to making a decision like that to help ensure that the step you remove did not provide something else down the line that is necessary for a value add step later in the process or in some other process. If it makes economic sense to remove a step that does build something of value for a future step, how will you adjust or add value for that future step?

There is nothing so useless as doing efficiently that which should not be done at all.

Peter Drucker

- And for each step you might ask the following:
  - Does this step add value to the customer? If yes, it is VA.
  - Does this step add value to the organization? If yes, it is BV.
  - Is there any value derived from completing this step? If no, it is NV.
    - If yes, is the value worth the cost of the step?

Although you are still in the planning stage of the assessment, after seeing the VSM you will probably start to consider some resolutions to any concerns that were raised initially which provided the impetus to accomplish an operational assessment.

Do not come to any decisions about how to fix the issue until you gain a full 360-degree view of the process and possible problem. All insights and perspectives should be used before making assumptions or decisions.

I once read that *decisions need only be made when you can't or don't take the time to look at the facts.*

As an assessor, an auditor, a consultant, or a person, we have a tendency to look for alternatives and answers once we gain the slightest inkling of the ineffectiveness or inefficiency cause. This is a normal trait. Even during a conversation, we normally listen with the intent of answering. Sometimes we don't realize the real content before we have made a decision. Many of us have experienced training in communication dealing with talking, writing, and lecturing, but there are very few training courses that focus on listening—really listening.

A lady from Canada by the name of Nejolla Korris provides some insight on the use of the language used to tell if the person is telling the truth or lying. Unlike others who look at body language and for specific tones, she looks at the words and what they really mean when used in the context that they were used. I believe that there is a website that provides you with some insight into what she and her organization do. The web address is https://www.youtube.com /watch?v=nfCKRNIhc9.

We as human beings have a tendency to listen to someone speak with the intent to answer rather than the intent to understand.

From the mind of Stephen Covey, "Seek first to understand and then to be understood."

In the next chapter as you review this process during fieldwork, you will be looking at the as-is VSM diagram and asking some of the following questions:

1. For each step in the process, does it add value to the customer or the organization?
2. If a step does not add value to the customer or the organization, then during the fieldwork, determine why do we spend the time and effort to accomplish that step?
   a. I have often found that among the steps in a process, especially a process in place for over 3 years, there are steps that were of use and might have been required in the past, but the value of those steps was lost over time.
   b. If you remove a step of any process, I recommend that you review the SIPOC matrix to see if any input or output from the step has to be moved to another step for processing. Or can we save costs of the material and resources without a loss somewhere else down the line?

3. If the step adds value to the business, does the business value now or in the future exceed the cost of that step?
    a. Future value may be the knowledge about the customer or other products and/or services that your organization has the ability and desire to provide.
4. Does the process provide a quality product or service to the customer?
5. Does the revenue provided by the customer exceed the cost of the product or service? (Note that the cost of the product or service includes the direct and indirect costs to the organization.)
6. If the revenue does not provide a suitable profit or break-even point, then will this product or service provided to the customer at a loss gain other more profitable requests from that customer (a loss leader)?
    a. A loss leader is a product or service used to attract or keep a customer that does or will provide the normal profit margins.
        i. Loss-leader products or services are used to become a single source vendor for a good customer.
(Consider the number of introductory pricing from Internet service providers, TV cable companies, and even employers.)

You will realize quickly that the diagrams developed during the planning stage which depict the as-is environment can be used during the fieldwork and reporting stages to show the comparison of the current environment or process with the recommended to-be picture should the business unit implement your recommendation or something similar. The pictorial view of the before and after may provide the impetus for the business unit manager to support your recommendations.

The VSM diagram may ultimately show the cost savings including time and effort, which equate to dollars.

A picture can be worth a thousand words.

Spaghetti Diagram: As-Is (Where)

Another great business management diagram that can be used to show the *as-is* versus the *to-be* environment is the spaghetti diagram. This diagram will show the movement of data and/or product as it traverses through the organization. It translates the movement of data or parts, and even logical movement, as a physical move from one person or position to another office or position. The idea and concept of a spaghetti diagram will clearly denote redundancies that may not be visible in a VSM or normal flow chart. A swim lane flow chart will provide some insight into the logical and/or physical movement across business units; however, the spaghetti diagram will provide it in a clearer picture of any redundancies or micromanagement. Appendix C is a typical swim lane diagram depicting a restaurant order. This type of diagram is similar to the Flow Chart, yet it excentuates the change of business unit or move from manual to automated processes. You may realize that the movement from Manual to automated as well as a pass off from one business unit to another adds to the probability of errors or communication issues. These moves across the swim lanes normally add risks.

As I mentioned earlier, each tool provides a different perspective of a business process and environment. The spaghetti diagram takes a spatial view of the process. The view dramatizes the complexity, redundancies, and possible inefficiencies and should help to provide a way to reduce handling and easier workforce communication as well as better resource allocations.

The spaghetti diagram is another great business diagram that can show the as-is environment as well as to illustrate the improvements based on your recommendations in a to-be spaghetti diagram. This along with the VSM should be used in the reporting stage. The business manager can then visualize the improvements using a picture to show the before and after process that is hopefully less confusing, less complex, and more efficient without any loss of quality or effectiveness.

Rather than using the EFT business process that shows only the movement within one business unit, we will choose another process that traverses more than one office structure or business units.

The purchasing process crosses over multiple business units and controls and, therefore, we will use it for this spaghetti diagram activity. For this activity let's look at the purchasing process for a multimillion dollar company at one of their divisions.

Procurement Process Narrative

The purchasing process starts with a request from a businessperson for a piece of equipment of some supply item. The employee completes a requisition form that he or she gets from the supply cabinet and provides the request to the supervisor for the business unit approval. The supervisor signs the form if he or she approves of the purchase. The form is submitted along with the supervisor's signature to the division group controller via office mail or the supervisor can scan the document and send it via e-mail. The controller reviews the proposed cost and rationale and if the controller approves the request, the form is sent to the purchasing supervisor. The purchasing supervisor assigns a buyer to find the product and supplier and then provides the requisition form to the buyer. The buyer uses the requisition form to complete a request for proposal to a number of appropriate suppliers with 1-week suspense for normal orders. Emergency requirements would have an abbreviated suspense date of 2 days. For extremely complex or new design requirements, they would allow the suppliers with up to 1 month to respond with a proposal bid. The average for a normal item would be 1 week and the overall average is 10 business days or 2 calendar weeks. When the buyer completes their supplier assessment and vendor negotiations, they enter a completed purchase order (PO) into the corporate purchasing system, which sends an e-mail to the purchasing supervisor requesting final approval. Once the purchasing supervisor approves the PO, he or she sends the PO to the controller, who applies the account funding code to the purchasing system and then mails the PO to the chosen vendor. When available, the vendor provides the ordered item(s) to the receiving department of the division and then subsequently mails the invoice to the controller for review and payment. In a few cases the invoice accompanies the order, in which case the receiving department will send the item and the invoice to the controller. If the invoice is sent separately, the receiving department sends the purchased item to the controller for validation of the order. The controller checks the item against the PO and enters the receiving certification into the purchasing application software system. The controller also reviews the invoice and, if approved, mails the invoice with a payment approval to accounting for payment. Accounts payable department arranges for and pays the invoice.

To illustrate the spaghetti diagram's power, you should start out with an actual floor plan to help depict the movement of information and/or products/items. If the business units are separated geographically into different buildings, towns, or countries, the floor plan will provide an even better description. This is especially true if we are dealing with data movement across the country or the world. It will even be helpful for those business processes that have been computerized or sent using a manual hard copy media.

For our purposes, we have constructed a fictitious floor diagram for the ABC Organization. We will be using Figure 4.4 as our spaghetti diagram. For ease of viewing I have placed a copy of the legend for the spaghetti diagram as Figure 4.4a and the spaghetti diagram itself with the legend on the right side as Figure 4.4b.

Purchasing process

1. Employee completes a purchase requisition form and gives it to his manager.

2. Manager reviews and approves or denies the requisition.

3. Manager sends approved requisition to the controller.

4. If controller approves the requisition, he adds the appropriate funding code.

5. Controller sends approved requisition form to purchasing supervisor.

6. Purchasing supervisor assigns a buyer.

7. Buyer assesses vendors and negotiates price and delivery requirements with vendor.

8. Buyer completes the supplier assessment and chooses a vendor.

9. Buyer prepares the PO for purchasing supervisor approval.

10. Purchasing supervisor sends approved PO to controller for final approval.

11. Controller applies the account funding code to the PO.

12. Controller sends the PO to the appropriate vendor.

13. Vendor sends item to organization's receiving department.

14. Receiving department forwards item to controller for validation of asset delivery.

15. Controller enters receipt into purchasing system.

16. Controller sends item to business manager.

17. Business manager provides item to employees.

18. Vendor sends invoice to controller.

19. Controller reviews invoice for approval.

20. Controller sends authorized and approved invoice to accounting.

21. Accounts payable pays the invoice.

(a)

Figure 4.4   (a) Legend.   (*Continued*)

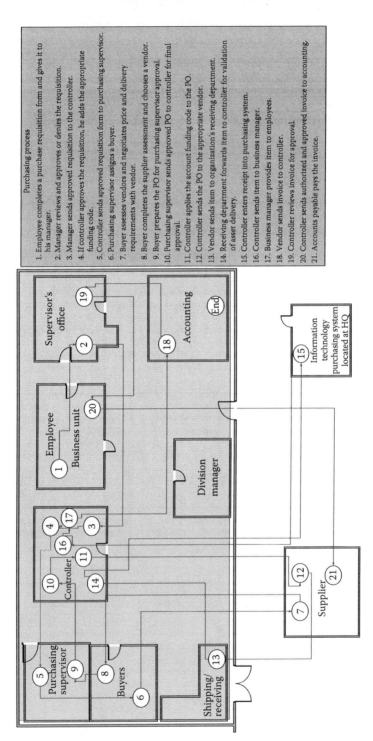

Purchasing process

1. Employee completes a purchase requisition form and gives it to his manager.
2. Manager reviews and approves or denies the requisition.
3. Manager sends approved requisition to the controller.
4. If controller approves the requisition, he adds the appropriate funding code.
5. Controller sends approved requisition form to purchasing supervisor.
6. Purchasing supervisor assigns a buyer.
7. Buyer assesses vendors and negotiates price and delivery requirements with vendor.
8. Buyer completes the supplier assessment and chooses a vendor.
9. Buyer prepares the PO for purchasing supervisor approval.
10. Purchasing supervisor sends approved PO to controller for final approval.
11. Controller applies the account funding code to the PO.
12. Controller sends the PO to the appropriate vendor.
13. Vendor sends item to organization's receiving department.
14. Receiving department forwards item to controller for validation of asset delivery.
15. Controller enters receipt into purchasing system.
16. Controller sends item to business manager.
17. Business manager provides item to employees.
18. Vendor sends invoice to controller.
19. Controller reviews invoice for approval.
20. Controller sends authorized and approved invoice to accounting.
21. Accounts payable pays the invoice.

(b)

Figure 4.4 (Continued)   (b) Spaghetti diagram of a fictitious organization and process.

For *legal* departments, please note that this is a fictitious process at a fictitious organization on a fictitious planet and any similarities between this and any organization with any legal standing is a complete surprise to the author, publisher, and anyone who is involved with the book, including the reader.

Many people don't consider the transportation delay for each computer transaction since you are normally dealing with communications that take less than a few seconds; however, as you traverse distances between the user and the data, you will realize that the delay is multiplied by the number of transactions as well as the message size and the distance. For a computer to provide data from one point to another point, a latency delay occurs in all cases. From the internal disk drive to the screen is quicker than from a file server located on the same segment of a computer network and even slower from the file server located in a different building, a different city, or, based on our global economy, a different country or continent. The latency delay can be negligible or can be so significant, it could impact the application, the network appliance, and the customer.

Although there is a latency delay for the disk head to position itself over the data or for the data lookup to occur on digital disk, the primary delay occurs from the transmission from the file or application source to the workstation or the PC which the user is employing. It is a matter of physics that electrons travel at a rate of speed not exceeding the speed of light. In addition, the protocol used to send and receive data has a latency effect to take the bytes and serialize them to individual bits to be sent across the telecommunication media. Please note that different media and different wire sizes or bandwidths will have an effect on the time it takes to transfer or receive the messages. We will discuss latency delays in detail in later chapters as we focus on the IT business environment and business unit support.

Once you have established the physical business locations on some floor plan or geographical map (real or imaginary), we can begin with the trigger that starts the process under scrutiny. Ultimately, we will be using a continuous line from the trigger throughout the process to the process completion without lifting the pencil from the paper.

Before you begin the lines, I strongly recommend that you establish the legend on the right side of, above, or below the floor plan laying out the steps which will be used for the spaghetti diagram. Use consecutive numbers to denote each step, movement, and business unit involved. If you do have to add a step while building the legend, it is easier at this stage to insert a number, or if you have completed the numbering, insert small *a*, *b*, *c*, etc. (for example, if you need to add three steps between 6 and 7, add 6a, 6b, and 6c). This may help you avoid doing a vast amount of renumbering should you be up to 45 before you notice the three additional steps.

Once the legend is complete, add the lines and number them as they are listed in the legend. Then incorporate that legend into the spaghetti diagram to the left or right of the floor plan, as shown in Figure 4.4b.

As you have a chance to review and assess the planning spaghetti diagram, you should start to gain an insight into some redundancies or multiple connections to the same person or business process.

If there are multiple lines from one entity to more than one entity, you can show those diversions as one continuous line stopping at the least handling stop first and then to the entity with the most moves along the way. An alternative should there be two specific lines of processes due to product differences, customer preferences, etc., you could build two entirely separate spaghetti diagrams so that the flow can be reviewed for each product line or major difference.

You will note that in the procurement diagram in Figure 4.4b, the vendor provided two things to the organization using two different lines: (1) one being the ordered item to the receiving department and (2) the other being the invoice to the controller. Since this was nearing the end of the process, I chose to split the item since there were no long-term lines from there. You could have just shown a continuous line from the vendor to the controller and then the controller's actions of entering delivery of the item then later the controller's action of approving the invoice, along with a line of action for delivering the item to the employee's supervisor and subsequently to the employee. If the diversity is quite different based on the specific product or business line or if the logical movements along two different paths rejoin each other later or start a second path on the same diagram and, when they meet, continue as one path once again,

- Is there a valid reason for that many visits?
- Is the visit to that business unit a control to help ensure accuracy and correctness, a lack of trust, micromanagement (go-for management style), or possibly something else, like fraud?
  - The go-for management style is a type of micromanagement style where the supervisor says "go for this"; when the person comes back, the manager then says, "go for that"; and so it goes on until the day is done.
  - This type of management style inhibits employee creativity and relieves the employee from any responsibility as they do not have a say in what and how anything occurs, nor will they ever gain enough knowledge of the business process where they could make decisions or help should that manager leave.
- Should we look into the rationale for each stop along the way to ascertain if some of the stops could be combined or even deleted?

Activity: Procurement Audit Planning

Using the procurement process shown in the spaghetti diagram in Figure 4.4b, let us look at other diagrams (Table 4.5) and consider the audit program and how we can improve either the customer satisfaction (effectiveness), the efficiency, and/or the economy.

- As you may note, the controller is a busy person when it comes to the procurement of items for the division.
- You may also note that the division manager is accountable for the total purchasing process.
- You may also note that the controller approves the purchase, distributes the newly purchased asset, and enters the item receipt to the PO system as well as approves the invoice for payment.
- Since the controller has both physical and logical controls of the newly acquired asset, is this some kind of control or would you consider it a SOD risk?

Don't jump to any conclusions based on just this RACI matrix. If you decide that there is a problem and present a recommendation based on this one view of the process, you may find yourself going

Table 4.5 RACI Diagram: Procurement Process

PROCESS	PERSON							
STEP	EMPLOYEE	UNIT MGR.	CONTROLLER	DIVISION MGR.	PURCHASING MGR.	BUYER	RECEIVING DEPT.	ACCOUNTS PAYABLE
1 Purchase request	R	A	I					
2 Business approval		R	R	A				
3 Division approval			I	A				
4 Vendor choice					A	R		
5 Build PO			I		A	R		
6 Issue PO			A	A	R			
7 Receive asset			I				R	
8 Distribute asset			R	A			R	
9 Post-item receipt			R				A	
10 Approve invoice			R	A				
11 Pay invoice			A					R

to the business unit too many times to be taken seriously. As we go along, you may find other things that could be combined with these thoughts that could present a better and more efficient and/or effective adjustment to the process. Don't forget: this is an operational assessment to improve the effectiveness, the efficiency, and the economy. Don't disregard your thoughts about the SOD concern, but set it aside until you gain even more insight into the process and possible root cause. Don't forget that you are still in the planning stage and have yet to move into the analysis phase.

The Customer

To be effective, you have to look at this process from a customer's perspective; therefore, you first have to determine who the customer is and what do they want.

If you are considering the employee as the customer, you are not wrong, but you are not quite there. Since the item is being purchased for a business reason, then that business unit manager is normally responsible for the costs incurred by the members and the business unit as well as the value that they provide to their customers.

I would probably put the business unit manager as the customer for our planning process.

Customer Requirements   Items purchased for a business unit may have different requirements based on the items themselves, including operational features, color, and size. Since we are looking at the procurement process across the organization, we won't look at the details of one order at this time. There are, however, some common questions we could ask the customers concerning the purchasing process itself and the satisfaction levels. We could build a survey to establish some customer service trends, etc. Admittedly, all surveys may have some subjectivity involved; however, take that into consideration as you assess the survey results.

The general customer requirements of a procurement process include that the appropriately requested item be provided and ready to use on a customer requested date at a reasonable cost in proper working order.

You could ask general questions to ascertain the business unit involvement to set up a segmented review based on many items or high-value items or rare use of the procurement process.

- In your opinion was the price for the item reasonable?
  - If the price was not comparable to what you expected, was it higher or lower?
  - If the price was not comparable to what you expected, was your opinion based on current research, past purchases, Internet search, etc.?
- Did the item purchased have the features and functionality that you outlined in your purchase request?
  - If not, were you consulted with respect to the change in features or of price?
  - Was the item usable for your business process?
    - If not, was the price reduced enough to satisfy your business need?
- Did the item that you request arrive within a reasonable amount of time so as not to delay your business use?
  - If the item arrived later than desired, was there a satisfactory explanation?
  - If the item arrived later than desired, did it affect your business plans and priorities?
- Was the purchasing unit responsive to your questions and/or concerns?
- Would you congratulate the purchasing team with a job well done based on your order(s)?

Please note that even though we are focusing on the procurement process during this activity, the same type of questions can be used for any activity as long as you focus on the customer for that activity. You should not focus totally on the IT environment in response to the IT involvement of a business operation; however, you can look at the interaction and the impact that the IT environment has on the business need to service their customers. If one business unit requires additional IT resources, an upgrade to the bandwidth or responsiveness of the infrastructure may benefit the total organization as you expand the capacities.

Everything must feed back to the organization's strategy and goals.

SIPOC Chart: Procurement Process

Table 4.6 is a SIPOC matrix of the procurement steps necessary to complete the purchase of an item for the business unit.

You may note that each step in the spaghetti diagram and/or the VSM diagram may not be depicted in the SIPOC diagram. The differences are normally attributed from the fact that each process may take multiple steps within the process using the same raw material or input (a.k.a. KPIVs) to create the output (a.k.a. KPOVs).

Always remember that nothing is accomplished in this world without a process; a process is one or more steps that can spawn other processes to complete its goals; and the spawned processes could return to the original process or go on without returning to the original process.

Based on the SIPOC diagram in Table 4.6, do you see redundancies or issues?

Table 4.6 SIPOC: Procurement Process

STEP	SOURCE	INPUT	PROCESS STEP	OUTPUT	CUSTOMER
1	Supply cabinet	Requisition form	Order an item	Requisition	Supervisor
2	Employee	Requisition form	Business approval	Approved acquisition	Division controller
3	Division controller	Financially approved requisition	Assign buyer	Approved requisition	Buyer
4	Vendors	Bids denoting cost and delivery time, features, and functions	Buyer analyzes suppliers	PO	Procurement application
5	Purchase supervisor	Approved PO	Division order	PO	Vendor
6	Vendor	Ordered item	Product delivery	Ordered product	Division controller
7	Division controller	Product validation	Enter receipt	PO receipt	Procurement application
8	Vendor	PO and shipping documents	Request for payment	Invoice	Division controller
9	Vendor	Invoice	Payment authorization	Approved invoice	Accounting
10	Accounting	Approved invoice	Accounts payable (AP) application system	Check	Vendor

Consider our definition of a process, which states that a process is one or more steps that take input or raw material and create output of a higher value to the customers.

As you look at each step, do you notice any areas that take a KPIV and provide the same KPOV?

If so, as you progress into the fieldwork stage, you should consider removing the step or combining the step with other similar steps to gain efficiency. This is especially true when you consider the number of controls that may have been put in place over the years due to defects in the process or some other rationale. We will be discussing controls and the risk appetite in further detail during the fieldwork stage (Chapter 5) and the control charting of an operation.

When considering the removal of a step or series of steps in a process, you need to understand the outputs from those steps to help ensure that you don't rob Peter to pay Paul.

Let us look at the VSM of the purchasing process shown in Figure 4.5, which depicts the current process including the average time for each step, the times between steps, and the total cycle time along with the process value time. Please note that the times are averaged and the average time for an e-mail to be sent and read was determined to be 12 minutes, whereas the postal service delivery time averaged out as 3 days or 1440 minutes based on an 8-hour day. Since we have no insight into the vendor processes, we cannot consider their process as either valued or waste. As you may note by the annotation in the step boxes, there are very limited number of (VA) steps in the process denoted by (VA) to denote (customer value add) shown in the VSM.

You may also note that I have provided an annotation of (Vendor) to denote the time that the outside vendor uses for the total process. Since these steps are out of our control, it is likely that we will not be able to improve those areas.

If we have a strong relationship with specific vendors, we may be able to build a supply chain environment with your major suppliers. The approach to supply chain management is enough to fill another book, so we won't cover that here.

As you will also notice, there are a number of steps that have (BV) in the description. The steps that include (BV) are considered business value adds. As I mentioned earlier, you probably

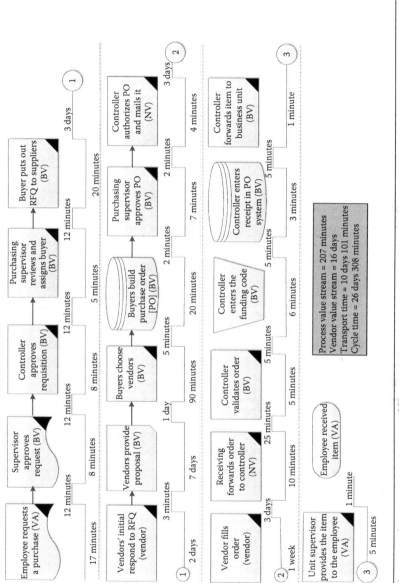

Figure 4.5 Value stream mapping—procurement process. RFP: request for proposal; RFQ: request for quotation.

won't want to remove any value add steps focused on what is CTQ and provided to the customer; however, most business value adds should be reviewed to determine if they are still of value or to determine if they can be combined to make them more efficient or effective.

As I see it, any process should be made up of two types of value steps:

1. Value add to the customer—A step to provide a quality product or service to the customer
2. Business value add—A control to help ensure that you can continuously provide the highest-quality yet economical product or service to those customers

As you see from the value stream mapping, you have a total of 206 minutes during the procurement processing cycle that adds value to either the customer (requestor) or the business out of a 26-day 303-minute process. Considering an 8-hour day, that equates to a total of 12,788 minutes for the average ordering process with an internal value stream including the vendor time of 7887 minutes or an efficiency rating of 61% efficiency. Based on this percentage, the process spends 39% in transportation time.

As mentioned earlier, any business value items should be reviewed and assessed to determine if the value exceeds the cost of the step.

Please realize that steps for complying with laws and regulations or protecting equipment and personnel from injury may override the ratio of cost to value of a step in the process.

3. No Value—These steps have no known value to the customer or business. If this is true, then it makes sense to eliminate this step; however, please check the SIPOC diagram to help ensure that we are not removing something that provides a resource for other future steps.

When I was a teenager in New York City, a lawyer there brought up the fact that the law stated that whenever a train car crossed a public street, they must have a horseman in front and behind the conveyance with a red lantern during the day and a lit lantern after nightfall. The lawyer also stated that there were many violations of this law on the west side of New York City near the docks and the police were not enforcing the law.

Needless to say, the warehouse owners and dockside folks hired riders and horses from the Central Park stables to ride in front and behind the train cars as they were moved across each city street until they could get the law removed.

The letter of the law doesn't always provide the value that the intent of the law is supposed to provide. When you consider the New York law about the horsemen and the trains, they were controls of that day. The horsemen with the lanterns probably saved lives and property back in the days of the horse and carriage, but the control was outdated long before it was finally removed from the law. Look at your organizations and determine how many procedures had value in the past, but are still intact and still part of the published procedures.

During audits that I can recall, I reviewed business continuity and risk management plans and found them totally outdated. The business continuity plans (BCPs) focused on the organization that had changed physical locations, software applications, and computer mainframe systems, yet the plans were still there and they were given to me as corroboration of their process during an audit and SAS 70 assessment.

As you review our VSM, you may notice that the controller is extremely involved in the procurement process and does have both physical and logical controls of both the distribution of and the funding for the purchase of any equipment or supply.

This does constitute an SOD risk; therefore, you should consider alternatives.

The Planning Data

It is now time for you to review the planning documents and jot down any thoughts that first initiated your assessment as well as a review of the perspective provided by the tools we used during this planning stage to gain insight into the processes and to help us develop the approach and the fieldwork questions to be answered during the assessment.

(The following space is intentionally blank so that you can provide your thoughts, ideas, and concerns.)

_____

_____

_____

_____

_____

_____

_____

_____

_____

_____

_____

_____

_____

_____

_____

_____

_____

_____

_____

_____

Now here are some of my thoughts as I reviewed the diagrams and matrices created by the Lean Six Sigma tools that we employed.

The RACI Matrix

- You can clearly see that the controller is involved in almost every step of the process. Why is that necessary?
- Ultimately, the division manager is accountable for everything that the controller, the purchasing manager, and the division controller do; however, he or she is not informed of any specific activity.
- You may also note that the division controller has physical control and distributes the asset to the business unit in step 8. The controller also posts the receipt of the asset in step 9,

which shows logical control, as well as performs the approval step for the invoice in step 10.

- It is my belief that if the division controller has the need to commit a fraudulent purchase as well as the rationalization that a fraudulent act is justified, then he or she could do so.
  - The division controller does have the opportunity and security permission to do so.
  - He or she could gain assets that should be the property of the organization.

The SIPOC Matrix

- Reviewing the SIPOC shows the use of a manual form called the requisition form. This has a cost to maintain, update, and store for the business unit's use.
- The requisition form appears to be the basis for the approval of those members interested in the budget and productivity as well as used by the buyer to negotiate with the vendors.
- I would also surmise that most of the data on the requisition form get transferred to the PO and into the purchasing system.
  - *Thought or consideration:* Would it be possible and feasible to have the requisition form be automated as part of the purchasing system and reduce data entry by the business unit manager, the division controller, the purchasing supervisor, and the buyer?

The Spaghetti Diagram

- Even the supervisor, the buyer, the purchasing manager, or the requestor doesn't have as many contact points in the process as the division controller has.
- The spaghetti diagram shows at least six stops in the division controller's office, *three times the number of stops in anyone else's area.*
- *Thought or consideration:* If the receiving department was held responsible for validating the packing list against the order, entering the receipt into the PO system, and sending it to

the business unit, the asset could be available for use about 35 minutes earlier for each division order based on the VSM.

- *Thought or consideration:* If the requisition was automated and included in the purchasing system, the account funding code could be entered by the controller to denote the financial approval and that could save another 11 minutes per order based on the VSM in combination with the spaghetti diagram. This would also reduce the controller's workload for each division purchase.

The VSM

- Since the VSM shows the *as-is* environment with the average time for each step as well as the average time between steps, you can combine your thoughts as shown above with other diagrams and matrices.
- In considering the main players in the procurement process, the VSM shows the receiving section using 10 minutes per order; the controller, 27 minutes per order; the purchasing supervisory, 12 minutes per order; and the buyer, 130 minutes per order.
  - Based on the times, the buyer is the main bottleneck in the process with the division controller the secondary bottleneck. (Bottlenecks will be deeply discussed during our fieldwork stage of the assessment.)
- Based on the previous suggestion about automating the requisition form as part of the purchasing system, the buyer's time may be reduced for up to 20 minutes, reducing the buyer's workload from 130 minutes to between 110 and 120 minutes per order.
- Allowing the receiving department to enter the asset receipt and send the asset to the business unit would reduce the controller's time by almost 10 minutes.

Based on some of our thoughts, I have a concern about the process as it pertains to the division controller. A number of diagrams and matrices show an overburdened division controller, especially if you consider a fairly large division and the number of people in the division that over the year may submit a requisition for parts, services, and/or supplies.

Caution: As we mentioned earlier in the planning stage, I have a high concern that the division controller has both physical control and financial and distribution controls of any asset purchased. This to me is a red flag and a definite SOD environment which could be leveraged to commit a fraudulent act by the controller. Please realize that a red flag does not constitute a fraudulent act. It merely raises a weakness in the process and system in which a controller could commit fraud. As you may be aware, the fraud triangle consists of opportunity, need, and rationalization. The SOD environment provides the opportunity. Based on that, I would recommend providing your concern and the lack of duty segregation to your fraud investigation team and gain their advice. They may be aware of the SOD, and if not, they may want to open an investigation or be more deeply involved during your operational assessment.

Don't forget that if you are an auditor using the International Professional Practices Framework (IPPF) standards, you are required to look for fraud during your normal audit. (See IPPF Standards 1210. A2, 1220.A1, and 2120.) This does not mean that you should start a fraud investigation; it means that you should have the professional knowledge and ability to recognize the red flags that may be prevalent in your industry or the frauds that have been prevalent in the type of business unit that you are assessing.

IT Support of the Business Unit

Before we proceed to the fieldwork stage, we need to discuss the IT environment and the impacts that the ITs have on the business process.

User Perception

Shortly after I retired from the military and started working for an international manufacturing company, I had the opportunity to take a class on data communications taught by Ken Sherman. During the sessions, I mentioned that I had designed some computer networks for my organization using 9600 bits per second (bps) synchronous modems, but our parent organization canceled the modem order and provided some 4800 bps synchronous modems that they had from a previously canceled installation. Ken mentioned that the speed, no matter what speed, may or may not be sufficient. He went on to say, *"What the customer perceives is your reality."*

The computer networking that we set up for the Unisys Corporation A series computers provided a local two-wire direct (TDI) 19,200 bps asynchronous connection for the local users and synchronous or asynchronous connections for geographically separated offices. Within a year following the installation, the division manager at one of the satellite divisions visited their host A series system in Michigan, and when he saw the response time at the local division, he became totally dissatisfied with the response times for his division. I received an urgent call to increase their throughput.

Since we recently replaced an older 4800 bps modem with some newer modems for our Canadian manufacturing plant with the same issues, I was able to upgrade the Milwaukee division's modem using the newer 14,400 bps modem as a replacement for the 4800 bps Codex modem. *Beauty is in the eyes of the beholder.*

It took us all night to get the new environment up and running, but by morning the users could no longer get a cup of coffee while waiting for the screen to refresh. Even though this modem wasn't as fast as the TDI lines they had seen, the division personnel were overwhelmed by the new response time. It was so successful; the division manager took us to dinner at one of the best restaurants in Milwaukee.

IT's Business

It is my belief that IT operations can be assessed based on two very different perspectives. The IT department is, in fact, a *business function* supporting many various customers; therefore, they can be assessed as a business unit with associated processes as well as from each of the organizational business unit's perspective and the impact and support that IT provides to each business unit and each automated process. In the next section we will focus on the IT environment in support of each business process and the impacts that it has on each. In a later chapter we will assess IT as a managed business unit and how the technology business processes as outlined by the COBIT framework. To those non-IT folks, COBIT stands for Control Objectives for Information and Related Technology. COBIT is the baseline framework developed by ISACA for IT management and

IT governance. It is a supporting tool set that allows managers to bridge the gap between control requirements, technical issues, and business risks in support of the IT goals. ISACA was previously an acronym for Information Systems Audit and Control Association; however, they now proceed as the association legally named ISACA.

Background

Before we discuss the IT interface in each business process, we should realize some history about the way business applications are built or at least were built back in the day. Back in the day, IT gurus and programmers were not heavily invested in the business processes. Don't get me wrong; some IT programmers understood the basic processes, just not the various nuisances of each process. As such, they rarely asked the question, "How can we improve the business process while we are developing the program?" They merely developed application systems that mirrored the manual process.

On the same token, the business unit personnel didn't know all the technological capabilities of the IT environment. Also note that many business units didn't want to add a training curve to their staff by major adjustments or reengineering of the process as the process was being developed. They wanted a seamless transition for the current business unit employees. Therefore, in many cases, the process, good, bad, or mediocre, was emulated by automation. Although the physical movement of data was faster, any inefficient steps/processes or single points of failure were still evident in the new expensive automation program. Once the program and associated processes were automated, the complexities to accomplish these inefficient steps were now harder to reengineer or change for the better, yet they were still needed by the organization.

The flip side of the business automation process has been to purchase off-the-shelf (OTS) application software and then have the local IT folks load it and set up the environment. As you probably realize, an OTS application is not designed for your specific operation, especially if you have a unique or strategic process as part of your business model. The OTS software is built for the overall populace based on a survey of various businesses and organizational processes; therefore, your business may not have been one of the models used.

If you expect OTS software to help you strategically, I would tell you that the software will increase your communication capabilities; however, everyone who purchased the same software has the same strategic process as you do.

There is an old proverb based on a study before the change of the century:

- To add security or controls for a process during the business requirement stage costs X.
- To add security or controls for a process during development stage costs 3 times X.
- To add security or controls for a process during the testing stage costs 7 times X.
- To add security or controls for a process during the implementation stage costs 10 times X.
- To add security or controls for a process when it is in production costs 100 times X.

As such, you realize that if you want to improve an automated process once the application is in production, you must get the change through multiple committees with differing agendas. The business unit and the CFO must understand the value of change before they will fund or become champions (white knights) helping the IT folks help the business unit. Even if the business unit changes their process, changing the programs or sometimes building new programs and processes is as expensive as the initial automation to build as well as an added expense to not disrupt the existing process until the full testing cycle is complete.

If you are using OTS software, you don't normally own the source code or the rights to adjust the software. You can request a change from the vendor and if the change is good for all customers, they may make the change. If not, your cost for the change will very likely be expensive. If the change adds to the quality and features that the vendor can sell, your costs may be less, but it is their decision and not yours.

Initially IT should not have asked, *"How does your business process work?"* but should have asked the question, "In an effort to develop a process that will enhance your business unit, *how should the process work?"*

In more recent years, IT has recognized the need for business acumen when automating the business processes and the business unit gurus have learned more and more about automation and computers. Do they know each other's world and, better yet, do they truly care?

To a degree, I would say that they are more aware and when they see an enhancement to their individual objectives, they will listen to each other. As always, the process and the interactions between IT and the business unit must build a win–win scenario or you won't create any synergy.

IT Support Goal

The goal of IT as it pertains to any business unit and business process is to provide the infrastructure to move the data and the associated application program to the businessperson so that the business can service their customers. Data access is a key to the IT service quality. Most business processes are not interested in how the IT gurus accomplish the task; they are interested in getting the data they need, exactly when they need these, in a format that they can use to make decisions and service their business customers. Do you know of any customers that wouldn't want what they want when they want it with the quality that they expect?

IT and digital technology provides the connectivity from the user to the application that can process the data and the data themselves.

Data are the key to the organization's use of an IT environment. I use the word *data*, because data do not become information until these are seen by a person who understands the data and can use these to make management decisions or service a customer. To IT, data are a series of bits, bytes, chomps, etc., which represent digits in a local language or computer control characters.

CIA and IT

Data are the core of the IT industry. The IT folks don't use data unless the data are about their physical technological environment. Throughout the IT age, the technologist has focused on three things (another pyramid) to measure their success. They sometimes refer to the trilogy (three areas of concern) using the acronym CIA.

- C stands for confidentiality. One primary goal of the technologies is to provide the data to the businesspeople who own or need to use those data as information to accomplish the tasks for the data owner and no one else.
- I stands for integrity. By this I refer to maintaining the integrity of the organization's data no matter what these are or how these are presented or acted upon. For example,
  - If the principal accumulates interest in a savings account, the data should have a correct and accurate measure of the authorized interest and an accurate mathematical update to the principal when the interest is added to the principal.
- A stands for availability. The data need to be available to the authorized users when they need or want to view these. The authorized user (IT customer) should be able to use that data when they need these and the data should be presented to them in a format that makes sense to that businessperson.

Communication is accomplished only when the symbols and the media used portray the same meaning to the receiver as it does to the sender.

The IT environment has a cost as it pertains to the business process as well as a cost to the organization for the IT resources, including the applications, networking equipment, and servers. The costs of providing networks, servers, firewalls, routers, computer gurus, etc., will not be included in this chapter. The technology resources as in people, wide area network (WAN), LAN, wiring, Fiber, and equipment will be covered in a later chapter.

Within this chapter, we will focus on the costs to the business process in consideration of the time to transfer data from place to place and to provide the data access.

The cost to the business application is the time that is required to bring the data and application information from the source to the user. The technological delays are normally referred to as latency delay.

When a business unit or process is considered, IT should be included in the initial planning process. The response time to present the data to the business unit person can ultimately affect the productivity of that businessperson and the business unit process. I would recommend that for the assessment, you look at the IT involvement supporting the business process as well as the impact on the process should the IT environment become unavailable. The business unit and technology management should consider the technical impact on the business to determine if the IT team should be involved in the initial business assessment as an integrated business process or if the technical integration does not warrant that involvement.

If the current or planned utilization is and will be negligible, I would recommend that an IT operational assessment would waste resources. In the following, I show some initial metrics to review prior to including an IT assessment within a business unit operational assessment.

Metrics: Business Dependency on IT

- Business unit impact on the organization and customers
- The number of transactions over a period for the business application
- The average dollar impact of computer transactions, if applicable
- The average message size per transaction
- The average messages over a period
- The application response time to requests (baseline versus current)
- The user response time for requests (baseline versus current)
- Revenue or budget of the business unit
- Network speed of LAN and any WAN activities
- Cost of business unit support (IT equipment and personnel)

Since it takes resources to accomplish any operational assessment, you want to determine up front or in the early stages whether the IT portion of an assessment can add value or it would be a waste of resources and dollars. Remember that the organization's success metric is net profit, which equals revenue minus operating expenses. Operating expenses include the resources to accomplish an operational assessment.

The information and related technologies moving business and/or customer data from an organization's centralized repository to the business user have a cost that encompasses the communications equipment and a time delay to get the data to the businessperson's workstation.

When my wife and I decide to visit my son and our grandchildren in Baton Rouge, Louisiana, we can use our global positioning system (GPS) to estimate our arrival time. The GPS uses the speed limits for the roadways it chose to estimate the arrival. The algorithm is based on adding the miles for all segments divided by the speed limit for each of those segments.

That type of algorithm works fine, except for the fact that we have to load the car, stop at stop signs, adjust our speed based on traffic, detours, heavy traffic tie-ups, stopping for nature breaks, refueling at gas stations, accidents on the road, and unloading at the other end.

Similarly, the data requested at the user's workstation must go through a series of steps that delay the data movement process. The delays are commonly referred to as latency delays. The fact is that the request must go through a serialization changing the request and any parameters for the request from American Standard Code for Information Interchange (ASCII) or Extended Binary Coded Decimal Interchange Code (EBCDIC) (the computer's internal code) to data bits for transmission (serialization). Then if packetizing is necessary to meet the maximum message size (based on protocol, etc.), there is delay to break up the message into the maximum allowable packet size (payload), at which time the message can be sent across the wire or transmission medium, which adds a delay for each mile the data must move. At the receiving end, the message bits must be recognized as data and the bits commuted to digits and placed in a holding area until the complete message has arrived. This could be directly dependent on the number of packets to be created at the sending side. Once all packets are received, the message must be serialized to build the electrical pulses into digital data. Then the parity and other checks are done to help ensure that the received message is truly equal to the message that was originally sent; the message can go to the application, which processes the message and then sends a response that goes through the same process of packetizing, serializing, and transmitting to the requestor. These delays are the main portion of the latency delays. To fully understand the process, we should recognize that to communicate across a network, the communication programming has a tendency to follow the Open Systems Integration (OSI) model developed by the International Organization for Standardization (ISO). Yes, you read it correctly. The ISO developed the OSI model. Say that fast three times.

The OSI Model

The data communication environment is based on the seven-level OSI model denoting the following:

1. Physical level—Transmits the serial bitstreams on a physical medium, including radio-frequency signals, LAN, WAN, wire type, and voltage requirements for transmissions. Hubs and repeaters work at level 1.

2. Data link level—Provides the transfer of units of information to the other end of the physical link (Ethernet [IEEE 802.3], token ring [802.5], point to point, etc.). Bridges and switches work at level 2.

3. Network level—Routes information packets across the network; network interfaces such as Internet protocol (IP). Routers and bridge router (brouter) combinations work at this level. Some marketers claim that their switches work at this level; however, the switches appear to be a combination of router and switch. The Internet is a series of networks connected via a mesh network of routers. Most public networks route traffic based on availability and response time; therefore, they check routes for congestion and waiting message traffic.

4. Transport level—Provides end-to-end data transmission integrity. Transmission control protocol (TCP) and user datagram protocol work at this level. Gateways work at this level to help ensure integrity as data move between IP and protocol conversions (mainframe, LANs, WANs, IP, etc.).

5. Session level—Establishes, maintains, and manages session between the user and the other entities (website, application, data source, etc.).

6. Presentation level—Provides data representation between systems. File transfer protocol, remote terminal control protocol,

simple mail transfer protocol, name service protocol, and simple network management protocol are portions of the TCP/IP suite of applications that encompass levels 5, 6, and 7.

7. Application level—Provides the user interface and specific services so that the user can attain the application services.

Each layer or level of the OSI model communicates across the network with the same layer at each node or entities; therefore, the session layer at the user workstation communicates with the session layer at the application or website server.

As you can imagine, each level or layer takes a certain amount of time to accomplish its process. For the sending node something is either checked or added (a header in some cases); then at the receiving end, something else is done to the message (removing the header and checking correctness, etc.). Although this may take a millisecond or microseconds, those portions of a minute add up when you consider the number of transactions and users online at the same time.

The time delay is referred to as a latency delay.

The speed of light is considered the fastest-moving entity in our universe. You realize this fact every time you hear the thunder that follows the lightning and realize that the lightning has missed you.

Communication wiring cannot equal the speed of light. Even fiber-optic transmissions can attain only about 60% velocity due to the electronics necessary to transform the data bits into light at the sending node and then at the receiving end, to morph the light back to electronic impulses as bits and bytes.

The physical layer is typically a connectivity medium of wire or fiber optics. The wire, depending on its construct (wire gauge, copper, aluminum, coax, etc.), can attain between 40% and 80% of the speed of light. Although fiber optics transmit light, they do so at a velocity factor of about 60% of the speed of light due to the electronics necessary to convert the bytes to light and then morph the light back to an electronic digital format.

No matter how fiber optics improve the technology and electronics, I doubt if they will ever reduce the latency delay to a negligible number.

Network Speed   Based on the speed of the LAN or WAN and the size of the message, you can gain some insight into the time it should take for that message to traverse from the sender to the receiver using a formula like [message size in bits]/[speed of the network]. This should give you an idea of the maximum message capacity. As similarly stated by the old saying "a chain is only as strong as its weakest link," the speed of the network message transfer is only as fast as the slowest link in the network.

If you have an Ethernet LAN with network interface cards running at 100 Mbps attached to a WAN with a 56 kbps speed and the other entity in the communication is across the WAN, then your maximum throughput is based on the 56,000 bps and not the 100,000,000 bps LAN speed.

Needless to say, this maximum throughput does not take into consideration the latency delays in most networks.

Also, realize that whenever a digital connection is established, the communication devices decide on a maximum transmission unit or MTU. The MTU is negotiated between the devices and greatly depends on the protocol that the devices utilize. Ethernet has a message maximum of 1500 bytes.

Latency Delays

The latency delay of networks is the overhead due to the diversity of a network. Throughout a network, the communication equipment must accomplish many network management routines plus the serialization of the message; the packetizing of a message, should that be necessary; and the routing of the single message or message packets across a wide area take time away from the maximum capacity.

A major portion of the latency delay is the propagation of the data messaging. The rest of the latency delay is due to the time delays for the file or application server to deliver the data and/or application executable to the user and their workstation or PC, laptop, phone, etc.

The propagation delay deals with the handling of the data to be moved or copied from one workstation to another node in the network or even the WWW. Data within a computer system or server are normally dealt with digit by digit or byte by byte where each digit or byte consists of 8 bits configured as either on or off bits. The computer uses a number of bits, normally 8 bits, to define a digit to denote 0 through 9, a through z, and a number of visible and invisible special characters. The computer moves the bits as digits from disk or some storage place to the main memory area so that the central processor can access those digits. The original computers could move data one digit at a time or 8 bits per move; later the IBM XT could move 16 bits or two digits until Intel provided a Pentium system that could move 32 bits at the same time. Their motherboard (backplane of the PC) could move the data from disk to memory and back with basically four digits per move. Later Digital Equipment Corporation (DEC) produced a chip that they called Alpha, which could move 64 bits with reduced instruction set computing (RISC) to replace their 32-bit VAX complex instruction set computer. RISC was embraced by IBM, HP, etc. DEC did license the use of the Alpha technology and they were acquired by Compaq, who subsequently merged with HP in May 2002.

Many people believe that computers are so fast that after you put something in, it is ready almost immediately. Can a computer compute a payroll and develop payroll checks and associated payroll lists ready for printing faster than a human can? Of course, it can, but not instantaneously.

Since many people see time as hours, minutes, and seconds, they have a tendency to disregard the considerations that you may be able to reduce the computing time by 2 ms. (For your edification, 2 ms equal 0.002 s.) What is the value of reducing something by 2 or even 5 ms? When you consider that according to the automated teller machine (ATM) statistics shown by Len Penzo, "Trends Today," in March 2, 2012, ATMs process approximately 900 ATM transactions with an average of $60 per withdrawal. The total number of ATMs in use is 2.2 million. If we reduce the communication speed for each transaction by 2 ms, you have 2,200,000 times 0.002 s, which equals 4400 s or 73⅓ minutes or 1 hour and 13 minutes. Please realize that a transaction normally takes at least two transmissions: the transaction request and then the authorization request by the computer in charge; therefore, the actual time savings over time could be 2 hours and 26 minutes.

Table 4.7   ATM Ownership

COMPANY	NUMBER OF ATMs
Cardtronics	32,856
Payment Alliance	26,000
Bank of America	18,426
JPMorgan Chase	14,144

In 1 hour and 13 minutes or more, we can handle more transactions for other customers, or we may find that by reducing the transaction time or communication time, we can continue to service our customer's needs with a more economical or narrower bandwidth. Who knows what you can determine if you have the metrics and common sense?

Table 4.7 shows the five largest ATM owners listed in 2012.

If the 12,353 Wells Fargo ATMs processed the 900 average transactions with a 2 ms reduction in response time, the processing would save 22,235.4 s or 6.1765 hours. What could your network and data systems do with an extra 6 hours each day?

Any savings for the individual business processes may or may not be as fruitful as the reduction shown in our ATM computations above. The savings or not would be directly dependent on the number of transactions over a time frame. This could be tracked on a continuous basis using a control chart we will be discussing in Chapter 5.

Serialization

Although a computer deals with characters or digits/bytes, those characters are transmitted through the communication network bit by bit. The act of taking the characters in the message and building the message content into bits to be sent is called serializing the message. The process then sends the message bit by bit across the wire or communication link. In addition to the serialization, most communication processes have a maximum message load. In other words, each message can consist of only a certain number of characters (8 bits per character). For a LAN running Ethernet, the message load maximum is about 1500 characters. If the message exceeds the maximum characters per message, then the message is divided into multiple messages for the transfer mechanism to handle. The division of the message into multiple messages is called packetizing. Each message packet is numbered so that the message can be rebuilt at the receiving end should the packets not arrive in the exact sequence that they were sent. When the message is received at the destination or sometimes at intermediate nodes (store-and-forward e-mail server, etc.), the message is reconstructed and a checksum number is tested against the original message checksum to help ensure accuracy (the I in CIA).

The division and reconstruction process itself delays the transmission. Since the sending communication controller is responsible for sending the total message and ensure that it arrives as it was sent, one or more checks are created at the sending communication device including parity and checksum totals of all the bits that were sent. The receiving communication device will normally respond to each packet with an acknowledgment of checked parity and checksum. The sending communication device in an X.25 protocol may not send the second packet until it receives the acknowledgment (AK) that the first packet is good. This occurs for each succeeding packet; therefore, the larger the messages, the more packets and the more AKs need to come back before the last packet is sent. A total checksum of some sort may be sent with the last packet to help ensure that the total message has not changed during any transmission. When the receiving communication device gets the last packet, it compiles the messages into the full message and computes the checksum to ensure that it equals the total checksum sent from the other end. If the checksums don't match, the sender starts all over again with a retransmission. If everything matches, then the physical transmission is considered complete and the sending device can transmit other message traffic.

To determine the time delay of the serialization of a message, you can divide [message size in bits] by [transmission speed in bits per second]. The result will provide you with an approximate serialization delay. Therefore, a 1500-byte message going across a T1 circuit (1,544,000 bits/second) would result in an 8-millisecond serialization delay [(1500 bytes × 8)/1,544,000 bits/second = 0.00777 seconds or approximately 8 milliseconds]. Note that the 1500-byte message must be transformed into bits by multiplying the bytes by 8 (8 bits per byte).

Packetizing

As we mention previously, messages that exceed the MTU must be divided into packets and transmitted across the medium separately then combined to reestablish the original message at the receiving node.

Cases 4.1 and 4.2 outline a couple of issues that I or my team encountered some years ago. Case 1 deals with the packetizing of a print file, where the process did not work efficiently to packetize a 1800 byte per disk block print file into a number of 300-byte messages for transmission over a dial-up line. The computer system appeared to packetize other text files appropriately, but the print files would take forever to complete the transmission to the receiving computer systems.

CASE 4.1: PRINT FILE PACKETIZING

When I worked in manufacturing we centralized the payroll system at the headquarters. The print files for the checks, check-to-bank listing, and pay listings were then transferred to each data center via the mainframe transfer application (remote job entry) using an autodial unit and a 4800 bps synchronous modem. This was the 80s.

Since we dealt with strict labor union rules governing late payroll deliveries, we had to have them ready on Thursday by 2 PM local time. If we were late, we owed the workers next week's salary equal to this week's salary, but they didn't need to work that next week. We almost missed it a few times due to the time that it took to transfer the files; therefore, the IT directory asked me to see if I could speed up the file transfer systems.

I noted that the print files on disk had multiple records per block totaling to 1800 characters per block, whereas the transfer mechanism was set to send 300 characters per packet. That meant that the mainframe software had to packetize each disk file (multiple blocks of data) to send and then rebuild the print file at the receiving end.

Rather than just increasing the modem speed, I built a program that I called Print Compression to repackage the print files to 300 bytes at the sending data center and another one named Print Expansion, which repackage the file to a normal print file.

I expected a 20% to 30% reduction in transfer time, but during the testing phase I found that the files that normally took 1½ hours took only 20 minutes to transfer, whereas the files that had taken 3½ hours took about 40 minutes to transfer. The mainframe program to packetize the message was too diverse to handle the print files efficiently.

You may note from the packetizing process that a large message creating a large number of messages with a response to each packet can take time from the requested transaction being consummated. Keep the message traffic as short and as sweet as possible.

All because memory and disk pricing has been reduced, it doesn't mean that you should use it all up. In today's "I expect it now" society, response time is as important as accuracy and correctness. Look at the number of people with smartphones in hand with thumbs working up a storm.

Case 4.2 shows that the packetizing process and the response to each packet can take up valuable time, which we cannot afford if we were to meet the VOC. The receiving end had to respond with an acknowledgement to each packet as it arrived before the sending node would send the next packet. Each individual response along with a final response that the total message or file arrived with the appropriate checksum added multiple message traffic for one large message being sent.

Please note that most modems use about a 5 ms delay from message transmission to become ready to receive in a dial-up scenario. That means that each packet will wait at least 5 ms for any AK or NAK (nonacknowledgment). Case 4.2 shows a case where we had to move 1 MB of data per minute to meet the customer goals and have the data warehouse ready for user access by 7:30 each morning (VOC).

CASE 4.2: TRANSMISSION SPEED IS NOT ALWAYS THE ANSWER

Over the years I have found that modem speed is not always the way to speed up transmissions or message traffic. While working for First Union National Bank, we had a timing issue with the data transfers from the various mainframes to the data warehouse that we were building. One of the parameters that we had to work with was the fact that the transfer of data could not be started until the end-of-night processing for each system was completed. The customer need was to have the data loaded to the data warehouse and ready for use by 7:30 AM eastern time each weekday morning. To accomplish this task, we needed to transmit a megabyte of data each minute from each of the computer mainframe systems. Although the bandwidth seemed to be adequate for accomplishing this feat, we determined that since each message required an acknowledgment by the receiving system prior to the next message being sent, the waits for each response appeared to be the major delaying factor. We discussed the issue with the technology teams working with the data communication handlers of the mainframe, the systems architecture team, and the network gurus and decided that it would not be detrimental to other business processes if the tracking would respond to every 10 messages for the packetized data transmission. The risk of doing this was that if any of the messages didn't transfer correctly, all 10 messages would have to be retransmitted. The mitigating factor was the fact that all the geographical locations for our data were digital communication lines; therefore, some of the retransmissions found in an older analog communications environment should not be prevalent in our scenario.

Transmission Lines

For many instances, people have a tendency to just increase line speed or equipment speeds to help fix slow computer response time issues, and in some cases, that may fix the issue; however, in some cases that may just be a waste of time and dollars. Admittedly, I designed my first LAN to employ Ethernet protocol and category 5 unshielded twisted pair telephone wiring so that when the 100 Mb Ethernet electronics were developed I wouldn't have to rewire the building to upgrade the data transmission speed to 100 Mbps.

For many years a LAN was comparatively inexpensive as opposed to a WAN. In many areas, the costs were high and the data would have to traverse over three or more telephone company (telco) lines to get to the destination. You would be charged a cost to cover your local telco as an interexchange carrier (IXC) charge to interchange your message traffic to your long-line carrier such AT&T, MCI, and Sprint.

The long-line carrier would add their cost and then pass the signal to the local telco at the receiving end and another IXC charge would be incurred to cover the transmission charge to move the data from the long-line vendor point of presence to your building and office.

Luckily, you would work only with the long-line vendor and they would compile all the charges into one bill as well as be your single point of contact for any issues, problems, enhancements, increased speed or bandwidth, etc.

Now with the digital environment for wide area connectivity, most of the lines across the country are digital circuits, which have reduced the error rates that were prevalent in the older analog systems and increased the network speed of most transmissions. If you do service some rural area of an international country with antiquated analog communication lines, you may have issues trying to provide high-speed data transmissions. Although most analog and all digital lines will transmit at 9600 bps if they are operationally sound, you can run into issues in some analog areas going above 4800 bps.

I did run into a situation where AT&T sold a state-of-the-art 19,200 bps Paradyne Modem to a subsidiary company of my organization and they asked me for assistance while I was in town with our manufacturing plant.

The word *modem* is a contraction of the word *modulate* and the word *demodulate*. A modem takes the digitally formatted computer data and modulates the data into a bit-by-bit radio-type frequency transmission that can be moved over telephone wires using a carrier frequency (high-pitched sound). The modem also demodulates the sound type signal back into digital computer data.

CASE 4.3: FAST DOESN'T ALWAYS MEAN FAST

While at a manufacturing plant, our national sales subsidiary asked me to look at their network. They purchased the fastest state-of-the-art modems they could find, yet their response time and throughput were less than adequate. The issue appeared to be the fact that the analog telecommunication environment in the local area could not support the higher speed; therefore, when the modem was set to 19,200 bps, there were a number of retransmissions. If fact, there were so many retransmissions that the actual throughput of the data went at a rate of 4,800 bps and less. I recommended that rather than setting the modem at the highest speed (19,200 bps), set it at 9,600 bps. A voice-grade communication line should allow that speed without difficulty. They did and their response times became totally adequate for their usage.

When they moved their office to a newer location in a more metropolitan area, they didn't seem to experience any issues with the higher-speed transmissions.

Routing across a WAN

Moving message traffic across a WAN requires routing from network node to node. Each router maintains a dynamic routing table and checks the next router to determine if it can handle more messages. The dynamic router can also learn new paths to get its message traffic to the appropriate destination. The average delay of a high-performance router has been gauged at about 200 milliseconds or 0.2 second. When you consider that an average backbone network has routers about every 800 kilometers, the distance between the sending node and the receiving node can have a major impact on the latency delays. Eight hundred kilometers equals about 497 miles. Copper wire going through a dial-up network has a latency delay as well. When the United States had mostly analog telephone services, the latency delay of the wired telephone system I had used an estimated propagation delay of about 4.5 milliseconds every 100 miles or 0.045 millisecond for each mile. The microwave of that time was considered to have about 5-millisecond delay per hop, whereas a satellite data transfer had about a 300-millisecond delay per hop. You should realize that since the microwave hop went against the D layer of the atmosphere, the distance between hops was much smaller than in a satellite transfer of data.

Business Continuity Planning

If an unforeseen or an unwanted situation occurs, the organization should have a feasible plan in place to deal with unplanned events. You could say that this is a part of risk management or just good sense. Although the probability of experiencing an earthquake in the East Coast is unlikely, the probability of having a hurricane, tornado, power outage, fire, or theft is fairly high. How will your organization deal with these natural, artificial, or systemic disasters?

Natural disasters happen all over the world in varying degrees and impact. Whether a natural disaster is a tornado, hurricane, cyclone, snowstorm, ice storm, etc., it directly affects your organization's ability to serve the customers. Whether it is a daylong snowstorm in North Carolina that inhibits the employees from getting to work or your customers from ordering or accepting deliveries or destroys your facility and the capability to produce your product or deliver your service, you need to consider this as part of your operational risks and create a plan to deal with the unplanned and definitely unwanted event.

For most organizations, the ability to continuously support the internal or external customer requirements is of the utmost importance. To continually provide for the customer, most organizations develop a BCP in an effort to stay in business. During the 1990s, there was a study using some organizations which had experienced contingency situations, such as an earthquake, prolonged electrical outages, tornados, and fire. The study concluded that the organizations which had not been able to continue servicing their customers experienced an immediate loss of revenue as well as a residual loss of expected future revenue with an average of 8.6% across industries. Although the article did not specify the exact percentage, it went on to say that financial organizations had a higher loss of future customers than other industries. When I worked in business continuity planning for the First Union National Bank (now part of Wells Fargo) IT division, I used to tell our business managers that "customers will stay longer if they love you, but when you cost them money the love becomes extremely rare."

To me, business continuity is

"business as usual under unusual conditions."

During the planning stage of the assessment, you should try to get copies of the business unit and/or technical BCP as well as the business impact analysis (BIA) documentation.

The BIA is a risk assessment to show the impact of each and every business process on the organization's ability to survive as an organization.

The BIA is used to develop the prioritization of each business unit based on the loss to the organization. In addition, the BIA would normally include those processes of which the business unit relies on as well as the equipment, information, special forms, and technologies that the business unit must have to succeed. Without knowing the prerequisites of the business process, the process could be established; however, it would not have the resources or mandatory requirements necessary for the unit to service their customers.

In many cases, the business unit could advise the organization as to when the equipment, forms, desks, etc., would be needed based on when the impacts would be felt by the business unit or the organization.

That is to say, an office with 20 workers may require only 5 desks, computer, etc., for the first 10 days, 15 desks in 30 days, and the full complement would not be required during a contingency situation. As for the technologies, 3 PCs and the application may be necessary within one business day and they would need 12 PCs by the last day of any month.

During the planning stage, I recommend that you review the BCP and determine the following:

- When was the BCP developed?
- Had the BCP been reviewed/modified within the past year?
- Does the BCP reflect the current business environment?
- Does the BCP reflect the current technical environment and application?
- Has the organization tested the BCP recently?
- Were all major aspects of the plan recently tested?
- Was the testing successful?
  - To me, the BCP test is successful if the plans worked as written for a diverse scenario or if the team used the plan with some adjustments and the adjustment were added to the plan.
  - Also, I recommend that the scenario for each periodic test be adjusted to help ensure that the plan is diverse enough to handle different scenarios.

Insanity: doing the same thing over and over again and expecting different results.

Albert Einstein

- Did the BIA provide insight into the process dependencies?
- Did the BIA provide the data used to prioritize the recovery or continuity planning process?
- Did the BIA reflect the same business unit positions as the annual or periodic organizational risk assessment done by the auditors?

The rationale for some of the questions is based on my experiences. While working for KPMG, I had two clients that had BCPs that were well written; however, the technology plans were based on an application that had been replaced during the prior year. In fact, one of the best documented BIA and business resumption plans was provided by a banking client. The bank used word processing software to do the BIA survey, prioritize the recovery plan, and provide a plan that even integrated each business unit and IT step in the processes. As I read the plan, I was totally elated to see such details. As I got to the evacuation plan, I was confused about the mention of the elevator. The building was a modern one-story structure. I went on to read through the application recovery and realized that the plan was based on a software application and database that they no longer used. The bank had converted to the Fiserv application when they moved into their new building, a one-story structure about 10 miles from their previous downtown multistory banking building. Needless to say, even though it was the best documented plan that I had seen to date, I had to rate the BCP as unsatisfactory. The plan did not reflect the current reality.

Planning Summation

Please realize that we should not provide recommendations based merely on the review of some of the planning tools. Unless you see a risk or issue that needs immediate attention for safety or functionality, I recommend that you wait until you complete most of your fieldwork prior to sharing your thoughts, ideas, and recommendation with your business partners or any senior leaders with a vested business interest.

Base your test plan on what you learned or surmised during the planning stage. You may find that there are valid reasons for the way the process has evolved over time which may discount your initial impressions or concerns. As we said earlier, "Seek first to understand."

Since one of the procurement customer concerns is the time that it takes to gain the asset, we should look at any redundancies as well as automating the requisition process to reduce duplicated data entry as well as automated business and financial approvals. Design your interviews to ascertain the key business member's assessment as well as the purchasing system application developers to ascertain the feasibility of your first thoughts about the requisition forms versus an online request form. Is that process feasible, economical, and efficient?

Similar to a risk and controls assessment, the controls and any adjustments to the process may have a cost; therefore, the cost should be weighed against the long- and short-term benefits. Get a better understanding of this during the fieldwork.

Now that we are building the assessment plan, we can start to move into the fieldwork phase of the assessment and the tools that may help us understand the business and customer issues as well as ascertain the bottlenecks and the capacities of the people, technical environment, and processes involved in servicing the customer.

5

OPERATIONAL ASSESSMENT FIELDWORK

As we move into the fieldwork stage of an assessment, we must revisit and base our testing and analysis on the problem(s) outlined in our project charter. If you were doing a fieldwork testing in an audit, you would focus your testing on the most serious risk and how the business is managing that risk. Similarly, in an operational assessment, you need to focus on gaining an in-depth insight into the root causes of the problem before developing any recommendations.

To help gain the necessary metrics (continuous or discrete), you need to gain an idea of the root cause. For any process, you can start your research with a failure mode and effect analysis or FMEA.

Failure Mode and Effect Analysis

The FMEA technique should provide you with a priority list of the possible failures and the effects each failure may have on the business process, along with insights into the controls currently in place as well as the possible outcomes or impacts on the process or the organization. You can use a brainstorming session to establish the key failure events that could occur to a business process. (More details about brainstorming will be discussed later in this chapter.)

The FMEA will show you the process dependencies so you can identify the critical key process input variables (KPIVs). You can also evaluate the risks associated with any defects. This may also show you the relationships between the different KPIVs and/or different processes.

To develop an FMEA, you must build a table to identify the following items:

- Potential failure modes—Ways in which the product, service, or process might fail

- Potential effects of each failure (consequences of that failure) and rate their severity
- The causes of the effects and rate their likelihood of occurrence
- Your ability to detect each failure mode
- Product of the three numbers together to determine the risks of each failure mode or the risk priority number (RPN)
- Ways to reduce or eliminate the risks associated with high RPNs

A sample of your severity rating scale might be as follows:

10. Injury to a customer or an employee
9. Illegal or against an industry regulation
8. Render the product or the service unfit for use by the customer or anyone
7. Cause extreme customer dissatisfaction
6. Result in partial malfunction
5. Cause a loss of performance likely to result in a customer complaint or reject
4. Cause a minor performance loss
3. Cause a minor nuisance; can overcome it with limited or no loss
2. Go unnoticed; minor effect on performance
1. Go unnoticed and not affect the performance

A sample occurrence rating scale is shown in the following:

RATE–TIME PERIOD	PROBABILITY
10. More than once each day	> 30%
9. Once every 3–5 hours	≤ 30%
8. Once per week	≤ 5%
7. Once per month	≤ 1%
6. Once every 3 months	≤ 0.03%
5. Once every 6 months	≤ 1 per 10,000
4. Once per year	≤ 6 per 100,000
3. Once every 1–3 years	≤ 6 per million
2. Once every 3–6 years	≤ 3 per 10 million
1. Once every 6–10 years	≤ 2 per billion

A sample detection rating score scale is as follows:

10. Defect caused by failure is not detected.
9. Occasional units are checked for defects.
8. Units are systematically sampled and inspected.

7. All units are manually inspected.

6. Manual inspection is done with mistake-proof modifications.

5. Process is monitored via a statistical process control (SPC) and is manually inspected.

4. SPC is used with an immediate reaction to out-of-control conditions.

3. SPC out-of-control conditions reacts with a 100% inspection, to find root cause.

2. All units are automatically inspected.

1. Defect is obvious and will be fixed prior to customer delivery.

Although the FMEA technique is primarily used in designing new products or services as well as for business continuity management, it is also a great tool to focus your thoughts about data collection that may be meaningful to our operational assessment. The impact of the KPIVs is critical to the process being reviewed. If we determine that changes in the variables correspond to the changes in throughput or quality, it can help point to the root cause of anomalies in the process (good or bad anomalies). For example, if a supplier delivers a KPIV late or the quality is slightly off, the norm and your throughput or defects are affected due to the timing or quality; then, you learn something that will help you improve the process.

Table 5.1 shows a typical FMEA matrix.

Root Cause Analysis (RCA)

Although the two root cause analysis tools that I recommend are different methodologies and could each stand alone, I find that using them in conjunction with each other provides a better perspective. I will start with the easiest method, similar to the way you might start. It is based on the interview of key personnel who are actually involved in the process. Although this should include process and business managers, I recommend that your interviews must include the person responsible for the step as shown in the RACI diagram. The frontline personnel know what happened; whereas managers and leaders have an idea of what happened and when. Using the five-whys technique during the interview may point to the root cause.

Table 5.1 FMEA = Failure Mode Effect Analysis

FMEA analysis		
Process	Date:	Start
Team	Date:	

PROCESS OR ITEM NO.	PFM	PEF	SR	PC	OR	CC	DR	RPN	RA	RESPONSIBILITY	TD	PAT	SR	OR	DR	RPN

Note. CC: current control; DR: detection rate; OR: occurrence rate; PAT: post action taken; PC: potential causes; PEF: potential effect of failure; PFM: potential failure mode; RA: recommended action; SR: severity rate; TD: target date.

The Five Whys

The five-whys technique in RCA uses a questioning atmosphere to first ascertain what happened and then using the effect to ask the question why to gain an initial real cause or possible symptom. Then, using the cause or symptom as if it is an effect, ask why to determine the cause of that effect. Continue this process until you cannot find a why that can be answered. The last cause is probably the root cause.

Although this is referred to as the *five whys*, it may take seven whys, whats, and whens to gain the root cause. Or it may take only four whys. When you can't use the cause as an effect, then you are probably at the root cause.

Problem and Concern: The Car Alarm Keeps Going Off

If you stop there, you might replace the car alarm (cost $550). After the installation, you find that the car alarm still goes off.

In lieu of replacing the car alarm, you ask the following:

- (**1st Why**) Why does a car alarm go off?
  - (**Answer**) A car alarm is designed to go off under the following circumstances:
    - Someone or something is tampering with the car lock.
    - The car is lifted off the ground as if to be towed away.
    - The door is locked by the remote key, but opened by the door handle.
    - The battery power is being removed from the car alarm.
- (**2nd Why**) Why isn't the alarm getting the appropriate power?
  - (**Answer**) The battery power is at 11 volts for a 12-volt system.
  - Stop there and replace the battery—You can pay $76.25 for the battery and half an hour of labor or ask why.
- (**3rd Why**) Why isn't the battery providing the appropriate power?
  - (**Answer**) The alternator isn't properly charging the battery. Is that why that "Alt" light is on?
  - Stop there and replace the alternator—You can pay $495 or ask why.

- **(4th Why)** Why isn't the alternator providing power?
    - **(Answer)** The drive belt between the engine and alternator is broken or missing.
    - You can pay the drive belt cost of $110 with labor and ask why.
- **(5th Why)** Why did the drive belt break?
    - **(Answer)** When maintenance was done on the car, we forgot to check drive belts.

Two issues become apparent in this example:

1. A drive belt powering the alternator should be installed (mechanics' issue).
2. The owner should periodically check the drive belts or pay someone to do it.

Needless to say, we showed the example starting off with the lack of battery power being the cause of the alarm going off. We could have asked other initial questions dealing with people being around the vehicle at the time of the alarm, the car being on a steep incline, or the car being jacked up to change a tire, etc.

This could have included additional questions before getting to the whys about the lack of power or limited power. My next-door neighbor had this issue with her dad's old car that no one uses due to an issue with its brakes. The battery started to go dead due to lack of use and, of course, the car alarm started going off on a quiet Sunday afternoon when her husband was out playing golf. My wife diagnosed the problem with four whys and disconnected the battery. The root cause was located and the issue was fixed.

Fishbone Diagram (Cause and Effect)

The fishbone diagram (Figure 5.1) is a pictorial view that segregates the possible causes of a problem into specific categories so that the possible root causes can be reviewed and help you provide a feasible recommendation or action plan.

In your fishbone diagram, you have to have at least six large bones coming off the backbone. The end of the backbone depicts the problem and the concern; then you would add the categories that house the causes.

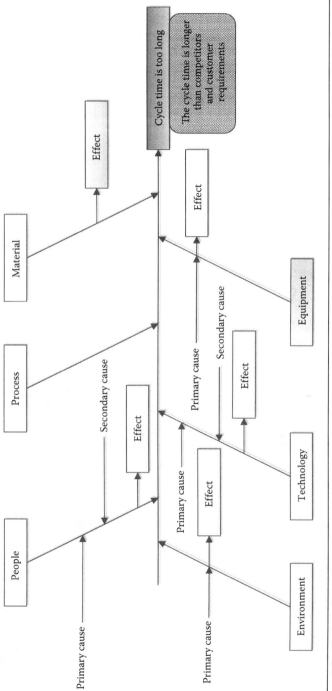

Figure 5.1 Fishbone diagram.

It is extremely helpful to denote the categories. This helps jog your thoughts. Commonly, I always recommend that the fishbone or cause-and-effect diagram be developed using a brainstorming session. By getting multiple people around a table or in a room to brainstorm, you can come up with a number of great ideas. When multiple people work together, they can synergize and create things far above the normal thought patterns.

The categories may be set up as shown in Figure 5.2 to denote the following:

- People—Anyone involved in the process
- Process—How the process is performed and the specific requirements or parameters for accomplishing the process, such as policies, procedures, regulations, and controls
- Material—Material used as input to the process (raw material, information, parts, and documents used in the steps to complete the activity)
- Environment—Includes the conditions of work environment, placement of the inventory, location, lighting, background sounds, laws, management, culture, and governance under which the process operates
- Technology—Any software, tools, technical spec availability, and supplies required to accomplish the goals of the process
- Equipment—Any hardware needed to move or adjust the raw material required to produce the output or support the people and process so they can complete the tasks correctly

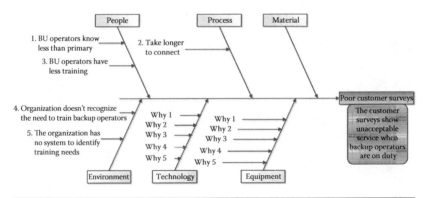

Figure 5.2   Fishbone–five-whys diagram. BU: business unit.

Needless to say, if you are working on something dissimilar to a normal process or if it makes sense for the process or issues to categorize them using different criteria and names, use what makes sense to the process and the organization.

If you were dealing with a problem where the lightbulb in the lamp doesn't turn on, you may choose to categorize each fishbone as *power*, *person*, *bulb*, *plug*, *wire*, or *lamp*. Then the causes under power could include power outage, popping of circuit breaker, bad wall switch, etc.; the causes for the lamp could include broken switch or missing switch. For the wire, the causes could include wire frayed by a cat, not plugged in, etc.

Don't forget that you can easily use the five-whys questioning technique to help build or establish a cause-and-effect diagram like the fishbone diagram.

Use the cause-and-effect diagram

- To stimulate thinking during a brainstorming of potential causes;
- To help understand the relationships between potential causes; this should help you build a Pareto chart, in the following section;
- To track which potential causes have been investigated and which proved to contribute to the problem.

Pareto Principle (80–20 Rule)

An Italian economist by the name of Vilfredo Pareto published a paper that declared that 80% of the land in Italy was owned by 20% of the populace. He also noted in this earthshaking dissertation that 20% of his garden peapods provided 80% of his peas.

Although you may not consider this as earthshaking, it has been noted that in business, 80% of your problems come from 20% of your customers; 80% of your sales comes from 20% of your clients or customers. The Pareto principle has become known as the 80–20 law of the vital few over time and exemplifies a normal distribution cycle. In reality, the metrics don't always compute to exactly 80–20 when you isolate the issues, the problem, root cause categories, or risk categories. The Pareto chart will provide the frequencies of all the major categories or root causes so you can prioritize your issue and work on the largest reduction for the concern to the left, and then fix the issues from left to right. The typical Pareto chart shown in Figure 5.3 is based on the reasons of people who arrive at work late or are late for meetings, etc.

The diagram is built by first putting the reasons or rationale of being late in order of the frequency of occurrences. Then you build a bar graph based on the frequency with the most frequent cause toward the left, then the next most frequent cause, and so on. The frequency metric is shown on the left side of the graph.

Then, you build a line graph showing the accumulation of each cause using the percentage of each frequency based on the total occurrences. The percentage scale for the line graph is placed on the right side of the graph.

As you project the line from the 80% scale on the right side of the graph to the accumulated frequency distribution point on the line graph and then project the line down to the individual root causes bar below the intersection point, you will realize that you can fix 80% of the issues by fixing the first three or maybe four causes based on the frequency of occurrences.

I do recommend that following your pursuit of the root cause, you look at the frequency of each event and/or category and put together

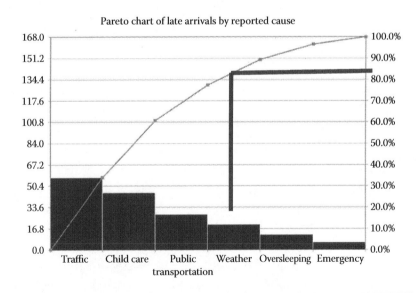

Figure 5.3   Pareto chart.

a Pareto chart. If you are using Microsoft Excel, you can go to the Microsoft website and find the instructions on how to use Excel to build a Pareto chart. The Microsoft answer section has a web address that will help you build the chart if you need it. The web address is http://answers.microsoft.com/en-us/mac/forum/macoffice2008 -macexcel/how-do-i-create-a-pareto-chart-in-excel/1c24c499 -4479-44cd-9e0c-9b81c9e76fc6.

Don't Jump to Conclusions

People have a tendency to jump to conclusions when presented with a problem; they target what they think as the most likely cause and fix it before they find the root cause. We as humans try to help or appear to be helpful based on the way we think we should act. We listen to someone with the intent of responding. We should listen to the person with the intent to understand. Once we understand then we try to be understood.

The cause-and-effect diagram is designed to help circumvent the natural tendency to jump to a conclusion based on a symptom by

- Providing a structure to understand the relationships between many possible causes of an issue or a problem;
- Giving people a framework to discuss and communicate possible areas for review;
- Serving as a visual display of possible causes, and as they are tested or discounted as the significant cause, they can be checked off;
- Helping members of the team to communicate and help to ensure that redundancies don't occur when testing for possible causes.

Construct a fishbone for each major problem. You may find similar causes for many of the current problems. This may help you prioritize your testing, by testing the most common causes for each fishbone problem. One cause may be the root cause of many problems. This would show you that the problems were symptoms of one cause. Test for the various causes and analyze the results of the testing. Verify the causes before developing recommended solutions. You can use various metrics to help analyze the cause and the effect. You could employ scatter plots, frequency plots, tables of results, etc.

If you are going to use brainstorming as well as the five whys, you will gain more ideas and feasible possibilities as the root cause.

Brainstorming   If you do employ brainstorming, please remember that you don't want to downplay the funny answers or inane statements during the session as they may spring ideas and thoughts from others that may be the perfect or near-perfect solution to the dilemma.

During any brainstorming session, you should allow and even promote levity as well as funny or strange approaches to the issue. This will also open the door to thoughts that are inane, funny, and thought provoking. This openness to all statements will normally open the attendees' minds to thinking outside the box. This openness can help develop great and ideal ideas from the levity. The ideal answers can come from a truly open brainstorming session.

Note: I am unsure of the truth and validity of the following; however, I will share the example as fiction or computer lore.

There is a story, sometimes called hearsay, about when a certain company needed more warehouse space; they got a great deal on an old General Electric (GE) warehouse. After they purchased the property, they found a number of computer systems from the much-respected old organization that had quit making mainframe computers. They tried to return the systems to GE, but GE stated that they were no longer in the mainframe business, and considering the *as–is* contract on the warehouse purchase, the acquiring company was now the proud owner of the computer systems. The company decided to have a brainstorming session in an effort to regain the warehouse space that they coveted. During the session, one of the participants said, "Let's set fire to the warehouse; collect the insurance; then build a new warehouse." Everyone laughed at the idea, but one person said, "Why don't we just have a fire sale and sell the systems?" They did and they sold the GE2000 computer systems to the military at discounted prices as the H6000 series computer systems. They also expanded their technical services by hiring the old GE technicians and added value to the air force, the workers, and their stockholders.

During most analyses, brainstorming can be used to quickly generate many great ideas in an effort to find root causes as well as possible recommendations. Brainstorming encourages creativity and collective excitement as well as a few raised eyebrows and hopefully a few laughs or giggles. Even an off-the-wall illogical idea brought up as a joke can generate new innovative thoughts with deep meanings. Although brainstorming can be accomplished by going around to each person who has something to say, whether it is meaningful, inane, or just plain funny or you can use the popcorn method, where anyone calls out ideas, no order, no negative feedback, and keep it up until no one can come up with anything; don't forget that any ideas that are meaningless are just discounted and those with merit are captured to a central board where they can be reviewed by all.

To accomplish the brainstorming session, I recommend that everyone hear the problem, then have a set number of minutes as thinking or contemplation time. Then the freewheeling can begin—don't hold back—no criticism or you blow the mood—hitchhike on each other's ideas—build more ideas because the more the merrier—post the ideas that might work even if they are far left or far right. The funny ones can be left out of the final considerations. Now moving back to reality and the cause-and-effect diagramming, the categorization has a direct impact on the brainstorming because it focuses your mind on a specific area of possible causes at a time.

Metrics

Management consultant and author Peter Drucker has been quoted as saying, "If you can't measure it, you can't manage it." However, I believe that what Mr. Drucker actually said was, "If you can't measure it, you can't improve it." I have never doubted Mr. Drucker's vision and common sense in business management.

Although I believe that you can improve something without measurements, I don't see any way to gain a sense of the degree of improvement until you can see some metric denoting *what it was* (As-Is) and *what it can be* (To-Be) following the process improvement. The measurement or metric should provide positive proof that the recommended change accomplished something. If you are going to help a business unit improve their operation, they need to be convinced that the change will increase their effectiveness, efficiency, or economic situation before they agree to go through the expense to follow or implement your recommendation. Please realize that any change to their process has an expense, even if it is just the removal of a step or implementing a minor adjustment like putting a left-handed person in place of a right-handed person to accomplish one step. People must go through a training phase to forget the old method and adjust to the new method. "People are by nature adverse to change unless they are the ones to decide on the change." Any adjustment or change made by a businessperson must be based on that businessperson's belief that the business and specifically his or her life will be better following the process adjustment or change.

$$\text{Belief} \rightarrow \text{Action} \rightarrow \text{Change}$$

The impetus of a business unit to accept, agree, and/or implement your recommendation is based on their belief that it will improve their position within the organization or their personal position. They must have a belief that the change will help them personally or professionally.

Since we are looking to improve something, we will need to find the current metric before we can measure any improvement. Once you have a baseline measurement, you can determine the percentage of improvement against the cost of the improvement. You always want to show a return on any investment. You may have to project the return on investment (ROI) over time against the initial and residual cost for the new process to gain payback and profit.

Since you need to review various metrics, we should take a moment to consider the type of metrics that you may encounter. The metrics that are normally used in control charts as well as other statistical analysis tools (Excel Analytics, SAS, Minitab, etc.) are segregated into two distinct types, discrete and continuous.

Continuous

Continuous metrics are normally obtained by a measuring system of some type. The data have a direct dependency on the quality of the measurement and the exactness required. Cycle time or the time it takes to accomplish a step may vary based on the person accomplishing the task, time of day, etc. Counts of nonconcurrence can be construed as continuous.

Discrete

Discrete metrics include percentages, counts, attributes, and ordinals. The percentage might show the proportion of times that you met the customer delivery date requests or the average percent of bandwidth in use within a network during the week as opposed to over the weekend. A count is changed when a specific occurrence happens during a certain period or when another variable is changed.

Some continuous metrics from a measuring instrument or calculation could denote the following:

- Elapsed time to complete a transaction
- Average length of a telephone conversation
- Cycle time for a customer order
- Substance purity (molten metal, etc.)
- Production rate
- Machine idle time
- Internal and external diameters
- Throughput or average throughput
- Late shipments

Some examples of discrete data may be proportions of the following:

- Late reports
- Incorrect invoices or paychecks
- Defective items
- Reworked items
- Damaged items
- Employee absences
- Incomplete orders or shipments
- Number of complaints
- Type of complaints
- Number of remedial maintenance (unplanned outages) compared to scheduled maintenance (planned outages)

For many of the metrics that may be in service as you read this book, the data (continuous or discrete) can be segmented to provide a more focused analysis or to review the largest impacts on your organization or your customer.

You might segment your customer base, each department, or external organizational interfaces. You might segment by time of day, day of the week, or week or month of year. This time difference may provide a wealth of information when you are dealing with staffing times as well as bottleneck assessments. You may look at the *where* factor when reviewing data. For example, most auto manufacturers don't have the financial sales to put all models in all colors with each of the various features in all dealerships or geographical areas; so they accomplish a thorough market analysis to determine the car purchasing habits of people in different geographical areas to determine their desires or buying requirements by geographical settings.

Do you realize that more red cars with higher horsepower sell in the Southeast than in the rest of the United States? It is not sure if this has anything to do with National Association for Stock Car Auto Racing (NASCAR) or the *Dukes of Hazard* or maybe just Daisy Duke, but more red high-powered cars are shipped to the Southeast than other areas of the country. They don't ship with all features to all the dealerships. They do ship to an area to help ensure that the spectrum of the most purchased colors and options are available in the geographical area. The dealerships have agreements to sell each other's inventory. That way, a corporation, as well as each dealership, has a win–win scenario. Even the customer wins since their desire will hopefully be filled by one of the area dealerships working together and they may even get a few extra options that they hadn't initially considered.

When I worked in network management, I gathered statistics on bandwidth, central processing unit (CPU), and disk utilization, etc. I then segmented the data by time of day, then again by day of the week, then by day of the month, etc. By seeing the data based on a visual chart with various perspectives, I could determine the peaks and valleys of utilization as well as research special events that caused certain variances. For those who study Lean Six Sigma, variance is something that you try to reduce. Variances in processes have a tendency to cause defects and waste. A standard operation has less variance than a nonstandard, haphazard, or ad hoc operation. The quality doesn't vary if the process is standardized. The quality may vary for other reasons, but if the process works the same each time it occurs, then there is limited opportunity for variance.

Using a segmented analysis, we could schedule certain high-utilization mainframe applications around the online customer's high or peak utilization time. We could then take less time for each batch application, reducing the impact on the online customer. We could also determine the true trend and the capacity in an effort to determine and qualify for upgrades.

If you look at the total utilization for a year or a month with no regard for the days of the week, weekend, month ends, end of quarter, or end-of-year processing, you may gain a sense of well-being that falls apart since you may not consider the normal variance in use throughout that year. The segmented utilization across the hours, the days, the weeks, and the months may show why users are complaining about response times or delayed computer reports during the normal workweek. It may only be the last or first week of the month, every month.

Since we gained a view of the network by the hour, by the day of the week, and the week of the year, we soon realized where our network bottlenecks were and why the online users in certain areas were continuously waiting for available network bandwidth or computer resources. We also noted the trends in use so that we knew where and when we needed memory or disk upgrades to service our customer base. We also realized that the items that we can schedule fit better at certain times or days of the month without adding bandwidth, computers, and other resources.

When I was a noncommissioned officer for a data center in the military, we measured the read and write counts for each disk file so that we could periodically realign the placement of specific high-utilization files near the disk heads. Most Disk Units read/write heads retract from the disk plate when not in use and then enter the disk plate area from the outside of the disk plate. This way, the checkerboarding that normally occurred during each day's process would be overcome every month as we realigned the files on disk. We placed the most used files closest to the platter edge and the least used files later in the load routine so they were further away from the disk head (platter edge). This helped us service the customers while awaiting a planned and much needed disk upgrade.

If you have a large customer base, it may make sense to segment your metrics by market, geographic area, industry type, order size, etc. This should provide you with some diverse information about your customers and their needs, wants, and desires.

When you gain some insight into the type of data that you want to assess, make a sanity check to help ensure that the data are specific and concrete based on the process for review; the data must be measurable; and the data must be useful to you and the customer. If they don't ring true to the customer and the process owner, then any conclusions that you share will not be acted upon by the business unit.

Once you determine the data, gain enough data to come to some conclusions or establish some trends. I normally like to have data compiled over 3 or more months; otherwise, it may be a snapshot of a small volume of work. If you tracked the toy-buying habits of the populace in the last quarter of the year and came to the conclusion that you needed to produce that many toys per quarter, you would be overproducing due to the holiday season in November and December. Base your capacity planning needs for automated teller machines (ATMs) or bandwidth in support of those machines on credit card use from November 15 through December 1, and you will have a lot of ATM idle time the rest of the year.

There are some common problems with some measuring systems. For the measures to be helpful, they must be accurate, repeatable, and reproducible; have stability; and have adequate resolution (Table 5.2).

Whether the problem is the area lighting to read a label, a dirty meter lens, or the dust or grime, the data must be read correctly and the data must be accurately measured to be helpful.

Table 5.2 Measuring

TEST FOR	HOW
1. Accuracy	Test for the amount of bias throughput by repeatedly measuring known quantities.
2. Repeatability	Have the same person measure the sample repeatedly to help ensure no measuring variance of the machine.
3. Reproducibility	Have multiple people or labs measure the same item periodically.
4. Stability	Have the same person measure the same item over time. Look for special causes that would account for any lack of stability.
5. Adequate resolution	Make sure that at least five distinct values can be ascertained or observed by various technicians.

Standardization or Anarchy

Standardization is what allows high quality to happen on a reliable and sustaining basis.

Standardizing is making sure that important steps and elements of a process are performed consistently by all personnel, systems, or machines. Without standardization, controls become difficult to manage. Anarchy is difficult to govern or manage.

Standardization reduces variations among individuals or groups. Variations can be viewed in two different categories. You have the normal variances that occur day to day, month to month, etc., and then you have the special variances, sometimes referred to as *anomalies*. An earthquake, a snowstorm in Charlotte, North Carolina, or a tsunami might be considered a special cause variance.

To help standardize practices and procedures, the process should be documented. If the process is complex, then it is imperative to document the process.

If you are going to use metrics to help improve the process, you should make sure that the process is unified and standardized. I might recommend that prior to employing any continuous monitoring or using any control charts, you should

1. Make sure that the process and the procedures are documented, especially if the process is complex;
2. Collect documents that represent the procedure;
3. Compare the documented procedures with the actual process;
4. Reconcile the actual practice and the procedure;
5. Ask why doesn't the process follow the procedures if the procedure is up to date;
6. Use the documented procedures once the procedures and actual process are synchronized;
7. Determine the appropriate metrics to show management
   a. When the process is working correctly
      i. Throughput
      ii. Customer delivery, etc.

    b. When the process is going out of control
       i. Reducing or increasing throughput
       ii. Nearing upper or lower limits
       iii. Adverse trends
    c. When the process is out of control
       i. Metric is exceeding the upper or lower limits
    d. When an event happens that affects the process
       i. Sharp increases or decreases not exceeding limits

Once the process is in control, you can start to look for ways to optimize the steps based on the new controlled process metrics and business needs, including the VOC.

Control Charts

At the onset of fieldwork for most audits, I ask two questions to the management:

1. How do you know when things in your area are going well?
2. How do you know when things are going bad?

If the management's position is to wait for the customer to tell them whether things are bad or good, then I worry about management's ability and their capability to manage the process or business unit.

In my mind, control charts of the appropriate metrics will tell you well in advance whether things are good or going bad. They can be used to help you and the management see trends before the customer complains.

Whether you are tracking risks, delivery performance, throughput, on-time deliveries, response times, or customer satisfaction levels, if tracked properly, you will see the current state, the projected state, and the past state. You will see whether you are meeting the goals of the process and the goals of the organization.

In the 1920s, a gentleman by the name of Walter A. Shewhart, while working for Bell Labs, developed a graphical tool to track key process metrics across a continuous period. Many key metrics could be captured and tracked to help determine the capability of the process. The capability is focused on the accomplishment of the process as it pertains to the goals of the organization.

The graphical metric capture could also be used to visually determine trends and anomalies (out-of-the-ordinary events). Whether you track the physical aspects of something you are building or the delivery performance of a service technician, the time-relevant chart will show trends and the actual response to a customer requirement. Mr. Shewhart stressed that bringing a production process into a state of statistical control where there is only common-cause variations, and keeping it in control, is necessary to predict future output and to manage a process economically.

Mr. Shewhart concluded that while every process displays variation, some processes display controlled variations that are natural to the process; while others display uncontrolled variations that are not present in the process causal system at all times. Six Sigma focuses on the reduction of the process variation to reduce the defects.

To develop and display the control chart, you must gain a series of metrics to show the normal state of the process. Over a reasonable period, you should see the normal variations of the business process. Based on the metrics, you should find an average or a mean metric along with a high and a low level that meets the customer's requirements. If there is no upper or lower level specified by the customer, then the upper level (UL) and the lower level (LL) should be set by the business unit. Similar to the risk appetite or risk acceptance level, the upper and lower levels should be set somewhere before they impact your organization or the customers. These levels should be the goals or standards to measure a normal desired operation.

We need to realize that when people and even machines are used, there will be a variance in the metric due to each person's physical and mental states at the specific time of execution including any other influences including the auditor asking questions, etc. The machinery may differ in speeds as well as due to the age or the current oil viscosity. These factors and others would denote the normal variations. In addition to different people and mechanized systems running slightly differently, other factors may influence the variations in metrics.

You will probably note some differences based on peak utilization or high volume of customer requests or even lower than normal volume of requests, weather conditions, scheduled maintenance, summer vacations, etc. These normal variations will be acceptable as long as the customer is satisfied.

There are also special causes that could occur as well. These special causes should be investigated as they could adversely affect the customer confidence and satisfaction. These special causes may or may not be acted upon to mitigate the impact on the customer.

The control chart shown in Figure 5.4 was developed using the organizational goal to ship diverse products to the customer on Day 10 with an upper limit of 21 days (3 weeks) and a lower limit of 1 day.

As you can see, the process went past the upper limit (out of control) on three occasions, and on 2 days, it was right on the lower limit. If I were monitoring this atmosphere, I would need to review each of the three out-of-control conditions to ascertain why it went out of control. A few possible reasons could be the following:

- New operator or equipment reset
- Backup personnel filling in for primary personnel
- Abnormal weather conditions or absenteeism
- Late delivery of materials, etc.

As Mr. Shewhart stated in his presentation, every process will have some normal variations due to a number of normal factors, such as the specific worker, machine, weather conditions, and humidity. He stated that you will have normal variances as well as special variances. The normal variance or event should be accepted and should

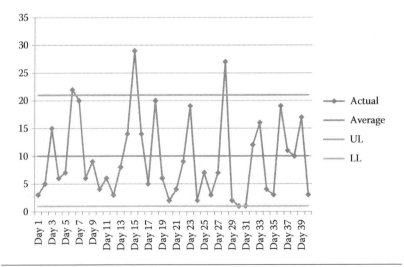

Figure 5.4 Control chart.

not require any special investigation or exception status. However, special variations should be investigated to determine the root cause. I recommend that when analyzing a control chart, you should check on any abnormal variations and try to determine why the variance occurred. If the metric appears to remain within sight of the upper or the lower limits, the variance should be reviewed to help ensure that the process is maintained within the UL and LL limits.

Mr. Shewhart identified four process states: (1) the ideal state, (2) the threshold state, (3) the brink of chaos, and (4) the state of chaos (out of control).

Whether you use the basic average or mean for the centerline and some measure required by the customer or business unit as upper and lower limits or maybe three sigma (3σ) above the mean and three sigma (3σ) below the mean for the lower limit, you should see a normal distribution of about 68% of the process (one sigma on either side). This means that for every measure above the mean, you will likely have one below the mean to offset or equalize the one above and maintain the average or the mean.

When a process is stable and in control, it displays common-cause variations—variations that are inherent in the process.

A process that is in control when based on experience and metrics can be predictive of how the process will vary (within the limits) in the future.

If the process is unstable, the process is considered to be influenced by special cause or major event variations. This nonrandom variation may be due to external factors; however, a sick person or piece of equipment could also cause a special variance.

If you see a number of measures above or even below the median without any in the opposite side of the chart, you should look into the process to determine why.

Multiple scores above or below without scores in the opposite area may indicate something different is occurring with the process. This may be a problem or it may be due to some other rationale, for example, the workers are becoming more efficient, the cost of raw material has been reduced, etc.

If the scores continue above or below, then the average is changing. I *do not* recommend changing the centerline if it was the average without first determining why the average process metric is changing. Is the root cause a part or a person that is not operating normally or following the documented procedures? Norms don't move unless something changes. If you find that the process has changed with regard to normal variances, I recommend that you investigate why before you adjust the mean, the UL, or the LL.

I do recommend setting some rules about the control chart assessment and abnormal variances in the data:

- Eight or more points in a row on the same side of the median indicate a process shift.
- If the data are symmetrical, it's OK to use the average centerline instead of the median.
- Six or more points in a row continuously increasing or decreasing indicate a possible trend.
  - Before moving the baseline, investigate why the trend is occurring.
- Start counting at the point where the direction changes.
- Too few runs indicate a shift in the process average, a cycle, or a trend.
- Too many runs indicate a sampling from two sources, an overcompensation, or a bias.
- Fourteen or more points in a row alternating up and down indicate a bias or a sampling problem.
- One or more points outside the control limits (UL and LL) indicate that something is different about those points (they are out of control).
- If a point exceeds three standard deviations on either side of the median, you should consider it out of control and determine why this has occurred.
  - If it is a special cause, can it and will it occur again? Find the root cause.
  - If it is a common cause, how can you contain this out-of-control situation?
  - Is the median changing toward this side of the control chart and will it be acceptable to the customer? If not, you must mitigate these instances.

Western Electric Rules

Western Electric set up a Six Sigma–style control chart baseline to indicate where the process metrics fall within three sigma above and three sigma below the goal or average. They set up a basic graph with a normal (average or goal) line and then an A, a B, and a C area above and below the normal line to signify the one sigma, two sigma, and three sigma areas as shown in Figure 5.5.

As you can see from the baseline, they have three zones above and below the average or norm. The norm could be the desired metric with the UL and LL as the allowable limits. For those metrics that do not have an imposed limit to service a customer, Western Electric used sigma to denote the metrics within the UL and LL. Area C showed the metrics within one sigma from the average or desired metric; area B showed those metrics between one sigma and two sigma; and area A signified the metrics between two sigma and three sigma from the desired or normal average process metric. This would provide for an allowable variance of up to six sigma. For those who study Lean Six Sigma, a variance of six sigma provides for 34 defects per million opportunities or 99.9997% error free.

Anything above the UL or below the UL would constitute an unacceptable or out-of-control condition. Since you will normally expect some variances across the three levels above and below the norm or average, the variance would be considered normal causes (people, timing, normal interruptions, etc.); however, Western Electric determined that certain trends or anomalies should be investigated to help

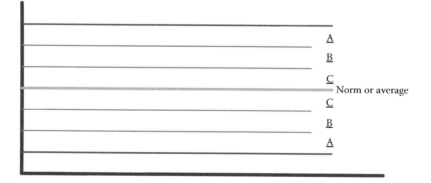

Figure 5.5   Western Electric control chart baseline.

ensure that a special cause is not going to send the process out of control.

They provided four basic rules:

1. Any single data point that falls outside the 3σ limit from the centerline (UL or LL) denotes an out-of-control metric and must be investigated to determine the root cause (Figure 5.6).
2. Two out of three consecutive points fall beyond the 2σ limit (in zone A or beyond) on the same side of the centerline (norm, average, or desired metric) (Figure 5.7).
3. Four out of five consecutive points that fall beyond the 1σ limit (zone B or beyond) on the same side of the centerline (norm or desired) (Figure 5.8) must be investigated.
4. Eight consecutive points that fall on the same side of the centerline (zone C or beyond) (Figure 5.9) must be investigated.

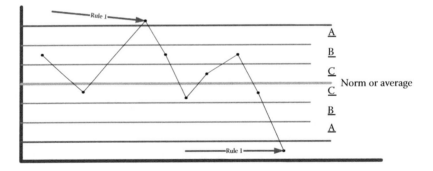

Figure 5.6   Western Electric rule 1.

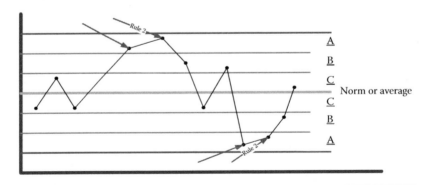

Figure 5.7   Western Electric rule 2.

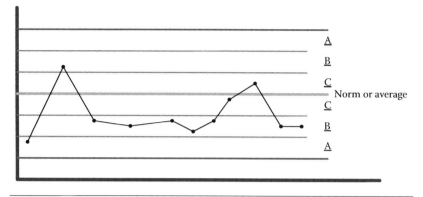

Figure 5.8   Western Electric rule 3.

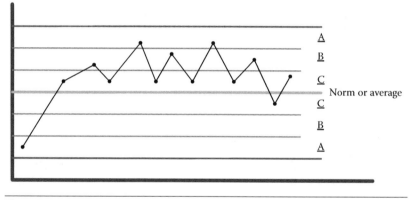

Figure 5.9   Western Electric rule 4.

When you look at the variances in rule 4 (Figure 5.9), you may realize that a normal variation based on the history and the baseline metric is not occurring. The variation appears to be moving the norm toward the upper limit. If your norm is based on an average, then the average may be moving or in need of adjustment; however, this new variance may indicate a part or a person who is not adhering to the established process, a part going bad, or even a person who is hung over or sick. I never advise an organization to move an average without first determining why the average is changing. Find the root cause and if then you realize that somehow the process has changed for the better, then and only then adjust the norm or average. If the root cause denotes a need for better training, preventive maintenance, a couple of aspirins, etc., then deal with the root cause.

Since all processes employ some sort of raw material, which is acted upon using resources to build something that has more value to the customer than the process costs, then you need to help ensure that the norms are not adversely going to affect the customer value and the quality or the costs.

Please realize that raw material is not just a manufacturing requirement. Internal auditors use existing reports, regulations, and interviews as raw material to accomplish an analysis of a business unit or process for the audit customer. A customer's deposit slip is a form of raw material used in banking along with withdrawal slips and checks. Deeds are raw materials used at the county clerk's office to denote real estate ownership. IT uses data provided by the business units as raw material to establish the database for use by the business units. The interpretation of the data is not part of the IT business process. They just report the data in a language and a format that can be understood, used, and leveraged by the organization. Not that many business personnel can understand the computer bit languages such as ASCII or EBCDIC.

If you are dealing with an external customer of the business unit under assessment, delivery performance is a key to success; therefore, I always recommend that the delivery performance is a key metric that should be tracked. You can track the delivery performance with respect to the following:

- On-time delivery (throughput or cycle time [efficiency])
- Customer acceptance for quality and satisfaction (customer survey results, rework, complaints, etc. [effectiveness])
- The cost (inventory and resources [economy])

If you review the IT interfaces to the business process, you may look at the response times for the business process, which can include user response times, application response times, and network response times. If a computer housing the application or the data is slow, then the total response time may be too slow for the customers. Remember the old saying "A chain is no stronger than the weakest link."

In the same respect, the IT response for a business request can be no faster than the slowest link. This is and can be a bottleneck or constraint that can be overcome.

The normal process for any transaction is based on a workstation sending a request to an application; the application, in turn, gets data from the database or some data repository and transmits those data to the originating workstation or some other node or workstation. In some cases, the data could be transmitted to a robotic arm that searches for some encoded resource and then provides that resource based on a pick list. In some cases, the robotic arm finds the magnetic media where the data reside, then loads the media into a reader for the user's access if they have the correct authorization for the data. The ultimate result is to provide the data in a format that the customer can understand within a reasonable time frame as determined by the customer.

As you consider the response time provided to the customer, please remember that "the customer's perception is your reality."

IT Control Charts

As you look at one business process, we are reluctant to set up control charts to isolate that specific business process or application; however, we may find more than enough global data used by the IT technicians that will assist in a business unit assessment within the normal IT metric collection.

Most computer networking, database, and server administrators monitor their equipment for various issues and activities, especially the utilization percentages and free and used memory and disk. Although the administrator may not think about or build control charts, they do save the data and review them to indicate and justify the need for capacity increases and updates.

In network management, most data communication equipment in today's market contain the simple network management protocol (SNMP), not to be confused with simple mail transfer protocol. Most network management equipment vendors provide their management information block (MIB), which shows the hierarchy of how their network management data are stored and how to traverse the data tree to the information that you would like to see or track. If you don't want to take the time to develop software routines to access the SNMP data, then just look for an application that meets your needs. In today's market, there are a number of vendors who have applications that will access the individual data from each of your network communication devices.

IT and the Business Process

Although IT is held responsible for data security in many organizations, we will first look at the IT effects on the normal business process.

As mentioned earlier, IT communication is not as instantaneous as people seem to imagine. There are a number of communication delays that affect the user's ability to obtain the computer data that they need. Among the delays, you have the following:

- Processing delay
    - This delay is between the receipt times of each packet for transmission to the point of putting it into the transmission queue at the sending systems.
    - On the receiving end, it is the delay between the receipt times of a packet in the receiving queue to the point of actual processing of the message.
    - This delay depends on the CPU speed and the CPU load in the system.
- Queuing delay
    - This is the delay between the point of entry of a packet in the transmit queue to the actual point of transmission of the message.
    - This delay depends on the load on the communication link.
- Transmission delay
    - This is the delay between transmitting the first bit of the packet to the transmission of the last bit.
    - This delay depends on the speed of the communication line or link. For a wide area network (WAN), consider the slowest link in the network (throughput cannot exceed the speed of a bottleneck).
- Propagation delay
    - This is the time delay between transmitting the last bit from the packet to the time when the last bit of the packet is received at the other end.
    - This delay depends on the physical characteristics of the communication link and the distance.
- Retransmission delay
    - This is the delay that results when a packet is lost or has to be retransmitted.

- This delay depends on the error rate on the link and the protocol used for retransmission.
  - You might recall the case where the 19,200 bps modem would provide a throughput less than 4,800 bps due to retransmission errors.

As you can see in Figure 5.10, the user enters a request for data or service from a web or application service on a server; the server in turn sends the application request to the database server; and the database server honors the request if the authorization to the data and the database are deemed to be authorized. The database server may have internal storage or rely on another server to get the data for the request as shown by a data repository service computer. Each server may experience the packet delays shown in Figure 5.10. The business request may experience normal delays:

- How fast the PC can build the packet or the transaction, how many windows on the laptop are open, or how much memory and/or disk is available.
- The network traffic may impede the transmission based on available bandwidth and current activity on the network.
  - The Ethernet runs as a carrier sense multiple access/collision detect (CSMA/CD) user network; therefore, when one node is transmitting, the others sense the carrier and wait; if two or more don't sense a carrier and try to transmit at the exact instance, they would sense the other carriers and they would retract their message, then wait a predetermined time based on an algorithm and their individual media access control (MAC) address so they won't collide again.
    - MAC is a unique identifier of each network interface card.
    - The address consists of 12 hexadecimal digits—the first 6 denotes the manufacturer or producer of the network interface card and the other 6 digits are sequentially numbered.
    - Each local area network (LAN) ties the MAC address (6c-62-17-72-ed-46, for example) to the Internet protocol (IP) address (192.168.1.221, for example).

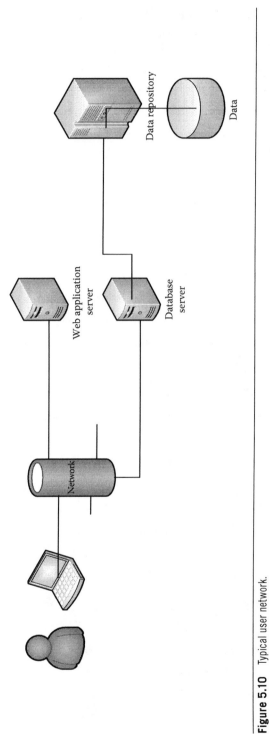

Figure 5.10 Typical user network.

- Following the wait time, the nodes would once more look for a carrier and, if the circuit is free, they would try to send once again.
- At the web, application, and database servers
  - You are again experiencing process, service, transmission, and propagation delays at each stop.
  - All servers experience multiuser congestion due to multiple users or programs requesting similar resources.
- The database service may also have an issue with the current authorized size of the database data area as many database management systems (DBMSs) preallocate the size of the database and tables.
  - If the DBMS is not set to automatically expand, then you might consider using a control chart to continuously track available space on each major table.

Although the delays may only be milliseconds or even nanoseconds, they can add up. If you are wondering what a nanosecond looks like, I would like to describe how Admiral Grace Hooper, the mother of common business-oriented language (COBOL), presented the concept during a briefing at the Strategic Air Command (SAC) headquarters.

When Admiral Grace Hooper addressed the U.S. Air Force members at Offutt AFB, Nebraska, SAC headquarters, she was asked, "What is a nanosecond?" She took a paper clip out of her attaché case and broke the paper clip into the smallest pieces possible by hand, and then she used a fingernail clipper to cut that piece in half. She then stated that if that piece of paperclip represents a nanosecond, then you can consider a Slinky 1 second, and she took a Slinky out of her case and held it up by one thin end.

Nanoseconds and milliseconds do add up, especially when you consider the number of messages and transactions going across your network and the Internet. You should consider the number of employees and customers that your IT organization services before deciding not to assess the IT environment.

The technologies are interfaced into most aspects of most organizations. Can your customer order a product or service from your organization and have it delivered without a technological activity? Very likely, the sales order information is transferred electronically; the work order is very likely online; and the shipping department very likely uses a technology to deal with the carrier as well as your organization to let you know that the order went to the customer so the billing for that order can start with an electronically created invoice, etc., etc., etc.

Please realize that most server administrators monitor available disk space, memory utilization, CPU utilization, and other statuses. You can leverage their work and control charts if they maintain control charts to help you with the assessment.

Queuing

If the server administrators monitor utilization over time for servers, disk units, etc., you can use the metrics to estimate the average queue size. One formula that I have used for many years in capacity planning is based on the average size of the waiting queue if you cannot control the arrival of requests (Poisson arrival). The average queue = $1/(1 - \%\text{ utilization})$; therefore, with an average utilization of 50% you can expect a queue of 2. The formula $1/(1 - 0.50) = 1/0.5 = 2.0$.

For 75% utilization, you can expect a waiting queue of 4 ($1/(1 - 0.75) = 1/0.25 = 4$).

As you will note from Figure 5.11, the average waiting queue starts to increase more after 30% and then even more at 50% until 80% = 5, 90% = 10, and 95% = 20.

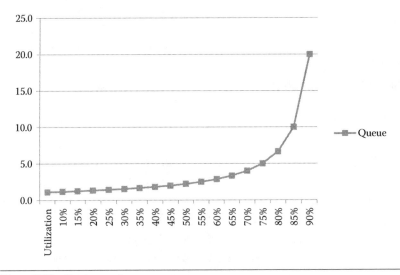

Figure 5.11   Queuing graph.

Many people find it strange that at 50% utilization, you can expect a waiting queue of 2. If you consider the fact that you don't control the arrival times of each customer request, an average of 50% utilization means that there are times when nothing is being handled, and then at other times, there is a waiting line (queue).

If you want to view a few approaches that dealt with the normal unscheduled arrival of requests, look at McDonald's, Taco Bell, Wendy's, and Burger King. At times, they are dormant and then they are inundated with customers and requests during the lunch breaks.

If you are looking at a CPU that exceeds 70% utilization, you are probably experiencing some slowdown in processing due to the system trying to share the CPU among many requests and a waiting list (queue) of almost 4. If you think that adding another CPU will cut the utilization in half, please note that it will not double your throughput. As you build a workforce or team, as you increase personnel, you increase the management necessary to keep the members coordinated. Similarly, multiple CPUs require a CPU to manage and schedule the workload between the CPUs. Therefore, the more CPUs you have, the more management time is used to coordinate the efforts of each CPU. Similar to the way any business unit works with an expanded staffing, the more the people, the more management and coordination is necessary to align the process toward productive throughput. This management time is not productive time, but the time is necessary to help ensure that CPU steps are not duplicated or missed.

As you consider the queue and the queuing, stop by at a McDonald's, Burger King, and Wendy's and look at the way each organization deals with the waiting customers and their waiting lines. McDonald's uses multiple lines with order takers/cashiers for each line; whereas Burger King and Wendy's appear to use one line with one order taker/cashier. Anyone handling money cannot handle unwrapped food. This means that in McDonald's and similar eateries, having four lines opened with a staff of 10, you have 4 employees who work with the customer and 6 employees cooking your food. On the other hand, Burger King and similar eateries employ one line with one order taker/cashier; therefore, if they have 10 employees on staff, 1 is working with the customer and 9 are working in the kitchen preparing your food order.

The major queuing at McDonald's occurs in the kitchen preparing the food while the customer orders have multiple queues so they get the orders in fast, but wait on the customer delivery.

Doctors' offices have a queuing system as well. Consider the last time you went to the doctor's office. You probably had a 1-hour appointment and actually met with the doctor for anywhere from 5 to about 15 minutes. Someone called you in to the inner sanctum just about the schedule appointment time and then the same person or another medical professional would take the height, the weight, and the other measurements. Following the preliminary measurements, you would be placed in an exam room and eventually someone else, probably a nurse practitioner, would come in and take your blood pressure and possibly a blood sample to test your average glucose levels for possible diabetes and other possible issues. Then after sitting in the exam room for a while longer, your doctor would appear and spend between 8 and 15 minutes with you discussing your health and possible issues or health risks. If you are in exam room 5a like I was recently, that means that they have a waiting queue of at least 10 or more people waiting to see a doctor. What room were you in for your last visit? How much time was spent with the doctor? What was the percentage of wait time during the whole visit? (This is an operational assessment and a good place for a VSM.)

Available Data   I recommend that you contact your IT server and network personnel and ask them what they use to monitor utilization and to help them accomplish their capacity planning for the servers and networks. If they are collecting data and have been over time, this will save you from reinventing the wheel.

If they wait for the customers to complain before they look for capacity or utilization metrics, then I recommend that you share any metrics and monitoring process that you deem appropriate in your operational assessment with the IT folks. They should be proactively working to help ensure that the business process does not fail due to their actions or inactions.

A friend of mine and coworker in a Corry, Pennsylvania, manufacturing plant described his IT job as "making sure that the business units didn't realize that they needed him or IT." His position as systems analyst was to make sure that the IT processes supported the business process no matter how their manufacturing process changed. He didn't want the business process to be the one to inform him of any issues, outages, etc. He was extremely proactive in his approach to the organization, so much so that the division management added him to the production meetings and the division leadership team.

If the IT division has an unlimited budget to buy what they want or need when they want to, they might just buy equipment and networking bandwidth as soon as anyone feels a slowdown. If not, I recommend that you help them develop their computer capacity monitoring and metric collection and reporting process.

That brings us to some common technology issues that can interfere or inhibit the user's data access and productivity. If you completed an IT FMEA during the planning stage, you might be aware of the following failure modes:

- Servers
  - Lack of memory or high utilization will inhibit response time.
  - CPU utilization over 50% causes a waiting delay for users; utilization higher than 80% or 90% may inhibit throughput to a degree that the application could time out prior to gaining the needed CPU response. This issue has been referred to as being CPU bound—similar to being spell-bound or muscle bound, it is so busy scheduling the multiple user requests that actual throughput is reduced to the nth degree. The CPU is inhibiting progress due to moving from one request to another and spending more time controlling the applications rather than producing results.
- Databases
  - Many DBMSs establish an allocation of disk space for each database table.
    - Some DBMSs can be set to automatically expand the table space by a certain number of bytes as the percentage of free space goes below a predetermined percentage.
  - If the DBMS is not set to expand, then is there a mechanism in place to alert the database administrator (DBA) of the need for expansion?

- For the nonautomated tables, the time it takes for the DBA to be alerted of the table expansion need and react to the limited space could inhibit the program from completing its tasks.
- Although many current DBMSs can expand the table space when needed, I am unaware of any that are set to remove the allocated table space.
  - Therefore, following a surge processing cycle, if the application goes into a linear search, then the DBMS may spend an inordinate amount of time searching through blank records before completing the search routine.
- Since the DBMS is an application, heavy request times will cause a waiting queue, especially if the users send a *select all* statement (structured query language [SQL] statement "SELECT * From ...") to the DBMS.
  - The database will select all records from the table or tables specified, which could tie up the database and disk repository while the transfer is occurring.

Queuing can occur in any portion in the IT environment; therefore, you need to become aware of the number of customer requests at the application, network, and server levels.

To gain some insight into the utilization and the load, you might consider starting a table to track each business unit, application, average message sizes, average transactions, supporting network, supporting servers, and utilization for each. You can use Excel or any other matrix establishment to gain insight into each business unit need and track the changes to the business needs. An example of a possible matrix is shown in Table 5.3. This doesn't encompass all you need to know about the business process to support it, but it does or should provide enough information to start with. Based on your organization and the business process, you will develop a knowledge base to provide the needed support and the assessment of your impact and opportunities to improve. Please realize that each business unit may employ multiple applications and services as part of their IT dependencies.

The matrix in Table 5.3 or anything similar is a living document and should be updated to help ensure that when you require the information, it is current and accurate.

Table 5.3 IT Business Unit Support

Business Unit

Business Unit Manager	Contact Number	E-mail
Business Unit Contact	Contact Number	E-mail

ITEM #	APPLICATION	# USERS	AVG. MESSAGE SIZE	AVG. MESSAGE PER USER	AVG. RESPONSE TIMES	NO. OF TRANSACTIONS	AVG. DISTANCE FROM SERVERS

Some questions that should be asked while building the business requirement document are the following:

- How many people or users will use the application?
  - Not just for the pilot program, although that information will help to support the pilot testing. You need to know the expected utilization to help ensure that the infrastructure will support the production environment.
- Where are the users located? LAN or WAN? Continental United States, Europe, or anywhere else like Brooklyn, New York, the world, or the WWW?
- Considering the user's workstation or PC, what is the normal message size?
- In response to the user's request, what is the average message size answer or answers?
- What should we expect as the number of transactions per hour, per day, etc.?
- What is the network speed of the LAN? Wi-Fi 54 megabits per second (Mbps), 100 Mbps, etc.
- What is the network speed of the WAN access line?
  - In many cases, the local access point to the WAN is normally the slowest network speed when considering the worldwide network.

My home network provided the information in Table 5.4 when using an Internet control message protocol (ICMP) ping, data upload, and data download requests from my PC via my home Wi-Fi network and Internet service provider.

Table 5.4 Home Network Baseline—PC

TEST DATE	DOWNLOAD (MB)	UPLOAD (MB)	LATENCY (MS)	SERVER NAME
8/26/2015 21:44	37.91	5.21	27	Rock Hill, SC
8/26/2015 21:49	43.92	5.39	30	Rock Hill, SC
8/27/2015 15:25	59.13	5.83	32	Rock Hill, SC
8/27/2015 15:38	51.86	5.82	27	Shelby, NC
8/27/2015 16:10	20.35	5.78	29	Conover, NC
9/1/2015 14:19	25.09	5.08	44	Charlotte, NC
9/1/2015 14:21	10.56	5.56	30	Rock Hill, SC
9/1/2015 14:23	21.49	5.86	35	Rock Hill, SC
Average	33.789	5.566	31.750	

As you may note, the PC has an average latency of 33 milliseconds to a server within 50 miles from my house. Please note that my Wi-Fi network is advertised as a 54 Mbps wireless connection; however, the upload and the download don't meet that speed. As you may know, every network has overhead within the network and a shared network shares time between nodes.

The more people conducting business, the slower the network will be servicing one specific node or workstation. You may also notice that the download speed far exceeds the upload speed.

Computers are controlled by a system program that tries to service multiple programs or execution requests. Since the mainframe and file servers service many other workstations and printers, the programming is designed to prioritize the output to a channel or line prior to opening up to receive a message. This way the computer frees up member and space so that it has the most available resources to service the incoming message or request.

Admittedly, if you have many customers with different desires and needs, the balancing act to satisfy them all becomes more diverse.

Consider Henry Ford's dilemma when the customers started to ask for cars that were just basic black. His mass production atmosphere changed. Later when automatic transmissions were available, the process became more diverse, then disk brakes, radios, AM/FM stereo, cigarette lighters, etc., etc., etc.

Business Support VSM

Now that you are aware of the network supporting the business process and maybe all your business processes, let's look at some metrics that may depict your organization's time impact on the business unit processes.

For customer value time as well as the time used for the customer transaction transmissions, we can use a VSM. Please realize that some of the transmission delays are based on the nature and the physical attributes of the elements involved; therefore, they may not be adjustable.

The fact is that the speed of light is approximately 186,000 miles per second in a vacuum; whereas a fiber or a copper connection can attain a speed of only 120,000 miles per second under perfect conditions. Please note that the natural condition of the elements still adhere to the laws of physics in the sense that a body at rest tends to remain at rest and a body in motion tends to remain in motion. That is one reason that a dedicated line using asynchronous transmission mode always sends a signal. The receiving end of the line accepts that signal and doesn't process anything until it received the start bit. That awakens the receiving end to pay attention and act on the message.

As you look at the digital communication, you may note that the absence of a bit (0) emits a voltage of 0.48 volts direct current (DC); whereas the active bit (1) emits a voltage of 4.8 volts DC. You may think that 4.8 volts is not a lot of voltage, but if you look at it with respect to the 0.48-volt (0) bit, 4.8 volts is 10 times the magnitude of the no-bit voltage.

As you consider this, we need to think of a digital message of a series of bits, some turned on (1) and some turned off (0). The voltage is normally shown as a digital wave as shown in Figure 5.12.

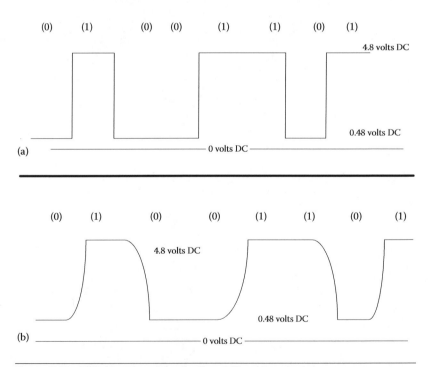

Figure 5.12 Digital wave form: (a) no inertia and (b) resistance to change.

As you may note in Figure 5.12, the digital signal wave form as shown in Figure 5.12a shows a specific and sharp up and down for the turned on (1) and off bits (0); however, the reality of the law of inertia is shown in Figure 5.12b, where the impedance to movement is skewed to form a more saw-toothed wave due to the normal resistance to change. The sawtooth wave in lieu of a digital block wave adds issues to the receiving communication devices. The electronic receivers are geared to accept the sawtooth signals.

All in all, you have a wire and/or fiber resistance to the movement of data across any network. The latency delay based on the miles traveled is approximately 0.82 milliseconds per 100 miles. This is based on the current digital communication environment that we have in most major U.S. cities as well as the long-line connections between each of the U.S. cities. Prior to the digital upgrades, the older analog communication systems across the nation we estimated about 4.5-millisecond delay per 100 miles. Those older systems used a mechanical switching device (X–Y switch) in lieu of the current digital integrated circuit chips; therefore, the mechanical movement was replaced by an electronic connection, which doesn't take the time to move relay switches.

While in the military, we reviewed the communications availability where we planned to place the first B-1 bomber and found that the communication available in that area used older aerial wires and mechanical switches in the telephone systems that supported the air force base; so we had to upgrade the local telephone communication to digital systems to support the rollout and maintenance system for the new bombers.

For our purposes, we will use the anticipated latency delays experienced in today's U.S. digital communication systems. If you work with unimproved areas in developing nations or extremely rural areas in the United States, you may have to use the older 4.5-millisecond resistance delay per 100 miles in lieu of our metrics in Figure 5.13.

Figure 5.13 shows a generic Ethernet LAN. Since most Ethernet LAN speeds range from 10 Mbps to 1 gigabit per second (Gbps) for a

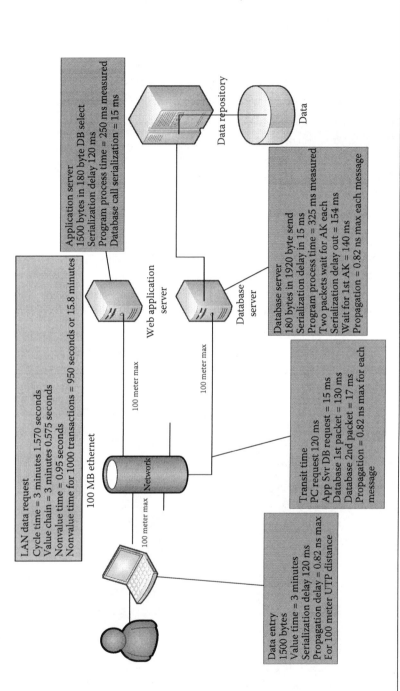

Figure 5.13 VSM LAN.

distance between each node and the hub of 100 meters (approximately 258 feet), the travel time is negligible, but the serialization delay may still be an issue. The serialization is normally computed by dividing the message length by the network speed. For our purposes, Figure 5.13 is computed using a 100 Mbps LAN.

You will note that the cycle in Figure 5.13 is 3 minutes and 1.575 seconds, the majority of which is the 3 minutes used by the data entry request. The value time includes the data entry and the server time used to answer the request.

Data Entry Screens

Based on this, you can surmise that within a LAN, optimization can be best achieved by reducing the data entry process without adversely affecting the accuracy and correctness of the data. As you consider the reduction of the data entry, you should also note that the smaller the message transmissions, the lesser time it takes for serialization as well as packetizing the longer messages. This should make us realize that only the information necessary to be data entered should be transmitted to and from the file or application servers.

To keep the message sizes more reasonable, most programs create a form and populate the form with known information. Using this approach, the known data are static and the data entry person need only enter the unknown information to the current application form. Then only the dynamic information entered by the user would be transmitted to the application or the data repository. This approach will reduce the message traffic, which reduces the serialization delay time, the transmission time, and hopefully, the need for packetizing the message. Don't forget that the predominant LAN environment in today's organizations is Ethernet and that Ethernet has a message load of approximately 1500 bytes. Any larger message would require additional overhead by the packetization of the message.

Please note that if you do fill the screen with information from the main server and were to use that information as part of your transaction, that data could be adjusted by a smart IT-oriented person.

CASE 5.1

I heard this from a somewhat reliable source; therefore, I can't state it as fact and the car manufacturer would not corroborate or refute the data: A car manufacturer built an online ordering system so a potential customer could put together their car or truck with their desired features, colors, options, etc. Then they could even pay online via a credit card or put some money down and pay the balance when they picked it up at their local dealership or at the factory.

Great thought—great marketing—great idea; however, poor execution. When they built the web application, the process would update the total cost based on each added option, feature, etc. Then the screen would be presented to the buyer so they can finalize the purchase and electronically seal the deal, including full or partial down payment.

It seemed great, except the total cost was part of the submitted contract with the data as part of the PC screen transmitted to the company. A smart user could actually use the View Source feature of Internet Explorer and adjust the total cost data to something they could afford, and then subsequently submit the order for a brand-new truck at a cost of $200 or something similar. They would then put it on their credit card, sealing the truck purchase deal. Once the first IT guy picked up his new truck with all the features and options that he requested, he let his friends know of this new and innovative website where they can purchase the truck of their dreams for a very reasonable price. Needless to say, others took advantage of the great deal. Eventually a person in accounting finally questioned the number of below–unit cost trucks that were being sold. They initially thought it was some giveaway that marketing and sales were presenting. The organization found and fixed the flaw by keeping the system of record on their site with an information-only field on the user's PC. The company lost some trucks but gained some training and knowledge about online web-based business transactions.

CASE 5.2

From a more reliable source: While working for a bank, I was asked to get involved with the bank's web presence. One of the corporate security folks found that in the new web-based banking application, the customer account information was transmitted to the PC or workstation after the user signed in with the appropriate user ID and password. When the authorized customer entered the transaction information and submitted the transaction, that person's account number, and all the other necessary information on the user's PC, was submitted to the application and was processed. The issue and concern that the information security had was that if that authorized customer knew any other person or business account numbers, they could change the account number located in the memory and then consummate a money transfer from the other account into one of their own accounts in this bank or a numbered account somewhere else in the world. The system automatically accepted the account number in the memory since theoretically the application put it there. Another system application could search for the user's account number in the memory and change that memory location to another account number. There was no control when the user executed a transaction to check the account number against the user ID to see if that user was authorized to accomplish any activity on that account. The program trusted the user and did not consider that an IT-savvy user could adjust the account numbers provided for that online session.

Although we did not have any specific evidence that someone had done this, it was a risk that was adverse to our risk appetite; therefore, we needed to change the system.

Another consideration that should be made when considering the data entry process is to gain only the information that the organization requires. A very complex or wordy data entry screen will be adverse to the attention span of the human animal. We may deem the amount of information requested too much and do our business somewhere else or put the entry process off for as long as physically possible. People purchase and carry smartphones so they can abbreviate everything. It is the now generation.

Most of us think that a 5-year-old child has an attention span of 15 seconds or so. To some degree, many people never outgrow their childhood.

If I give my wife a birthday, anniversary, or any other holiday card that has more than a few sentences, she will glance at it, gain the gist of it, and not take the time to actually read it. Anything I hand her must be concise and to the point. To that same degree, if you present a screen full of questions to a potential customer, they will lose interest after the first few fields and either enter something short or quit and go somewhere else.

Try to make the screens presentable and uncluttered. If you do require a lot of information, use multiple screens and present the important information on the first and possibly the second screen. Reduce the time that people, especially customers, have to spend on data entry if possible at all.

Organizational Network Transmissions

The network in Figure 5.14 merely shows a LAN using an Ethernet hub to amplify the signal strength. Since the hub works at the physical level of the Open Systems Interconnect (OSI) model, it doesn't need to serialize the bits to data or the data to bits; the hub merely amplifies the signal quality. The 100 meter maximum distance of category 5 twisted pair wire will have a maximum propagation delay between 4.8 and 5.3 nanoseconds per meter or up to 538 nanoseconds for a full 100 meters; therefore, the maximum distance between the two nodes in the LAN would be negligible (approximately 1 millisecond) when compared to the serialization delay or the data entry or the time that is expended by the application, web, and/or database servers; therefore, we will not include that in the LAN optimization. I do have a tendency to consider every communication device to delay the signal by 1 millisecond, whether it operated at the OSI level 1 or level 7. The physical level still has to take the signal, amplify that signal, and then broadcast the more powerful signal out of the other ports.

As we have mentioned earlier, each of the servers and network may slow down when memory, disk space, CPU, or bandwidth utilization is over 75%. As we saw in the utilization curve diagram in Figure 5.11, each time you have an unplanned arrival of orders or customer requests (Poisson arrival) and when the utilization exceeds 50%, the queue of 2 waiting requests will start to shoot up like a hyperbolic curve, doubling to 4 at 75%, 5 at 80%, and 10 at 90%.

The wait time for any queue is directly proportional to the instruction execution time and the number of average requests ahead of the latest request. As you will see later in this chapter as we review the PROCESS section and Process Analysis, when you buffer a process step, the cycle time or process cycle for that item increases while the

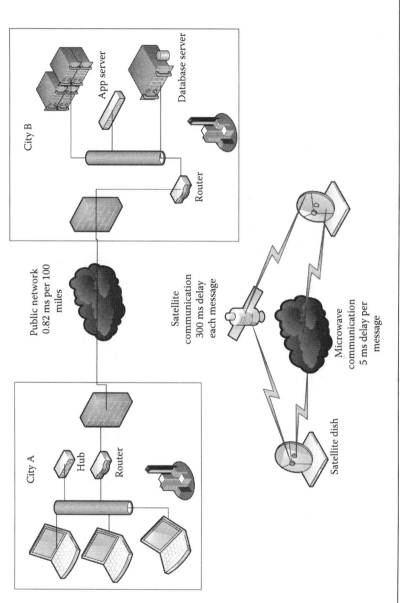

Figure 5.14 Typical WAN.

value stream remains the same. In the case of building a queue for a step that is the process bottleneck, you will find during the analysis stage that the throughput will be at a maximum level even though the cycle time for the last request is longer than accomplishing one transaction at a time.

Since the majority of the process time is used by the data entry and the servers, we need to determine whether the user interface, the server, or the application causes any unnecessary delays due to queuing. Data serialization should not differ whether the node receiving or sending the data is an application or a database server or the PC initiating the request; therefore, we will be looking at the servers for their responsiveness.

Utilization Assessment

To assess a server or the application they execute, we first look at the utilization of each to isolate or prioritize where to start. You can use a Pareto chart to prioritize the assessment steps. If the average utilization is above 50%, then you may consider assessing the highest utilization first, then the next highest, etc. For those of you who are unaware of the Pareto chart and the Pareto principle, also known as the 80–20 rule, the principle states that 20% of your activities accomplish 80% of your productivity; therefore, 80% of your problems come from 20% of the root causes.

For those of you who have programmed computers or developed new processes, did you find that 20% of your program actually accomplished the task and the rest of the program (80%) were controls helped to ensure that the process did not fail and that the program maintained the accuracy and correctness?

If you deem that the utilization of any server or network exceeded the 50% to 75% upper level boundaries, then you need to look internally to determine if the internal processes of the service were exceeding a reasonable timeline. If you take a baseline measurement of process and service times when the system is installed, you can review those metrics at any future time to determine the differences and trends as well as capacity issues. If you continually or even periodically track the measures, then you will see any trends or some anomalies prior to them causing customer discontent, major concerns, or late deliveries.

In an effort to view and collect the control chart data, you can employ a protocol analyzer like a sniffer device or an online program to capture the request from a specific workstation as a controlled environment test. You can also look at the server end and obtain the time that the input transaction arrived and when the answer to the query was sent back to the workstation.

As I mentioned, whenever you develop a new system or program, you should capture a baseline of the server, network, and workstation response times to build a baseline that can be used to determine the trends. This way, as more personnel use the device or network, you can see the changes, the trends, and the capacity utilization and expand the capability before the lack of capability or resource adversely affects your business process or the IT status within your organization. Proactive capacity planning will help to satisfy the business needs and not show the IT division as a bottleneck to productivity.

The network speed can be baselined without an enormously expensive equipment and time. A small business or frugal shop can determine a baseline network speed by using the following unscientific test:

- Transfer a specific file from one point to the furthest point to determine the throughput for the network.
- The basic formula for the calculation is (Table 5.5)
  - [Message size] * 8/[network speed] = [time for transfer]
  - The message size is in bytes.
  - You multiply message size by 8 to determine how many bits (8 bits to the byte) it is.
  - The network speed is in bits/second.
  - The time for transfer is calculated as if there is no other traffic in the network.
  - Other traffic will or can inhibit the time to transfer.

Table 5.5 File Size and Network Speed

FILE SIZE	EXPECTED NETWORK SPEED	EXPECTED TIME
12 Mb	10 Mbps	9.6 seconds
120 Mb	100 Mbps	9.6 seconds
1,200 Mb	1 Gbps	9.6 seconds
67 Mb	54 Mb Wi-Fi	9.9 seconds

- Since you may not have the access to pinpoint 9.6 or 9.9 seconds, I recommend that you approximate it with a 10-second completion time.
- If you find that the baseline is a major difference, then use the formula to determine your current throughput based on your controlled test of a specific file size.
  - [Net speed] = [message size] * 8/time
  - For instance, if the file is 12 Mb and the completion time is 22 seconds, then
    - Net speed = 12,000,000 * 8/22
    - Net speed = 4.3636 Mbps throughput
  - This could be caused by other traffic using the same network leg along the way.
- Once you have established the actual bandwidth and throughput, you can use this as a baseline for future assessments.
- If the baseline bandwidth will not support the anticipated need of the organization, then this is the best time to assess alternatives to decrease the delay and bottleneck before you have a significant number of users.
- Then build another baseline to be used for future trend analysis and fault isolation.

An old friend of mine and IT analyst for a Corry, Pennsylvania, IT operations unit used to say, "Our job is to make sure that no one knows we are needed." "The less they call for help, the more productivity; and IT helped them attain that productivity level."

Now that you have the knowledge to assess a small network for a small business venture, let us take a look at a larger organization with multiple divisions in geographically separated environments.

WAN Environment

To gain a better insight into the WAN environment and the equipment used to connect each node on any network from various LANs, you need to determine the appliances used to effect the connectivity. Each Firewall, switch, router, DSU/CSU, etc., add a latency delay. I normally use at least 1 millisecond for each appliance as well as the natural serialization and distance delays. The OSI model can help you understand the node to node interface. This is especially true as you consider the appliance working at the network and session level has a higher latency than a physical of data link level.

OSI Model   Since the local hubs in a LAN work at the physical layer of the OSI framework, they don't need to read the message or any headers. The hub just boosts the signal strength and sends each message out all available ports as if it is a broadcast message. Some organizations try to minimize the traffic on each leg of the hub by using switch appliances to send each message out a specific port to reach the address on that port. To accomplish this LAN routing, the switch opens up the message and works at the data link level of the OSI model. The time it takes to open the message includes the serialization. The switching delay can take from 30 microseconds (0.000030 second) to 1 full second. In addition, you probably require a router and if you are connecting to or through the public network environment, you will want a firewall as well. The router works at level 3 of the OSI model and will add a serialization delay as it routes the message toward the correct IP address. The firewall normally opens the whole message to look at the message content; therefore, I would consider a 750-millisecond to 1-second delay for each message plus the serialization delay.

As I alluded to the above, the OSI model is an environment set up by the ISO; therefore, it is sometimes referred to as the OSI or ISO model. The OSI framework consists of a seven-level framework where the information at each level is used by the same level in the receiving environment. Each header or information is a standard that can be read and understood by the same level for a different platform.

The ISO model framework (Table 5.6) allows many different and diverse environments to communicate with other unlike networks, computers, and applications.

As you consider the ISO model and the network in support, we need to consider the long-line telecommunication devices used in a WAN. Each time the digital signal is opened to read the address or message content, you have the act of serialization. Even with the store-and-forward atmosphere of a mail server, the file is opened and the sender and receiver addresses reviewed (for mail, it would be the mailboxes; for routers switched, etc., it would be the IP or MAC

Table 5.6   OSI/ISO Framework

LEVEL	NAME	DESCRIPTION	PROTOCOLS, STANDARDS AND LINK CONTROLS
1	Physical	Electrical interface bitstream, physical medium, method of bit representation, voltages, etc.	Hubs—physical examples include Ethernet, FDDI, V.35, V.24, RJ45, etc.
2	Data link	Error detection, flow control on physical link	Switches—transmission protocol, MAC layer, logical link control, PPP, ATM, IEEE 802.5/802.2, HDLC, and frame relay
3	Network	Network addressing: routing and advanced switching	Switch/router—virtual circuits for transmitting node to node include AppleTalk, DDP, IP, and IPX
4	Transport	End-to-end error control—circular redundancy checks, etc.	Ensures data transfer; includes SPX, TCP, and UDP
5	Session	Authentication level permissions, session restoration, reconnect, etc.	Manages and terminates connections between applications; includes RPC and SQL
6	Presentation	Coding into 1s and 0s, encryption, compression and expansion	Transforms data presentation to application and vice versa; includes ASCII, EBCDIC, TIFF, GIF, PICT, JPEG, MPEG, and MIDI
7	Application	Message format into end-user usable information—From data to information provides the customer interface	WWW browsers, NFS, SNMP, Telnet, HTTP, and FTP

Note: ATM, asynchronous transmission mode; DDP, distributed data protocol; FDDI, fiber distribution data interface; FTP, file transfer protocol; HDLC, high-level data link control; IEEE, Institute of Electrical and Electronic Engineers; IP, internet protocol; NFS, network file system; RPC, remote procedure call; TCP, transmission control protocol; UDP, user datagram protocol.

addresses). The serialization delay is measured by the size of the message in bits (characters including spaces ÷ speed of the network segment = serialization delay (normally in milliseconds). For example, a 1500-byte (Ethernet maximum) message would equal 12,000 bits; when this is divided by a 100 Mbps LAN, it would equal a delay of 120 milliseconds for serialization. The transmission or the message would take 120 milliseconds at the senders end plus 120 milliseconds at the receiving computer plus a transport time of approximately 1.76 milliseconds if both the sender and the receiving computers were 100 meters (maximum distance) from the Ethernet hubs.

As you can see in Figure 5.14, there are more appliances at work and we now have to be cognizant about the distance to be traveled by each message. Figure 5.14 shows only two geographical environments; however, if you are considering Chase Bank; Bank of America; a state, city, or federal government; Bon Secours Hospital Systems; and many other organizations, the diversity increases and so do the delays. Each site will have at least one digital service unit (DSU)/chanel service unit (CSU) or modems, routers, firewalls, etc. Each device has a protection factor and a programming that may add to the message delay. In Figure 5.14, I show a microwave connection as well as a possible satellite interface between sites.

A router, a switch router, or a firewall, etc., would be required to open each message as well. Therefore, you will consider the serialization delay in each case. Also note that the modem or DSU/CSU (for digital communication) would not require the serialization delay. They work at the OSI level 1 and 2 layers. Also note that the modem or DSU/CSU may use a different network speed for the transmission from the local network to the communication company's network. Most modems transmit up to 19,200 bps; whereas digital DSU/CSU units normally start at 56,000 bps, which equals one channel in a T1 and the DSU/CSU could handle a T1 (1,540,000 bps or 1 Mbps) as well.

While in the military, I was approached by one of our captains and a senior supply sergeant. They informed me of an issue that they encountered during a worldwide military exercise. The supply sergeant was in a tent somewhere in the world trying to use their computer equipment; however, the transaction-level processing failed to work. They were able to build a transaction file on their workstation and send the batch file to the computer system in support of their activities; but they could not get a transaction to work.

I asked where the supporting system was located and how their communication link was set up. They were able to mention that they were in a tent and had a microwave connection from where they were to a military installation in England. From England, the message was transmitted via satellite to Washington, D.C., where it was then sent via satellite to a Midwest military base and then through a landline for approximately 450 miles to the supporting air force base. I realized that the delays encountered by the transaction process timed out each time it was transmitted. The wait time for a message acknowledgment or nonacknowledgment was normally set to 5 milliseconds. At the time of the military exercise, we estimated about a 5-millisecond delay for each microwave transmission. The microwave bounces an electronic radio signal off the ionosphere and has a normal delay per message of about 5 milliseconds. Adding to that propagation, you have the two satellite shots: one from England to the United States of America, followed by another satellite transfer from the East Coast to the Midwest and then 450 miles via copper wire. Since the average satellite shot has a propagation delay of around 300 milliseconds, you have an additional 600-millisecond and another 20-plus-millisecond delay for the 450 mile landline. (Please note that in the 1980s, many telephone companies had the old mechanical X–Y switches and we estimated the latency delays for copper at about 4.5 milliseconds per 100 miles.)

Since most data communication controllers had a 5- to 25-millisecond wait-for-response setting, each message was timed out and then subsequently resent after the timeout. The data file batch transmission was a larger message so it was handled differently. Since the file exceeded the normal 1500 bytes, which is the maximum Ethernet message size, the message was packetized and each message had a header denoting where it belonged in the full message. Each piece of the message in a separate packet had an individual number in sequence. These packets could travel across different paths parallel to each other; therefore, the sequence number provided the means for the receiving device to put the message back together. Whether the packet was a retransmission of that packet or the original transmit, the receiving computer would accept only one transmission with a sequence number, then the receiving station would respond to the sender stating an AK for that sequence number. The sender would then send additional sequence numbers until it receives AKs for all those packets that were sent. Since each packet had additional information that even the second or third retransmission may have sent, the first attempt might have been acknowledged as accepted and looking good with an AK. Then the sender would start sending the next packet until all had been accounted for. I recommended that the next time they do a worldwide exercise, for them to change the timeout at the host computer system wherever, they go to at least 1400-millisecond wait time. This will slow down the system at times waiting for workstations that were powered off, but the geographically separated workstations should negotiate a better wait time and less retransmission.

Before we start our analysis and share ideas of how to optimize or solidify your operations, we need to consider the control chart and the data that can and should be reviewed to present a clear picture of the IT environment and capacities.

Data Collection

Control Chart Analysis   In an effort to share some ideas about using control charts to help analyze the IT environment and capacity, we should start with a known baseline. Like always, if you don't know where it is, or what it is supposed to be, you have no reference as to any improvement or out of the ordinary events.

As I mentioned earlier, whenever you build or establish something new such as a new system or program, install a new piece of equipment, start dealing with a new vendor, etc., you should build a baseline to denote the effectiveness, the efficiencies, and the cost. The effectiveness should denote or at least outline the qualities, features, and functionality of the product or service leaving the new process. You might even show the material used to complete the process, which could include the quality of material used, if known. When we speak of the efficiencies, show the throughput across a specified time frame, such as 25 units per hour and 140 units per minute. And last, but certainly not least, the cost: what did the raw material cost and the cost of labor (qualified technician versus novice, etc.)? You may consider listing all KPIV and key process output variable (KPOV).

Since we are interested in the user response times as an IT goal for the new or improved application, I would like to show you a total fictitious baseline denoting the user workstation response times along with the network bandwidth, application or web server, and database server utilization metrics in Figure 5.15. Consider that most baselines are captured over a short period following the implementation or change of a process; for our purposes, we will imagine that the metrics shown in Figure 5.16 are the average metrics captured during the normal workweek (Monday through Friday) for the month and a half following the implementation. As you can realize, an organization that employs their workforce during a day shift very likely has limited activity after hours and

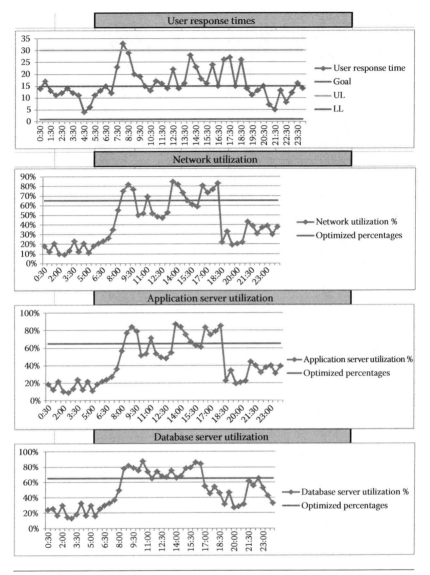

Figure 5.15   Baseline metrics.

on weekends. They do run a nightly workflow following the end of each workday to process any outstanding transactions and build the appropriate reports as well as the nightly data and server back-ups. The backup routines normally start each night around midnight. The backups during the week are updates to the full backups accomplished each weekend.

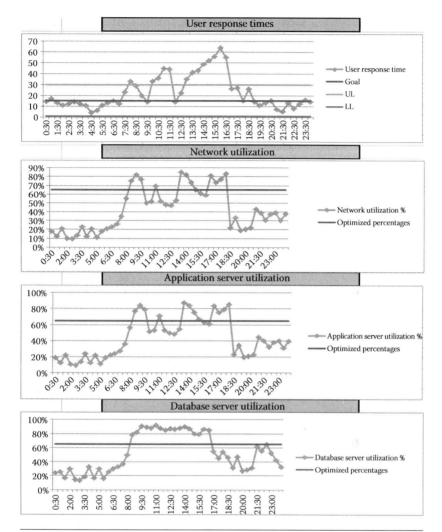

Figure 5.16   Customer complaint—slow response times for easy transactions.

Based on the queuing theory that we discussed earlier, this organization has determined that 80% utilization was too high and 20% utilization was too low. Organizational leadership believes that based on the waiting queue, they would like to have an optimized utilization of 60% to 70% because that would allow for two to three resources waiting for service and they felt that it would balance the cost of the resource with the time to wait for services.

Some thoughts about the baseline data capture are as follows:

- Did you notice the lull between 12:30 AM and about 7:00 AM?
- Why is there a lull between 11:00 AM and 1:00 PM?
- Since the organization mainly works during the daytime, what do you think is going on after 6:00 PM?

You may notice a relationship between the user response times, network traffic, the application or web servers, and the database server utilization. As people send transactions, the activity levels are affected. Please note that the user response was timed from the transmit to the application response. The response time for the acknowledgment of the transaction averaged about one-third to one-fourth of the time. In other words, the free cursor came back an average of about 5 seconds per transmit. Please remember that most transactions take four messages:

1. The workstation-requested transaction
2. The acknowledgment that the message was received (AK or NAK [nonacknowledgment])
3. The response from the application or data areas (data or a notice of completion from the database or application)
4. The workstation's response letting the database or application service know that you acknowledged receipt of the data or, if the data were not discernible, the NAK to let the sending server to retransmit the information

Although we are merely viewing the baseline data in Figure 5.16, it would be great for the organization to continue capturing these metrics to help proactively determine trends, anticipate growth, or investigate abnormal activities.

Let's look at a specific day's metric as part of a daily production review by the IT business unit. This would entail a person comparing the normal day-to-day activity against the metrics captured for the last operational days' workload. On this particular day, there is a slowdown noticed by many of the application and database users. In fact, the call desk received a number of calls from users who thought their workstations were hung for the day shown in Figure 5.16.

Control Chart Assessment 1

- What do you notice as you review the control chart?
- Does the control chart stay within the normal parameters or centralized around the mean or corporate goals?

Take a moment and jot down any of your observations:

_____

_____

_____

_____

_____

_____

_____

_____

_____

_____

_____

_____

Observations/Perspective of Assessment 1

- I totally understand the customer help desk calls and concerns about having a frozen workstation.
- The response times look like that, for most part of the day, the average response times exceeded the upper limit parameters.
  - If I only had this metric to review, I might start looking at the network or each individual workstation for the root cause of the slow response time.
  - I might test for a shorting wire. If it was an old Thinnet Ethernet or coax, I would probably suspect a terminator cap dislodged.
  - I might also look for a virus or malfunctioning PC.
- Since I do note that the database server responses also exceeded the upper expectations, I would adjust my research to the database server.
  - If the database continually has four or five waiting requests due to the 80% and 90% utilization, I can understand the user wait times for data-oriented requests.

- My first thought would be to ascertain if the server just had some sort of upgrade for hardware or software.
- If not, I might look into the log to determine what the users are asking from the database system.
- When I come across a number of query calls that look like Select * from PayFile, followed by a number of other "SELECT ALL (*)" from other database files, I recognize that our anomaly appeared to be caused by an untrained user or someone attempting to commit a fraud.
  - If this database has the organization's history, then a "SELECT * (ALL)" would ask the database to provide all records and all fields in each record from the specified table. If the organization was 25 years old, then the database would have to send every pay_file record in the file.
  - If the user sent a number of these queries, then that user may have been the cause of all the customer trouble calls.

As mentioned earlier, the larger the message, the more overhead (packetizing) and delays to transmit the message, not to mention the time that is expended extracting all the records into a file to be transmitted to the workstation.

Users need to be trained to understand that by preparing a concise request, the database and application activities will provide the information quicker. If the request is a "SELECT * from TABLE" with many records, then it might be wise to schedule those types of requests in the evening where the computing resources and services are not in high demand by everyone. We always tried to schedule major resource jobs after hours so the online workers and the customers will not have a major impact due to busy resources.

Most auditors are aware that senior leaders don't like verbose reports. They would like to know your recommendation and why it is important to do something. Be as concise as possible.

Control Chart Assessment 2   During your operational assessment, you look at another day's data and see a different yet similar abnormality. The activity just doesn't appear to be a normal day's data.

As you review Figure 5.17, please place your observations and notes in the following lines.

_____

_____

_____

_____

_____

_____

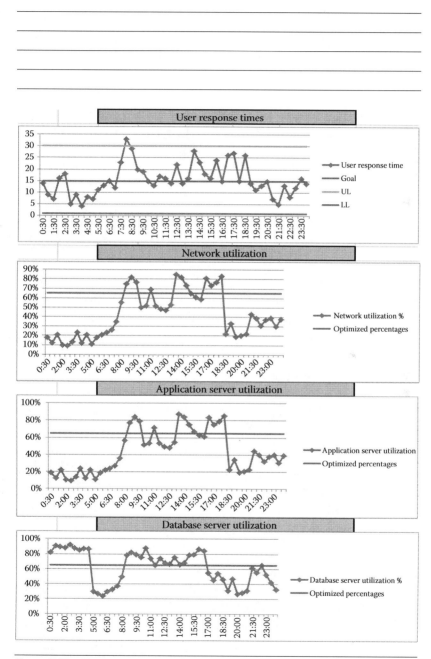

Figure 5.17   Control chart—Assessment 2.

Please realize a similar issue shown in Figure 5.17 was encountered during an audit of a major bank.

Some questions for your consideration as you review these control charts are as follows:

- Is the scenario similar to the one shown in the previous control chart assessment?
- What are the differences between assessment 1 and assessment 2?
- Do later graphs denote a rise in utilization across the board, for one server or the network used by the business application?
- Are there common similarities, anomalies, and outliers?

Observations/Perspective of Assessment 2   There is a similarity between the database activity in the wee hours of the morning (after midnight), yet there were no adverse help desk calls about poor response times due to the fact that a limited number of people were using the network or the database service. Needless to say, if I were doing something questionable or illegal, I would probably do it when I wouldn't disrupt the normal operation or get other users' attention; therefore, they would not react and stop my queries before I attained my goal.

Another train of thought might be that I as an authorized person wanted to do some large database queries and didn't want to either disrupt other authorized users or take more processing time than it should while running by itself. I then scheduled an after-hours execution of the query.

Going back to the role of a hacker, he or she wants to download all available HR information as well as the vendor master file, customer information file, accounts receivable and payable, and any proprietary organizational information, including proposed mergers and acquisitions. If I were a hacker, I would want to get any information (data) that can be sold for a profit without even leaving my house or the office.

Many intrusions are scheduled during off-hours. When I worked in manufacturing, many of our divisions closed down from Christmas to New Year's as well as the whole weekend following Thanksgiving. As I entered the data center following one of those long breaks, I found that my network-monitoring system showed all transmission lines as red blinking icons. The management system could not communicate with any other network devices. Further investigation showed that someone had tried to gain access to my various systems, but since we had some proprietary mainframes and operations, they were unable to match the protocol or formats. They were versed in UNIX and tried to gain information from our UNIX-based networking devices and the one silicon graphics system, but the network equipment and software impeded their access to gain information or any of our proprietary designs from what we could ascertain.

Also, while doing an audit for a major bank, I was doing a word search for security violation words in the computer and network logs and found a number of user ID and password responses showing that the username or password does not match our records during the off-hours and weekend log times. Further analysis showed that each time it occurred, the same logical connection used various user IDs with two different passwords. Then it would try a different user ID with two passwords and then tried another user ID.

- When I looked at the user files, I realized that the person doing the hack did know many of the employee's names.
- Some of the passwords looked like birthdates, pet names, children's names, children's birthdates, etc.
- I could not ascertain whether this person or group trying to gain access actually knew the bank employees or whether they did some phishing prior to attempting a login as an authorized user.

We never did find the perpetrators. It looked like the hackers tried for about a week or two and then quit. I never heard whether they returned for another attempt at entry into the bank's data areas, as I left the organization some months later.

Other Graphical Charts

There are other graphical charts that can help you with the operational assessment. You still require meaningful metrics captured at reasonable normal and abnormal times.

Bell Chart   I believe that most people have seen and maybe have used the bell chart, as shown in Figure 5.18, the old chart that is used by

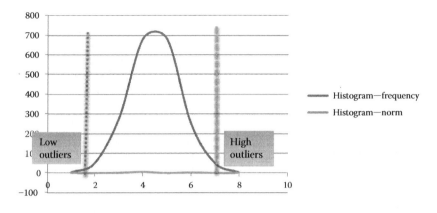

Figure 5.18　Bell chart to find high and low outliers.

educators to plot the grades of the students. The bell curve provides an A for the few students on the small populated right side of the curve and an F for those few students on the extreme left of the bell curve. The majority of the students at the top of the curve and within one standard variance comprise approximately 68.4% of the students being scored. The bell curve is a standard variance diagram used for the Six Sigma views as well. That one standard deviation approximated two sigma. At two sigma, you are one-third toward six sigma.

Scatter Control Chart　I have found that the scatter control chart can be a useful and powerful tool in finding process differences and anomalies. You may also find it very useful while looking for fraud red flags. For those readers who are auditors, the International Professional Practices Framework (IPPF) 2120.A2 for risk assessment requires that the auditor consider the fraud risk in all assurance audits. IPPF 2220.A2 states that internal auditors must consider the probability of significant errors, *fraud*, noncompliance, and other exposures when developing the engagement objectives.

As you review Figure 5.19, you will see two scatter charts. The diagram in Figure 5.19a shows a number of metrics outside the normal metric stream as denoted by the dark gray circle. Figure 5.19b shows a different set of metrics; however, you should note that in this case, there are two breaks in the metrics.

The one in the middle appears to be not a part of the normal data progression. Something occurred to cause the break. In some cases,

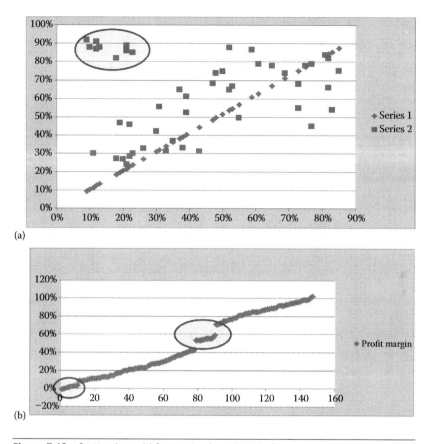

(a)

(b)

Figure 5.19   Scatter charts. (a) Scatter view for outliers. (b) Outliers could be buried somewhere else. Ask why.

you may see a normal high as well as a normal low; however, you may note a few times where the data fell between the high and the low, yet nothing to denote the differences. As with any suspected fraud or the Western Electric rules for control charts, research the differences. Why didn't the numbers fall in line?

For fraud, it is a common tendency to look for all purchases that are in round figures. The organizational cost for this item with tax and transportation comes to $3834.00. Since most item costs end in 99¢ or 98¢, add tax, and it rarely adds up to an even dollar figure. Is this a fraud or abnormality? This is definitely an abnormal total.

People have a tendency to do things that will quickly and easily return results. As for the security professionals, they need to secure all holes in the infrastructure, servers, and databases; while the perpetrator only needs to find one way to enter and get what they want.

Simple Network Management Protocol

As you progress in your understanding of the business process needs, then you can employ SNMP to inquire into most communication and computing devices. For each computer or machine, you will normally find logs telling what is happening, some of the anomalies that have happened, capacity utilization, and average used or free memory. When I needed a disk upgrade at a military data center, I first had to prove that we were effectively using the resource. To optimize the resource, I first looked at the size of the files and how often the files were being accessed, the file messaging to read or write, etc. Then, periodically, we dumped all the files to a backup environment, cleaned the disk area, and loaded the files in the order of their use so that the most used files were the first ones loaded; therefore, they resided closest to the disk head parking area, then the next most used file, etc., etc.

This semimonthly process provided the business unit customer with the fastest access to their data and reduced the normal checkerboarding that occurs within most computer disk units. Checkerboarding causes the disk head to move from one portion of the file to another open area of the disk unit to read the next and then somewhere else for the next record or segment.

So I would recommend that you determine any anomalies or security rejects that occurred on any piece of hardware; then decide how often the files are accessed and who is accessing those files, etc.

All in all, I would look at any application counters, exceptions, methods, and service states as well as CPU, memory, disk configuration changes, audit logs, and any other information that is available from that vendor. Note that each vendor provides an MIB description so that you can use most network management systems, including SNMP, to look for throughput information and issues dealing with security or limit anomalies. For an example of the Cisco environment, you can use http://tools.cisco.com/Support/SNMP/do/BrowseOID .do?local=en&translate=Translate&objectInput=1#oidContent to gain access to the MIB for Cisco equipment as shown in Figure 5.20.

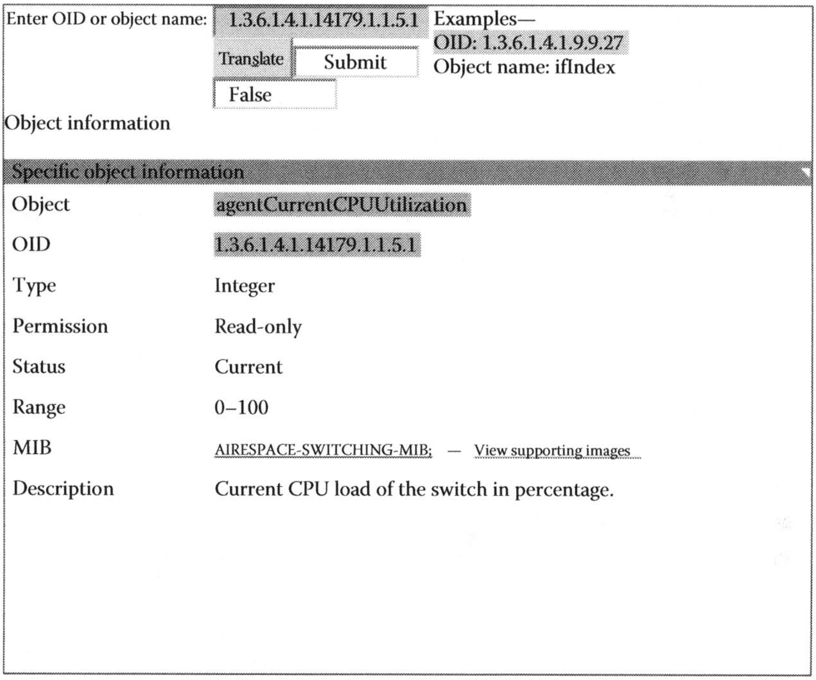

Enter OID or object name:	1.3.6.1.4.1.14179.1.1.5.1	Examples—
		OID: 1.3.6.1.4.1.9.9.27
	Translate Submit	Object name: ifIndex
	False	

Object information

Specific object information

Object	agentCurrentCPUUtilization
OID	1.3.6.1.4.1.14179.1.1.5.1
Type	Integer
Permission	Read-only
Status	Current
Range	0–100
MIB	AIRESPACE-SWITCHING-MIB; — View supporting images
Description	Current CPU load of the switch in percentage.

Figure 5.20   Cisco MIB—CPU utilization.

I might recommend that you do an Internet search for the equipment manufacturer and SNMP using Google; Bing; Moe, Larry, and Curly's new web crawler; etc., to gain information of your vendors' MIB.

Using the SNMP MIB for Cisco, you could use the tree-type structure to traverse to the field of information that you are interested in and then look up utilization statistics. The object identifier or OID is the object name and the tree traversal is 1.3.6.1.4.1.14179.1.1.5.1 as outlined in Figure 5.20.

As you review each available metric, determine which metrics will help you determine the root cause or best method to assist the business unit in achieving their goals and strategies.

IT Security

For each business process that involves ITs, business managers have had a tendency to hold IT responsible to ensure that the data are true, accurate, and available to the business personnel and, if authorized, to the customer and the business partners.

Since this responsibility entails some sort of security process that is normally not included in the business requirement documentation, the IT guru has to imagine or research the security requirement necessary for the automated environment.

Normally, the initial business requirement documentation fails to include the necessary security environment and to outline the authorization to the data based on roles. The business units have a tendency to rely on the IT professional and/or the corporate security officer to make or facilitate those conversations.

Although many business unit personnel view security as a one-dimensional environment similar to a firewall, in reality, the technical security environment is a multiple-layer atmosphere. The computer user must traverse multiple architectures prior to the user gaining access to the organization's *data. Data are the valued asset of any organization.* Data provide the necessary information for the management to make informed decisions as well as educated guesses, in lieu of just making a wild guess.

Decisions need only be made if there is no time to gain the facts.

As shown in Figure 5.21, the security architecture begins at the outer physical layer. There was a time when each authorized workstation was located in a protected area of the organization so that only authorized personnel could gain access to that controlled physical room or cubicle. In today's environment, the user can be anywhere in the world; the physical layer has been usurped under the guise of helping the organization communicate and do great things from anywhere in the world.

What once was the backplane of the mainframe is now the worldwide communication network, physically bringing the data that once resided inside the computer and directly connected to the backplane or the motherboard of the mainframe to the worldwide communication network.

This does allow the user to be a valued employee, a prospective customer, or even a potential perpetrator of a fraudulent act to gain equal access to the physical layer housing the organizational data.

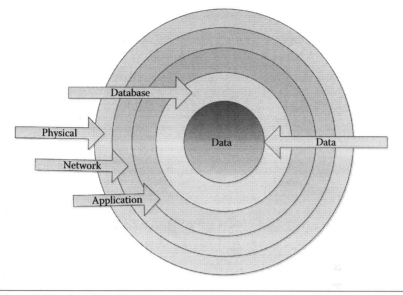

Figure 5.21   Security architectures.

The physical protection layer of protection has been surrendered for employee and customer conveniences.

Once the user has access to the physical layer of the architecture, the network layer is the next security level that is encountered.

As you may have noticed in the ISO matrices, the first two layers in the ISO model deal with the physical connections and include the electrical connectivity as well as the appropriate protocols.

Physical Layer   As mentioned above, the physical network security used to rely on a wire connection between the mainframe that is connected to the workstation (computer terminal).

Network Layer   Most networks relied on the workstation name or MAC to authorize the device access to the network. Most mainframe computers used a network configuration file to declare the network and each communication line showing the protocol, the speed, and the connection type along with a poll list showing a two-digit communication address so the mainframe could poll each workstation when the mainframe was ready to send something to that device or it would poll the device to see if the device was ready to send something to the computer system. As LANs became popular, most mainframes would dedicate a communication circuit to handle a gateway for non-mainframe protocols. The gateway acted on level 2 (data link) of the OSI model. IBM used to employ systems network architecture (SNA) protocol; whereas Unisys (once called *Burroughs*) employed a poll/select protocol. Now, they would use a gateway to connect to X.25, frame relay, cell relay, token ring, and Ethernet. Later, they started to use the newfangled business feature called the Internet.

LANs (Novell, Microsoft, etc.) employed a similar network security with access lists for devices connecting to the networks. Initially, the LANs would accept the devices; however, there were provisions to let the network administrators control the device access and most large organizations do control the workstation access. They provide permission to those PCs, laptops, and other devices and keep track of their utilization and activity. Many organizations automatically disable any workstation that hasn't been used for a specific period (90 days, 6 months, etc.).

For user access to the mainframes and LANs, the environments use a user access list where the user's ID and password are kept in a secure file so that when a user tries to access the network he or she is challenged to provide a user ID and a password. Some systems also require a biological key card and other personal information. The user's answers are checked against a secure data area and, if correct, they are allowed to use the network based on the permissions attached to that user ID.

Application Level   Each application is normally placed on some sort of server or mainframe. The mainframes and file server have similar user ID password along with biometric and/or additional personal questions before letting the person have access to the application. The application has an additional access control list where it houses each authorized user, their permissions, and any security requirements for those permissions. An open application in support of the Internet customer presence may be open to the Internet server possessing the application permissions to support the customer. The application then will retrieve the data from the database. Many applications have the ability to receive request and service workstations without involving the server that supports the application. Some applications have the ability to answer requests or process transactions using a similar protocol as the web servers. By listening for a transmission control protocol (TCP)/IP packet while employing a specific port, it will communicate with the user without server security. It relies on the application security to deal with the users.

Database Level   The database is normally housed on a file server with similar security as shown in the application level. In addition, the DBMS may have an additional access control list where it specifies the authorized user IDs, any passwords or security, and data access permissions to read and/or write at the database table, row, and/or field levels.

The database can accept a general user ID and password provided by the application software or individual user IDs or a combination of those user IDs.

Most DBMSs can service customer requests without involving the file servers that support the database system. Similar to the application calls using a TCP/IP port number, most DBMSs will respond to an SQL query or request. The standard port for an SQL call is 1433; however, an organization can use other port numbers between 1024 and 5000. If a nonstandard port number is used to add additional security, the database, as well as the user, must set up and use the same port number. Otherwise, the query will not be heard by the database. It will respond only to the port number chosen in the configuration file.

Data Layer   Since the data reside as a file on a server or within a table within a database, once the file access or database access is provided, the data will be provided in accordance with the security listed on the file server for a file or the DBMS for a database table or record.

Overview   If the Internet user gains physical access to the organization's public presence, they are probably allowed to enter an area that I refer to as the *organization's demilitarized zone* (DMZ).

This public access area normally houses a web server and the user can exchange information with web services open to the public. If the Internet user answers some questions or sets up an account correctly, they may be viewed as nonthreatening and allowed to interact with the DMZ web applications. The web server is normally designed to act on the user's behalf to send information through a firewall to the internal network and an application or database service designed to share public information or act on the public user's behalf. Any user external to the organization should never be allowed open access to the organization's inner sanctum or, as I refer to it, the *corporate network*. They should work through the DMZ environment. The authentication of the external customer or even a business supplier/partner is not an open invitation to share all information or to provide complete access to organizational data and facilities.

Normally, the DMZ service provides only predetermined access to certain information and no more. This way, if an IT guru and hacker extraordinaire gains complete control of the web server in the DMZ, he or she will still gain only a restricted access to the inner sanctum. The only messages allowed through the DMZ firewall would be the ones authorized to most customers. Although this could still be dangerous, the authentication and authorization of the web service should be fairly generic and hopefully nonthreatening to the organization.

For the web service to access a specific account or move dollars, additional security for that specific user is added to the web service authentication and subsequent application authorization based on the internal application and security data structure. For that to occur, the person must know something like a customer's user ID and password. They may also be required to have something else, like a security key, a universal serial bus (USB) plug-in with a security response system, fingerprint, or some additional security questions. Typically, an organization's security team would like to enforce a security process that includes but is not limited to something the user knows, something the user has, and something the user is. For the prospective customers, this is hard to develop and enforce.

The only truly secure system is one that no one can access.

The firewall between the DMZ and the organizational network should help to ensure that only certain messages to specific internal servers are allowed through the firewall. In many implementations of public web access, they normally place a firewall between the public worldwide network (WWW) and the web server area referred to as the DMZ. Then in most cases, you should encounter another firewall between the DMZ and the organization's internal application network.

In addition, you may find that within a well-planned organizational network, there is a division between the application servers and the database servers as well as a division between the internal users (employees) and the application and database servers. That way, you have some protection from an internal employee or a contractor going rogue and doing something that adversely impacts your organization. Recent surveys have shown that the security risks are not just from outside people or organizations; many of the bad things and fraudulent acts were perpetrated by internal trusted employees.

The internal user's workstations, scanners, printers, etc., would be part of a main network segment as shown in Figure 5.22. This multitier network, separating the user's network from the data, helps to inhibit someone who is on that network's authentication list from doing something unauthorized or unintended to the application or database servers that was not an authorized command script. If the data and the users were all on one network, the network access list may not inhibit a disruption of the operation or access to proprietary data whether it is due to an accidental access or with the intent to commit some fraudulent act. This separation may also protect those

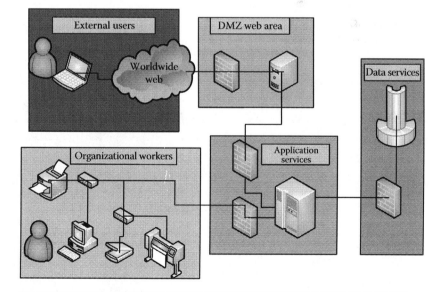

Figure 5.22   Typical organizational network.

multiuser servers from an unauthorized program or a virus being introduced to the application or database by a user's laptop, etc. The unauthorized program might have the capability to attack specific services and disrupt or steal data. This tiered network would help to inhibit certain types of transactions from going to the application or database servers.

Whenever the organizational network touches the public area network, even within a dedicated line, there should be some protection afforded to the data in transition.

I once had the opportunity to visit the dial central office of a telephone company and my escort took a set of earphones and connected it to a circuit to let me hear a conversation between two elderly ladies. Apparently, they called one another each day to discuss their latest dates and sexual encounters. As soon as I looked at the headphones, I realized that people in that organization could have just as easily connected a no-load protocol analyzer like a sniffer to a dedicated data line to see what my organization was sending and receiving. That was when I started looking into encryption for our organization. Most dedicated circuits traversing over long distances are merely a four-wire line that traverses your local telco office, a long-line carrier's circuits, and then through a local telco office at the other end.

We used to think that fiber lines were secure because someone would have to break the circuit, insert something into the fiber line, and then reconnect the rest of the circuit. The break would be seen and the IT folks or the organizational security could be made aware of the issue. Now there is equipment that will view the signal through the fiber line when you make a right-hand turn in the fiber; therefore, you no longer need to break the circuit, even temporarily.

Then there are other ways to send data. Many homeowners use radio-frequency Wi-Fi for their house network. For the most part, current wireless Wi-Fi provides up to 54 Mbps network speed. If you have the advanced system that provides both 5 and 2.4 GHz, you can attain a higher local speed, because it can use both frequencies to transmit and receive as opposed to the normal one 2.4 or 5 GHz for communication. Most people don't get 54 Mbps for downloading or uploading data. The speed depends on your Internet supplier and the number of other people who use the same communication link on your block, area, etc. My home computer speed will actually download a file at approximately 50 Mbps, but the upload speed is approximately 5.5 Mbps and a ping of about 30 milliseconds for a server more than 50 miles away.

The Fraud Red Flag

For any fraud red flags that were found during the planning phase, I recommend that you share your initial concerns with a fraud investigation team to determine if

- They want to get involved;
- They want you to stand down so they can do an investigation;
- They are interested in helping you develop some tests;
- They would just like to review your fieldwork testing; or
- They didn't believe that they were needed.

For our purposes, we would probably filter or segment the purchases made by the division so as to sample those purchased items that could be used by a private person for personal gain. Then we would traverse the paper trail from the business requisition, the resulting purchase order (PO), the receipt, the financial budget code, the invoice, the general ledger, and the vendor payment to help ensure that everything was copacetic. This should test to see if there was any foul play or signs of fraudulent activity for personal gain.

The Process

To improve a process, we need to use the information gathered during the planning stage and vet our understanding of the process and the goals of the process with the business professionals.

Don't ever lose sight of the goals. The goal of the organization may be to make money or accomplish the mission within an affordable budget.

We need to remember this point and revisit the ideas and the concepts governing the process and the process capacities as well as process throughput and constraints.

Each of us is a consumer of something. At some time in our life, we buy something; therefore, understanding the customer is not some unearthly process. As a consumer, we make most of our purchasing decisions based on our perception of price, product, and service.

Product and service include features, functionality, and availability. If I needed a parka to help keep me warm during a trip to Alaska above the Arctic Circle this winter, I don't want to buy one that will be delivered the following March. Having the product available when the consumer wants or needs it is important. Many organizations wait for the customer demand or order prior to building the product or service. Many organizations cannot fulfill all the orders within a reasonable timeframe following the customer order or demand cycle; therefore, they build the product based on expected demand. Many times with a new product, they build it while marketing builds the demand through advertising and other marketing approaches. Look at the toy industry. They start designing and building next Christmas's toys shortly after this Christmas.

Another thing that we need to be aware of is that the person doing the work and completing the tasks is the person who really knows what is happening. The manager, the director, the vice president, etc., may believe that it is working in one way; in fact, those managers may have developed and documented the procedures; however, you may find that the current line workers weren't aware of the published document. An adjustment to the procedures being accomplished may have occurred due to a previous process improvement study or a production line recommendation which proved fruitful. If you ask senior leaders and then ask the production line personnel and find that there are two different procedures, then please be aware that one hand doesn't know what the other hand is doing. This will affect efficiency and effectiveness.

While auditing a small design and construction organization as an external auditor, I was testing to determine how the IT department and the organization handle personnel job changes within the organization, new hires, and terminations. In a discussion with the chief of personnel, he showed me a three-part form and informed me that they use the form for new hires, position changes, and terminations. The form is completed by the HR department and the second and third copies are sent to the accounting department so they can adjust any payroll changes; then accounting sends the last copy to the IT and they add the user, change, and/or remove access to the organizational data and the business applications.

When I met with the IT director, I asked to see the forms and he asked, "What am I talking about?" He has never seen the form. I talked to accounting and found that the form included pay scale so they destroyed the third copy of the personnel form.

So I asked the IT director, "How do you know when a new person is coming on board?"

He said, "Normally, the new person's supervisor calls and lets me know the date of hire and what permissions the person would need."

So I asked, "How do you know when a person moves to a different job in the organization?"

He answered, "Normally, the gaining supervisor lets me know about the move and what access permissions will be needed. Then I contact the losing supervisor to determine when to remove the worker's permissions and authorization."

Then I asked, "How do you know when a person is terminated?"

He answered, "I am normally invited to their going-away party."

I tested the systems and didn't see any issues with terminations, change of permissions, or new hires. The informal process worked great, but the procedural manual needed revision.

Thing are not always what the senior leadership imagines.

Process Analysis

As specified in the prior sections, the process to be assessed should focus on the delivery of the product or the service to the process customer. Any process improvement recommendations shouldn't reduce the functionality or the feature critical to the customer quality requirements.

Since the KPIVs including raw material and resources are costs and the KPOVs represent production, we can measure production based on how many products or services are performed over a period (throughput). Please note that the following example does not include any transport time between each step, yet in reality, there may be lead and lag times as well as transportation time.

Example

Figure 5.23a shows a process with four specific steps. The total processing time that adds value is an average of 30 minutes from start to finish. This will provide an output throughput of two processes per hour if the customer requests come in one at a time.

You may note that the worker doing steps 2, 3, and 4 are idle while step 1 is being processed. Then, workers doing steps 1, 3, and 4 are idle while the person assigned to step 2 is in progress. This scenario occurs each time the process begins.

You will also notice that step 3 takes the most time to complete than any other step. This is and should be considered the bottleneck

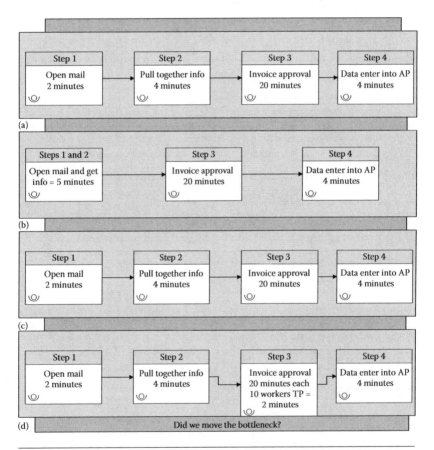

Figure 5.23 Throughput analysis: (a) current four-step process – value time = 30 minutes, throughput = two per hour; (b) combined steps to improve the process – value time = 29 minutes, throughput = two per hour; (c) mass production – value time = 30 minutes, throughput = for first hour, two per hour, and three per hour thereafter; and (d) hire nine more invoice specialists – value time = 30 minutes, throughput = 15 per hour.

of the process. You may have heard the old saying that the chain is only as strong as the weakest link. The same is true when you think about process throughput. No matter what you do to the rest of the process steps, you will never be able to have a throughput faster than your bottleneck step. Since this bottleneck step takes 20 minutes, the best throughput you will ever obtain is no more than three per hour. Dr. Eli Goldratt explains this law in his book *The Goal*. His book also reminds you about the need to focus on your organization and business goals and not to focus on unit costs as a goal.

If you automated the three other steps so that the combined steps only took 1 minute, your value time will be 21 minutes and your throughput will still be two per hour. If you didn't require the three other steps, then your value stream would be 20 minutes or three per hour.

- If only one item is sent through the value chain, the total time is 27 minutes.
- The minimum theoretical time it takes for the process of the requestor's perspective is 27 minutes.

Figure 5.23b shows the process of combining step 1 and step 2 to save resources as well as time. Although you reduce staff by one, which reduces personnel costs, the throughput remains the same. The value process takes 29 minutes, but the throughput is still two per hour. Automating or reducing any step other than the bottleneck will add future capability but it would not increase throughput.

Figure 5.23c shows what will happen if you take Henry Ford's concept of mass production should you be able to warrant a continuous procession due to the incoming customer requirement. By adding more requests, you keep all resources active as well as providing a waiting queue for the bottleneck. You never want to have a bottleneck that is idle. That is a total waste of time adding no value to the process.

If you have the invoice requests, this continuous process will add to the cycle time (work in progress) for each individual request; however, the value-added time will remain the same, but throughput could increase to three per hour. This is accomplished by keeping the bottleneck active. As long as the bottleneck is continuously productive, your throughput could equal the time it takes to accomplish the bottleneck step.

In other words, you can have an output of three per hour or every 20 minutes if the bottleneck is kept active.

If there are more items in the value chain, we employ Little's law (inventory = throughput * flow time), where *throughput* is the throughput of the process and is equal to the slowest step in the process and *flow time* is the average time that a typical flow unit spends within the process boundary.

Continuous processing is effective only if the load or the need can support the continuing process. If not, you might consider utilizing the resources somewhere else until you can establish a number of processes that run together. That way, you may be able to take advantage of the continuous processing advantages and throughput.

By using Little's law, we can evaluate the following loads into the process as

$$\text{Inventory} = \text{throughput} * \text{flow time};$$

therefore, inventory ÷ throughput = flow time.

Using that formula, we get the data shown in Table 5.7.

Please realize that, although the delivery performance increases with the throughput increase, each process except the first one spends more time waiting for a process step. In fact, the efficiency ratio is computed by using the value-added time divided by the flow time.

Therefore, the efficiency ratio of processing one item is 30/30 = 1 efficiency ratio.

If the fifth request enters the queue with four ahead of it, the fifth item processing will be completed in 100 minutes; therefore, we compute the efficiency ratio as 30/100 or an efficiency ratio of 0.3.

For an inventory of 100, the efficiency ratio for the 100th request will be 2000/30 = 0.015.

- If when your invoice is received there are four invoices in the queue and one has just started, your invoice will wait until the fourth invoice (first in–first out) moves to step 2 for your process to begin. The total time or cycle time to complete those

Table 5.7 Flow Time—Efficiency Ratios

QUEUE	THROUGHPUT	FLOW TIME	EFFICIENCY RATIO
1	Two per hour	30 minutes	1
5	Three per hour	1.6667 hours or 100 minutes	0.3
10	Three per hour	3.333 hours or 200 minutes	0.15
100	Three per hour	33.333 hours or 2000 minutes	0.015

five items is approximately 100 minutes with only 30 minutes of value-added time.

Figure 5.23d shows the value stream and the throughput if the requirements warranted hiring 9 more invoice reviewers. Using 10 workers to accomplish the 20-minute process would provide a capability of throughput for step 3 as 2 minutes apart or 30 invoices per hour. Did we remove the process bottleneck? No.

We did move the bottleneck, but not remove it!!

The bottleneck moved from step 3 to steps 2 and 4. Now that we have the capability to process step 3 every 2 minutes, we have to wait for 4 minutes for the triage clerk to provide the detailed file for the PO.

When you add capacity and speed to the bottleneck, you will find that you may remove that step as a bottleneck, but the next slowest step will then become the bottleneck. For our exercise, we have two 4-minute steps, so we created two other bottlenecks; but we did gain a throughput of 15/hour from the initial 3/hour (Table 5.8). We have also changed the flow time and efficiency ratio.

You will note that we have added personnel costs to the process by hiring nine more workers; however, our capacity and productivity are greatly increased due to the adjustment in throughput. We are more productive; however, our inventory is up as well.

Resource Reallocation

Another option to increase throughput without hiring nine more employees would be to reutilize your resources.

For this exercise, we used four people, each accomplishing one step. As you reviewed the exercise, I am sure that you noticed that during the first 2 minutes, persons 2, 3, and 4 were idle; during the next 4 minutes, persons 1, 3, and 4 were idle, etc.

Table 5.8 Adjusted Process; Adjusted Efficiency Ratio

QUEUE	THROUGHPUT	FLOW TIME	EFFICIENCY RATIO
1	2 per hour	30 minutes	1
5	15 per hour	75 minutes	0.4
10	15 per hour	150 minutes	0.2
100	15 per hour	1500 minutes	0.02

These are the possible solutions:

- Option 1: Train all four employees to accomplish all four steps; this would require training, but no additional personnel. This would increase the throughput from three per hour to seven per hour.
- Option 2: This option would be to schedule each employee to do a specific number of steps and then move to accomplish a different job, such as in the following:
  - Person 1 does step 1 five times, then does step 3 twice, then back to step 1 for another five processes, and then does step 3 again twice.
  - Person 4 does step 2 five times (20 minutes), then does step 4 once, then step 2 twice, then step 4 once, and continues to do step 2 twice and step 4 once. The throughput would move to 10 minutes after the first 20 minutes or six per hour after the first 20 minutes.
- Additional options could be used as well without increasing the number of workers; however, you may have to increase the pay scales of the nonspecialist workers now accomplishing specialized steps. This is especially true if you are involved in a heavily regulated industry or a union workforce.

Bottlenecks

- Most processes with multiple steps will have at least one bottleneck.
- If a process bottleneck is idle, the throughput and productivity is at a standstill.
- Any process where the average times for the steps are not equal will have a bottleneck.
- Reducing the time it takes to complete a step other than the bottleneck may provide future capability or reduce the value stream; however, it will not increase the throughput.
- The throughput will always be directly dependent on the bottleneck step.
- Always queue the work so that the bottlenecks are continuously busy.

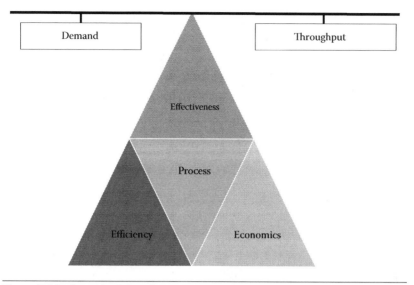

Figure 5.24 Demand and throughput.

- When you consider that the process goal is to provide the customer with something, the process will be a bottleneck until the customer's *demand is equal to the throughput* as shown in Figure 5.24.

Fraud Red Flag Testing

Based on the fraud red flag that we saw in the planning stage for the procurement process (spaghetti diagram—Figure 4.6), we tested any POs that could be used for personal use or personal gain and found that all items were distributed to the appropriate business units and were still in inventory or disposed of after they were used. Additional interviews of division personnel determined that the process was developed when PC prices were extravagant and since the division controller needed a PC to produce the monthly, quarterly, and yearly financial consolidation and reporting required a PC. Since the division controller was also responsible for the divisional spending and budget, it made sense that his computer be used for the approval and disposition of the purchased items. The budget was not available to provide computer workstations in all departments. Therefore, the centralization of the purchase process was assigned to the controller in an effort to curb excess spending.

Since the cost of a desktop workstation has been reduced due to new and faster technological production, this process could be adjusted to increase efficiencies, yet maintain budgetary controls. The costs of workstations have been reduced since those times and the controller was totally open to our recommendations to move many of his non-accounting activities to areas where it made sense to occur. As you review the VSM (Figure 5.25), the spaghetti diagram (Figure 5.26), and the SIPOC matrix (Figure 5.27), jot down your thoughts on how to improve the purchasing process using the available technologies.

_____

_____

_____

Since the assessment planning feeds the fieldwork stage, we will use two of the planning figures to assess and possibly improve the procurement process. We will use the VSM.

Procurement Process Analysis

As you review the VSM, the spaghetti diagram, and the SIPOC matrices, you might provide your observations and possible solutions on the following lines or on a separate piece of paper.

_____

_____

_____

_____

Process Observations

- Other than the vendor analysis, the data entry steps consume a majority of the time to complete the process.
  - The employee builds a requisition (17 minutes).
  - The buyer uses the requisition to build the request for proposal (RFP) (20 minutes).
  - Finally, the buyer uses the requisition and the RFP to build the PO (20 minutes).
  - The data information used to populate all three data entry processes used a total of 57 minutes; most of this information is duplicated information from the original requisition.

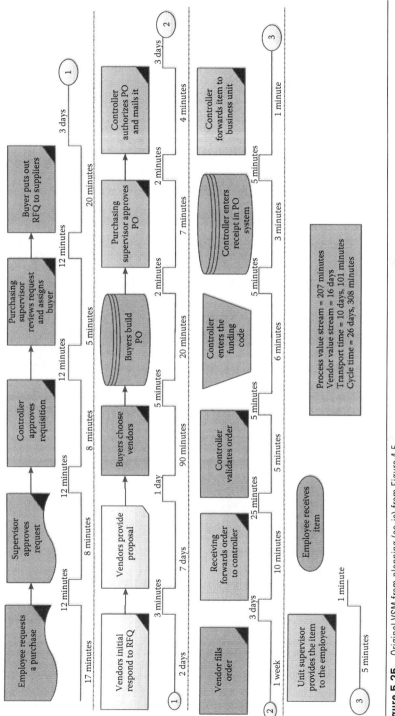

Figure 5.25 Original VSM from planning (as-is) from Figure 4.5.

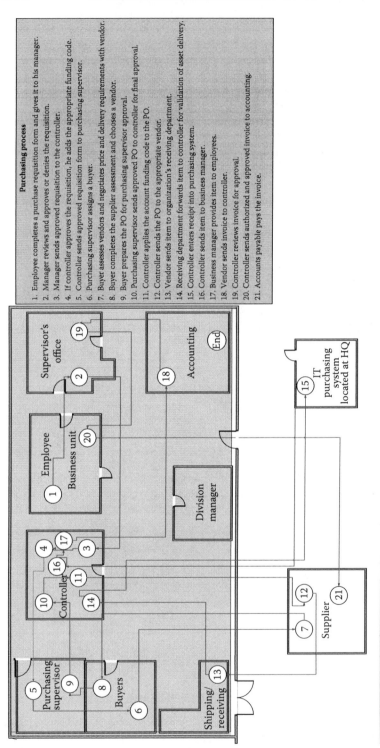

Purchasing process

1. Employee completes a purchase requisition form and gives it to his manager.
2. Manager reviews and approves or denies the requisition.
3. Manager sends approved requisition to the controller.
4. If controller approves the requisition, he adds the appropriate funding code.
5. Controller sends approved requisition form to purchasing supervisor.
6. Purchasing supervisor assigns a buyer.
7. Buyer assesses vendors and negotiates price and delivery requirements with vendor.
8. Buyer completes the supplier assessment and chooses a vendor.
9. Buyer prepares the PO for purchasing supervisor approval.
10. Purchasing supervisor sends approved PO to controller for final approval.
11. Controller applies the account funding code to the PO.
12. Controller sends the PO to the appropriate vendor.
13. Vendor sends item to organization's receiving department.
14. Receiving department forwards item to controller for validation of asset delivery.
15. Controller enters receipt into purchasing system.
16. Controller sends item to business manager.
17. Business manager provides item to employees.
18. Vendor sends invoice to controller.
19. Controller reviews invoice for approval.
20. Controller sends authorized and approved invoice to accounting.
21. Accounts payable pays the invoice.

Figure 5.26 Spaghetti diagram—purchasing process (as-is).

Step	Source	Input	Process Step	Output	Customer
1	Supply cabinet	Requisition form	Order an item	Requisition	Supervisor
2	Employee	Requisition form	Business approval	Approved requisition	Division controller
3	Division controller	Financially approved requisition	Assign buyer	Approved requisition	Buyer
4	Vendors	Bids	Buyer analyzes suppliers	Purchase order	Procurement application
	Division controller	Financially approved requisition			
5	Purchase supervisor	Approved PO	Division order	Purchase order	Vendor
6	Vendor	Ordered item	Product delivery	Ordered product	Division controller
7	Division controller	Product validation	Enter receipt	PO receipt	Procurement application
8	Vendor	PO and shipping documents	Request for payment	Invoice	Division controller
9	Vendor	Invoice	Payment authorization	Approved invoice	Accounting

Figure 5.27   The SIPOC matrix from planning (as-is) from Table 4.6.

- Since supervisors and managers are normally responsible for their operational budget, is it necessary for the division controller to be involved in every purchase?
- If the buyers have done due diligence during the purchase of similar items or equipment, shouldn't the RFP process and vendor choices be optional?
  - Saving the buyer's time of 1 hour and 50 minutes and an 11-day process.
- Considering that the division controller has six activities for each item purchased in the division, where does he or she find the time to accomplish his or her financial responsibilities?
- Since the order is received by the Receiving Department, it would make sense that they enter the item receipt into the purchasing system to alleviate the "segregation of duties" concern as well as reduce the non-accounting workload for the controller and increase their accountability or purchased items.

Opportunities
- If the data entry process beginning with the employee who recognizes the need for the item is able to trigger the procurement process by directly entering the data into the online

purchasing system, then the supervisor could review the requisition and the justification online and approve or deny the requisition without having to file paperwork

- If the cost of the requisition is within the manager's budget, then the application program could be set to allow the supervisor's approval to authorize the creation of the PO.
  - The supervisor could add his or her authorized funding code (checked by the PO system).
- If the requisition costs are not within that business unit budget, then the approval can be done online by both the supervisor and the division controller.
- Once the controller or the supervisor approves the online requisition, the application program could automatically build a baseline PO and alert the buyer.
- When alerted about the PO for a new or unique purchase, the buyer could build the request for proposal (RFP) using the PO data and send it to a number of eligible vendors.
- When alerted by the PO for a purchase that is similar to prior acquisitions, the buyer can choose the vendor and electronically send the PO to the procurement officer for final signature and send the PO to the vendor.
- In addition, with the computerization of the requisition form, you will no longer require storing the blank forms or file the completed requisition forms, thereby saving costs for printing and storing forms.

- Moving the responsibility for checking and distributing the received package from the division controller to the receiving department
  - Reduces the workload of the division controller;
  - Allows the department that receives the package to check it thoroughly and enter the receipt into the purchasing system database so the accounting department will be aware of the supplier's delivery in accordance with the PO for invoice processing;
  - Segregates the purchasing and approval process (logical control) and the physical asset, thereby setting up a segregation of duties (SOD) environment (reduces the opportunity for someone to commit fraud).

- Maintain an integrated purchasing system that tracks each order from requisition to the pass off to accounting for invoice payments. The integrated PO system should
  - Allow for electronic sign-off by the appropriate supervisors and controller, when necessary, based on budget, spending authority, and/or expense versus capitalized purchasing;
  - Track the vendor pricing, delivery performance, and department satisfaction for the vendor's previous orders;
  - Categorize each vendor as to the type of service or products provided;
  - Reduce the need for RFPs and the vendor time for responses.
- With the two systems shown above, I estimate that the internal process value stream will be reduced from 207 minutes to between 73 minutes and 143 minutes, as savings of between 30% and 64% staff hours.

Process Considerations

- While assessing the process, look for the wastes due to complexity, transportation of data or products, over- or under-inventory, waiting time, overcontrols, overprocessing, and movements.
- Consider the process with respect to the following:
  - Reduction of inventory levels → Reduce capital investment in inventory
  - Ways to reduce time-to-market → Increase revenues through increased sales
  - Reduce equipment downtime → Increase capacity
  - Reduce rejects or reworks → Decrease material cost and increase ROI
  - Speed up delivery time → Increase revenue

Remember that most customer purchases are based on product, service, and price.

- If the IT department will develop data entry screens, keep them uncluttered and inviting; otherwise, people, including potential customers or contributors, will shy away from getting involved.

- If you do require a lot of information to proceed, then put the data fields to be completed on two or three pages. I don't recommend any more than three pages; otherwise, people will not want to use the entries.
- Validate the data entry as they enter it or as they try to move to the next page, if possible.
  - Users don't want to complete screen 3 and press Submit, only to find that they have to return to screen 1 and fix an error, then traverse through the other screens to submit the data a second time.
  - This is especially true if your system finds only one error at a time.
- Prepopulate as much data as possible from your customer or user data profile so that the user will have to enter only what is absolutely unavailable to your organization.
- If you have customers, maintain a customer information file to help ensure that you are able to understand their needs and not just fill a specific request.

Note: If you are a pharmacist filling a doctor's prescription, a record of your customer's other medication may save that client from a drastic and possible fatal reaction to the combination of chemicals.

- If you determine that a step in the process is to be removed or adjusted, please remember to review the SIPOC matrix to determine if that step produced an output that is necessary for another step or another process.
- For every process,
  - Identify the customer and determine what you need to know about the customer;
  - Collect and analyze reactive system data, then fill in the gaps with proactive approaches;
  - Analyze the data to generate a key list of customer needs in the customer's language, not your jargon, acronyms, etc.;
  - Translate the customer's language to a CTQ list;
  - Set the specifications to adhere to the CTQ;
  - The control charts should have CTQ limits for quality, delivery performance, price, etc.

- For IT WAN environments, review the message traffic at strategic points.
  - At critical areas, look into adding a redundancy port to share the load or act on the primary entry area should the primary access point fail.
  - If the load is excessive at any point in the necessary network, add bandwidth or build a load sharing service.
  - If the cost of adding bandwidth is either too expensive or not totally warranted (more bandwidth would help with the response time; however, the cost for the next step up in bandwidth doesn't meet the advantages of adding the extra bandwidth), then you may look for different noncompetitive organizations to share a bandwidth upgrade to T1, T3, etc.
    - For a manufacturing division in Mexico City, the monthly financial data were transmitted via a dial-up line with inadequate response time and excessive noise, which caused almost continuous retransmissions.
      - So we contacted the Bank of Mexico to see if we could pay them to rent some of their wide bandwidth to alleviate our issues as well as increase the bank's revenue and ROI.
    - Use a chart to outline the average message length per application and the normal network traversal (if feasible, use a network management system to build a control chart for each port or line used for the production atmosphere in support of the external customer traffic as well as internal organizational traffic, including e-mails and any other communication method used to conduct the day-to-day business).
    - Recommend that you track the bandwidth utilization and the message lengths per application as well as per communication line.
- Remember
  - "Seek first to understand; then to be understood"— Stephen Covey, PhD (1932–2012), *The 7 Habits of Highly Effective People.*
  - "Quality in a product or service is not what the supplier puts in. It is what the customer gets out and is willing to

pay for. Customers pay only for what is of use to them and gives them value"—Peter Drucker (1909–2005), who wrote 37 books on business and management. He was awarded the Presidential Medal of Freedom in 2002.

The OSI Model

- OSI level 1—Physical interface matters
  - The physical interface must meet the IEEE standards for Ethernet and the various environments traveling over the Ethernet environment (Security Monitoring devices, video, etc.). Incorrect wiring or electrical power can result in multiple failures.
    - Bad cabling (opens, shorts, crossed pairs, split pairs, etc.) are showstoppers
    - Misconfigurations and incompatible technologies proprietary (vendor specific) versus standards
  - The Ethernet hub works at level 1 and transmits any message received to all other ports. It does no routing; therefore, it works electronically as a broadcast to all nodes on the network it services.
- OSI level 2—Data link coding and decoding
  - OSI Level 2 sets up the type of communication used for the transmission of data.
    - Whether it is point-to-point, fiber, ATM, token ring, Ethernet, frame relay, etc., each protocol has a different framing for the message to be sent and received.
    - The serial delay and message sizing is declared by the transmission protocol used for the data link. As I have mentioned earlier, Ethernet has a maximum message length of 1500 bytes.
    - Some protocols have fixed length messaging, while others have variable length messages.
  - Since OSI Level 2 works at the protocol level, it supports gateways from one protocol to another without any specific serialization delays.

- The gateway can take a fiber link to a wired Ethernet, Ethernet to SNA, token ring to Ethernet, Ethernet to Unisys poll select protocol, etc.
- OSI Level 3—Network level provides for switching and routing technologies
  - The serialized decoded message is viewed by the switch or router to determine where and which port the message should be sent in an effort to reach the appropriate receiver (IP address).
    - The OSI Level 3 processes reduce activity on all ports by sending the message through ports that the routing table has determined.
    - The routing table is a designated and learning process, where the administrator can set up specific ports to handle specific IP addresses, but the router also has the capability to learn new routes.
      - If a router receives an unknown IP address, it broadcasts to all ports and listens for the AK. Once the AK is received, the router adds that address and probable network to the receiving port.
      - The router does have a capability.
    - The switch is normally a one-IP address-per-port process; however, the newer switches have been set up to work as switch routers and could be used to route WAN addresses.

We will not discuss the rest of the levels, for you will probably not add value to the delays or the throughput. I will say that based on my experience, Level 4 transmission control protocol (TCP) and user datagram protocol (UDP) work much faster than Novel's SPX transmission. Novel's IPX for file and print services across a LAN were extremely fast for its time; however, Novel was extremely slow across a WAN.

We will not review the other OSI layers (5, 6, and 7) since they vary and are widely dependent on use and application for each session. They focus on the user's application and on the application session (layer 5—NetBIOS, SQL, etc.), presentation (layer 6—encryption, ASCII, GIF, JPEG, MPEG, etc.), and the end-user application (layer 7—e-mail, web-based HTML, FTP, etc.).

Business Continuity Management

This portion of the assessment tries to answer the question "Is the management planning to continue their business during adverse or abnormal conditions?" For the technology team, business continuity management directly supports the A in the acronym CIA (confidentiality, integrity, availability). Continuity management helps to ensure that the data and the technologies are *available* for the business processes to continue processing. Needless to say, the cost to provide this service is based on the recovery time required by the business unit as well as the current data necessary.

There are two factors that should be provided by the business unit; however, the cost of the two factors should be recognized by the business process.

The two factors are the following:

- Required time objective (RTO): The RTO is the interval of time from when the contingency situation is declared until the business unit has the facility to accomplish their business processes. The question to ask is, how much time can pass from when the declaration of the contingency situation to when the business process can/needs to resume operations?
  - If the RTO is long, the cost is comparatively low, but if the RTO is low; whereas, if the business unit must be recovered quickly, then the cost is high.
- Required point objective (RPO): The RPO describes the interval of time that might pass during a disruption of service before the quantity of data lost during the period exceeds an agreed-to threshold.
  - Due to an unwanted event, how much data can you afford to lose without having serious or devastating consequences?
  - Totally up-to-date data are considered *high availability*, which may require duplication of all data in a geographically separated facility as the data become available or as it is created.
  - The cost of duplicating data across geographically separate facilities requires duplicated resources and high-speed transmission facilities.

I always recommend using a supply-and-demand curve to depict the RTO, the RPO, and the impact.

The costs in Figure 5.28 depict a typical environment against a baseline cost of *x*.

As the time for RPO and RTO gets longer, the costs go down. A question to ask the business unit and the technology folks is, have they matched the business process impact (revenue, lost business, customer dissatisfaction, etc.) with the recovery time and point costs?

There are normally five phases to the business interruption event as shown in Figure 5.29:

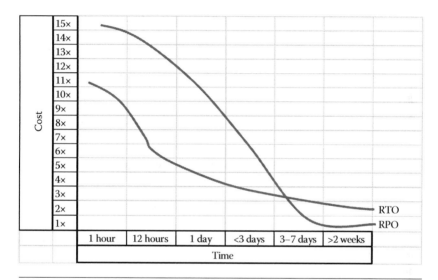

Figure 5.28 RTO–RPO representation.

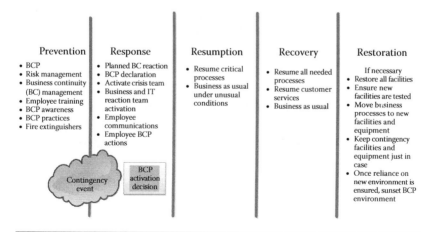

Figure 5.29 Contingency planning.

1. Prevention—Are processes in place to prevent or mitigate the impact of the contingency event?
   a. How do they protect the organizational assets (manage risks)?
   b. Business continuity management
      i. Business continuity plan (BCP)
      ii. Safety classes
      iii. Crisis committee
      iv. BCP testing
      v. BCP awareness program
   c. Safety programs
   d. Fire alarms
   e. Fire suppression systems
2. Immediate response
   a. Crisis management to contain the damage and activate the BCP if needed.
   b. People and property safety—People first then property.
   c. Knee-jerk reaction to an event can be more detrimental to the organization than a thought-out plan.
      i. In case of fire, liquid could help; but if the available liquid is volatile, then the situation is worsened.
         (1) Water on a grease fire has a tendency to splash the grease and increase the danger.
      ii. Baking soda works better on a grease fire than water.
      iii. Fire extinguishers work better to subdue fires rather than many other liquids, especially kerosene.
      iv. Water doesn't do well when you have electricity involved.
         (1) We used to use halon, but that has switched to FM2000 or something similar.
   d. Determine the critical applications and processes and prioritize the recovery.
      i. Organize the necessary steps to recover in a checklist or something similar to preclude having to make hard decisions while under duress.

3. Resumption—Resuming critical processes
   a. Resume time-sensitive operations at an alternate site if necessary.
   b. Determine critical needs of the employees and customers.
4. Recover—Recovering most or all business processes
   a. Business as usual under unusual conditions.
   b. Restore customer services under unusual circumstances.
5. Restoration—Restoring operations for long-term production
   a. Repair or replace facilities, equipment buildings, and personnel if necessary.

As we mentioned in the assessment planning stage, you should review the BCP as well as the business impact analysis (BIA). These documents must be based on today's environment, today's business needs, and the technologies and applications supporting the business processes in place today.

The BIA should reflect the following:

- Each business unit process requirements.
- The prioritization of application or process recovery must focus on the organizational needs.
- Each business process input requirement along with the source should be listed to preclude not providing the resources of a high-priority function because a lower-priority function that creates that input was not deemed important.
  - The list could be made be available through the use of a SIPOC matrix.
  - When converting a bank's BCP from one application to another, we did an undated BIA and found that the main trigger for most of the bank's processes relied on e-mails from the customers and other bank processes; yet during the prior year, the e-mail server in their backup facility was removed to save money.
    - If they did not reinstate the e-mail service at the contingency site, they would have the facility to accomplish the critical process, but not the impetus or trigger to get the process started.

OKLAHOMA CITY BOMBING

When I think of the five phases of a disaster, I remember the Federal Credit Union situated within the Federal Building located in Oklahoma City and the employees who lost coworkers and friends on the morning of April 19, 1995. During a contingency or dire event, people don't have time to think; therefore, they relied on the survivors and their BCP with checklists to reconstruct their business processes and to service their customer, clients, friends, and owners, many of whom were people and family members of the people who worked in that building.

- Did the prioritization process include the input from all business units as well as the approval or at least the understanding and the acceptance of the prioritization?
- Since business continuity management is based on an economic reality, did the organization match the cost of the BCP process for each business process against the impact on the customers?

As you review the BCP, you should try to determine if

- The business unit and the IT department agreed on the recovery prioritization.
- The steps used to accomplish the recovery are feasible.
- The steps and approach are flexible enough to use during different situations.
- The steps necessary for the continuity of services are known to the people who need to accomplish those steps.
- The BCP has been tested for various possible scenarios (fire, storms, frozen water pipes, strikes, or other events that precluded employee attendance, explosion, widespread communication, or electrical outages, etc.).
- There are plans to use an off-site location to meet and conduct business should the normal site be unavailable.
  - If so, does the site get power and communication from a company different from the organization?

- Are the off-site systems and/or equipment compatible with the organization's equipment and systems?
- If public transportation is shut down, will the plan work?

Do you think the BCP will achieve its goals?

To help with your testing, I would recommend that we start with an FMEA. The FMEA could be done in conjunction with the process workers to help you understand what they believe could happen as well as you share what you believe could happen. If you find that their possibilities are well thought out and they were involved in developing the BCP, then that would definitely be a great sign that they are doing it right.

Your agreement with their FMEA would indicate that you believe that they are also doing the right things.

Fieldwork Analysis

The ultimate goal of any assessment is to help the business unit and the organization by providing either assurance or corroboration that they are doing the right things or recommendations on how to improve their process and operations. In many cases and for many of the assessments that I have done over the years, the results showed that in many areas, the business units were doing the right things the right way; however, they could improve their processes. Most organizations are so dedicated and focused on the production atmosphere that they don't take the time to look at the changing environment and changes in the customers as well as the minor adjustments that they have done to the process. When a normal business unit considers a review of the process, they envision a major project with training, outsourcing, new applications, new equipment, etc.; therefore, they don't or can't expend that many staff hours to even start. Using an outside team, like the auditors (internal or external) or a cross section of internal personnel, they get a different perspective of their own operations. All processes can be improved; and based on the dynamics of the business environment, all processes need to be adjusted and improved.

While the business needs change, most people do not reengineer their process. They may add or adjust one thing or another, but then the original efficient process is no longer that efficient; yet the business need is growing due to the business growth.

As we analyze some of the business processes using the VSM, SIPOC, RACI, and spaghetti diagrams, we can see some possible improvements areas.

Purchasing Process

Looking at the purchasing process VSM in Figure 5.25 and the spaghetti diagram of the process as depicted in Figure 5.26, we can develop some process adjustments now that the cost of computers has been reduced to almost a commodity level; therefore, they are more affordable.

The VSM showed us a process value stream of 207 minutes with a cycle time of 26 days, 5 hours, and 8 minutes. The spaghetti diagram in Figure 5.26 provides a view of 21 steps with seven stops where the division controller's involvement was necessary due to the lack of computers. The redundant steps involving the division controller appears as a waste of his or her valuable time and salary. Although the stops were the controls necessary in the past, we do not believe that they are of value with today's desktop PC costs, networking, etc.

Problem or concern: The problem and our primary concern with the purchasing process based on what we see in the VSM (Figure 5.30), RACI, SIPOC, and spaghetti diagrams (Figure 5.31) is overburdening the division controller with work that can be feasibly accomplished by other personnel equally well at a cost per hour that is below the controller's pay scale. A secondary area of concern with the current process is based on the lack of SOD within the process. When one person has physical control of an asset as well as logical control of the distribution of that asset, it provides a person or a position with the means or opportunity to commit a fraudulent act and remove the asset from the organization. As you may recall, the fraud triangle consists of need, opportunity, and rationalization that the act is justified.

Since during the fraud portion of the assessment, we concluded that there were no fraudulent purchases on the part of the controller or anyone using his PC; and considering that PCs, especially desktop PC workstations, can be purchased for less than $300 per

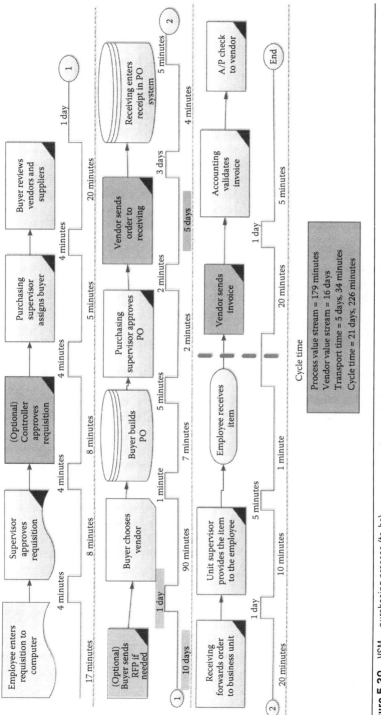

Figure 5.30 VSM—purchasing process (to-be).

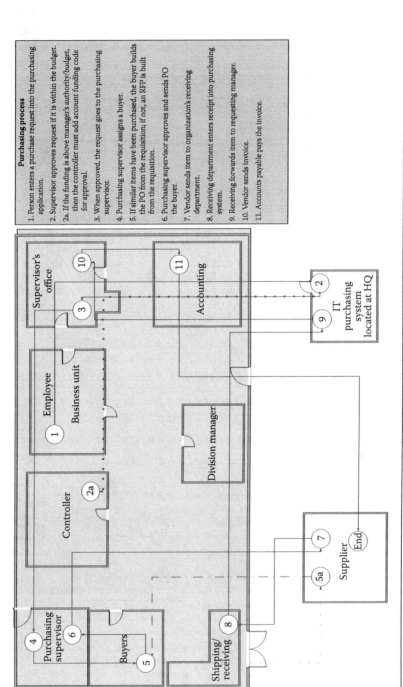

Purchasing process

1. Person enters a purchase request into the purchasing application.
2. Supervisor approves request if it is within the budget.
2a. If the funding is above manager's authority/budget, then the controller must add account funding code for approval.
3. When approved, the request goes to the purchasing supervisor.
4. Purchasing supervisor assigns a buyer.
5. If similar items have been purchased, the buyer builds the PO from the requisition; if not, an RFP is built from the requisition.
6. Purchasing supervisor approves and sends PO the buyer.
7. Vendor sends item to organization's receiving department.
8. Receiving department enters receipt into purchasing system.
9. Receiving forwards item to requesting manager.
10. Vendor sends invoice.
11. Accounts payable pays the invoice.

Figure 5.31 Spaghetti diagram—purchasing system (to-be).

unit and considering the number of purchases that the organization accomplished per week, month, and year, the placement of the PCs in receiving, etc., is warranted.

Possible recommendations: The new process would incorporate the following:

- Adjustment in the purchasing application to allow all division personnel to create an automated requisition in lieu of creating a requisition form
- Adjustment of the requisition software to allow each manager to approve up to a specific monetary amount based on their budget and budget code so the controller won't need to approve all requests (reduction in controller's workload and value time)
- Ensuring that the application tracks vendor performance and applies customer surveys to all business unit purchases to establish the vendor price, product quality, delivery performance, and service after the sale
- The purchasing software including a survey of the buyer to determine service before the sale, issues, etc.
- Addition of a PC workstation in the receiving department so they can enter the receipt of the package/asset (reduction in the controller's workload and addition of an SOD as opposed to the as-is process)

The recommended new process steps are as follows:

1. The requestor enters a requisition into the purchasing application.
2. The application requests for the unit manager's approval.
   a. If the manager has the budget and approves the request, the application applies the business unit funding code and alerts the purchasing supervisor.
   b. If the business unit doesn't have the budget or if it is a capital investment, the requisition goes to the division controller for approval or denial (*optional*).
   c. If the controller approves the requisition, he or she adds the funding code or the capital investment code.
   d. If denied, the alert goes back to the supervisor (*optional*).
3. Once the requisition is approved for purchase, the application program alerts the purchasing supervisor.

4. The purchasing supervisor chooses the buyer to handle that purchase.
5. The buyer looks for a vendor using the purchasing application to determine if a vendor has been chosen for that asset in the past or if the buyer can create an RFP (application provides the requisition data for the RFP) and send it to multiple vendors.
6. The buyer picks a vendor based on product, price, and past service or anticipated delivery performance and service.
7. The buyer sends the PO to the purchasing supervisor for final approval if the item exceeds $xxxxx.00.
8. Depending on the purchase amount, the buyer or purchasing supervisor sends the PO to the vendor.
9. The vendor sends the asset to the receiving department.
10. The receiving department enters the receipt information into the purchasing system.
11. The receiving department sends the asset to the business manager.
12. The vendor sends the invoice to accounting.
13. The accounting department reviews the PO and the receipt and pays the invoice.

The recommended process adjustments should reduce the following:

- Number of steps from 21 to 11 with 2 optional steps dependent on the purchase price and/or capital investment
- Asset delivery cycle time (not including the vendor actions) from approximately 10 days and 5 hours to about 5 days and 5 hours
- Wasted transportation time from 10 days and 94 minutes to 5 days and 34 minutes

The costs of implementing the recommended process adjustments include one desktop PC and the adjustment of the use and business settings in the purchasing application.

IT Considerations

As you consider the IT environment in support of the business process for your organization, I would like to share what Dr. Ken Sherman told me when I attended his class on data communication.

Your customer's perception is your reality.

Ken Sherman
Author

This brings us back to the VOC, the response time that each and every business application user receives, meets, exceeds, or falls short of the customer expectation. Like any business, the IT environment must add customer value while showing an ROI. The ROI may not be monetary; yet someone does need to pay the bills.

As you review the LAN and WAN in support of the business process and the users, you should concern yourself with two things:

1. Is the user satisfied with the performance and the speed of the automated process?
2. Do the trends show that upgrading the responsiveness of the network is or will be needed in the near future?

To ascertain the user requirements for each application, you can develop matrices to track the number of users, the normal message size, and the normal messages per day, per hour, per week, and per day of the month. For this, you could track the utilization of the program, network statistics, server, and communication statistics to build the matrix. I have provided a matrix in Table 5.9 that could be used to help develop your control chart approach.

As you should be aware by now, the latency delay of any network is directly related to the bandwidth (network speed or throughput), the size of each message, and the distance that the message travels.

When you review the wants and the needs of the customer (business network and application user), you must consider the cost to satisfy the needs. Just like in a car lot, if the customers can afford only a certain amount of money, they don't go to the Bentley automobile dealership.

The customer needs may be satisfied and may be some of the wants or desires as well at the Ford, Chevy, and/or Dodge dealerships. The same is true for the IT environment.

The customer wants a certain response time for each user. Physics and the cost of communication lines will tell you that the costs to

Table 5.9 Application Norms

DIVISION

DIVISION MANAGER

IT UNIT   CONTACT NUMBER   E-MAIL

CONTACT   CONTACT NUMBER   E-MAIL

ITEM #	APPLICATION	# USERS	AVG. MSG SIZE (BYTES)	CONCURRENT USERS	NETWORK TYPE	AVG. TRANSACTIONS/ PERSON/DAY	AGGREGATE NETWORK SPEED	AVG. DISTANCE FROM SERVERS	AVG. BITS/ HOUR	REMARKS	SERIALIZATION DELAY (MS)
1	ABC	57	180	48	LAN	60	100 Mbps	100 m	2,880	Ping range: 28–99 ms	0.028125
2	DEF	49	483	36	WAN	85	56 kbps	1500 mi	3,060		0.054642857
3	HIJ	12	2,400	7	WAN	22	56 kbps	585 mi	154		0.00275
4	KLM	37	678	35	LAN	42	10 Mbps	100 m	1,470		0.014355469
5	NOP	134	1,400	110	LAN	65	54 Mbps	100 m	7,150		0.069824219
6	QRS	2300	424	225	LAN	37	100 Mbps	100 m	8,325		0.081298828
7	TUV	24	375	24	LAN	85	100 Mbps	100 m	2,040		0.019921875
8	XYZ	84	450	75	WAN	63	256 kbps	450 mi	4,725		0.139957031
9	E-mail (msg)	2400	85	575	WAN	72	1 Mbps	450 mi	41,400		0.525796875
10	E-mail (F-XFR)	2400	3,258,560	575	WAN	54	1 Mbps	450 mi	31,050		0.303222656

provide equal service to the local (same building and floor) user and to the user thousands of miles away are not equal.

For a long-line connection, each increase in speed has an additional cost; yet the more distant, the more costs. A simple four-wire voice-grade line analog or digital has a cost per distance (usually referred to as the interconnection exchange cost [IXC]), plus you need the connection from each of the local telephone companies servicing the server and the user.

Since the service cost is based on the expected speed, the higher the speed, the more the costs; the longer the distance, the higher the latency signal delay. The art of the data communication business is to balance the user needs with the cost of providing those needs. The user's wants or desires cost extra. What can the user accept that the technologies can deliver without going over the budget?

There are a number of organizations that believe that if the system slows down, just add resources to the process. Normally, increasing the network speed (in bits per second) costs more and does increase throughput, which reduces response times; however, it doesn't always help the end user.

Since many applications are now web based, let's look at the hyper-text page loading. A study presented in an article by Mike Belshe on May 24, 2010 (mikebelshe.com) provided the data shown in Figure 5.32. It concluded that data transmissions speeds up to about 5 Mbps add value to the page loading time (PLT) of a web based application at an acceptable percentage. The study also shows that the PLT of a web-based page does not improve at the same rate than it had with speeds less than 5 Mbps. This data allude to the fact that the ROI to

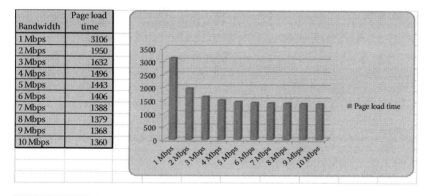

Bandwidth	Page load time
1 Mbps	3106
2 Mbps	1950
3 Mbps	1632
4 Mbps	1496
5 Mbps	1443
6 Mbps	1406
7 Mbps	1388
8 Mbps	1379
9 Mbps	1368
10 Mbps	1360

Figure 5.32   Page load time (milliseconds).

increase the speed above 5 Mbps may not be of value to each user. We must realize that a network speed affects all users on that network; therefore, the number of concurrent users on a network should help guide us to the economically realistic speed to support the users.

Since the user response time and delays are adversely affected by the message size, network speed, and distance, let's take a look at the response times of messages based on distance. The same study shown in Figure 5.32 also tested the message round-trip time as shown in Table 5.10.

The rationale for considering the round-trip time is based on the time-out function in most data communication activities and appliances. If the sender does not receive an AK or NAK from the intended receiver, then the sender will initiate a retransmission of the original message. As I mentioned earlier in this chapter following the ISO model, I presented an issue supporting a tent somewhere in the world.

If you are planning to use a control chart in an effort to periodically or continuously check the response time of an application, the service, the application, etc., I do recommend that you begin with the furthest geographical unit from the mainframe or the application service area.

Normally, the farthest geographically separated office will receive the longest transmission time or response time. If you compare the trends between the furthest area and the closest area, they should be trending similarly, unless something is affecting one area or building while not affecting another. To explain it a little more clearly, as new users come aboard, business needs expand, traffic will also expand, and load on the application service will also increase; therefore, all trends should show a slower response if the issue is the application

Table 5.10 Round-Trip Time and Distance

TO	DISTANCE (KM)	DISTANCE (MI)	RTT VACUUM (MS)	RTT IN FIBER (MS)
Durham/Raleigh, NC	196	121.79	1	1.52
Atlanta, GA	386	239.85	3	4.56
Washington, DC	529	328.71	4	6.08
Nashville, TN	549	341.13	4	6.08
New York City, NY	855	531.27	6	9.12
Denver, CO	2197	1365.16	15	22.8
Mexico	3232	2008.28	22	33.44
Los Angeles, CA	3417	2123.23	23	34.96
Brazil	6519	4050.73	43	65.36

Note: RTT: round-trip time.

or file server. Whereas if the LAN response goes up without a trend in the wide area response times, then there may be changes in the LAN that need to be addressed. If the response time is increasing for just one satellite office, then we can focus on the link to that office as the root cause. If all satellite offices experience an increasing response time, then the WAN appears to be the congestion point.

As I mentioned earlier, milliseconds and microseconds may not sound like very much; but you need to consider how many people use the environment. If the perceived experience is time consuming to the customer, then will that customer even bother to deal with you?

The same is true with the internal users. If the response time appears to be or is perceived as too long for the user, they will not be satisfied or they will find alternatives.

IT Bottlenecks and Slowdowns

During the analysis, you may determine that your bottleneck is within the server, the workstation, the LAN, or the WAN; but what can we do about it?

Some ideas are listed in the following:

- Measure the server, network, and database allocations correctly based on the needs of the application user and probably growth.
- Minimize the message traffic by using the shortest message size.
  - This can be accomplished by using a form of nonupdatable data and then have the application transmit only the updated (new information) data.
- Load sharing can alleviate an overly worked server or overburdened network.
  - If you do need to load share, it may be advantageous to place the additional environments in geographically separated areas.
  - Proper geographic placement will reduce the propagation delay caused by the distance between the user and your main site.
    - Example: With a main site on the East Coast, the placement of a load-sharing environment near the West Coast will save approximately 2100 miles with

a propagation delay of about 1722 milliseconds or 1.7-second delay each way.

- Load sharing in geographically separated places will also reduce the single point of failure when viewed from a business continuity management perspective.
- Database load sharing: Most DBMSs in today's market allow the application to share the database.
  - Placing a subsidiary database in a local area can alleviate the WAN latency as well as reduce the bandwidth congestion for the WAN.
  - In most cases, you set up *one* master database as the system of record, and then parse out the data to subordinate databases to house either some data or all data as a subsidiary to the master.
    - The secondary databases can contain all the data, one or more product lines, geographically separated customer support information, etc.
  - If you are working with a wide-area group of users, you can position subsidiary databases at specific geographic areas to provide quicker service to those users.
    - The subsidiary database will provide answers to all queries. This should suffice to handle all reads locally; the write or updates coming from the users must update both the subsidiary and primary databases.
  - If an update or write command is transmitted and deemed authorized by the database security, then the activation can be either asynchronous or synchronous.
    - Synchronous update will suspend the acknowledgment of the transaction as completed until both the primary and subsidiary databases are updated; therefore, the primary will update and then update that record within the subsidiary database.
      - This approach will tie up the user's cursor until both database updates are completed and then acknowledged.
    - Asynchronous updates may update the subsidiary and set up a transaction to update the primary system of record database before acknowledging the transaction.

- – If that transaction does not update the system of record database for whatever reason (communication outage, system or network crashed, etc.), the data update will not be truly consummated.
  - – The user will not receive a total confirmation; and although they will get their cursor back to do something else, the application should be programmed to send the user a message advising them that confirmation will be provided once the process is completed.
- For Internet users, you can set up multiple web servers geographically separated across the nation or across the world based on your user community so that distance doesn't become a deterrent to your productivity or your user's confidence in your organization's ability to support and service them.
  - Even if the support is for internal organization personnel, dissatisfaction with the services can lead to unnecessary outsourcing.
    - – Whether your business process is IT, HR, etc., if an outsourcing agency can provide better services at less cost, then the organization may outsource your business unit.
    - – I have heard of some organizations where almost all business units were outsourced.
- There was a time when your long-line telecommunication diagram would be set up with a delta wiring scheme with AT&T as one side of the triangle, Sprint as a second side, and MCI as the third side of the triangle. That way, if one organization had a major outage, you would still have data and voice communications.
  - The fallacy in that thought pattern was that the major long-line carriers rented each other's circuits; therefore, you would never be certain that the line your data were traversing was that vendor's line.
- Most major data centers know that they should have two entry points provided by two different telephone offices so that the data center communication would not be disrupted by one dial-central office or for that matter one backhoe.

- The same is true for electrical services; most major data centers arrange for two electrical inputs on two sides of the building provided by two different electrical grids so that if one grid or that pesky backhoe causes an issue, the other side or grid will provide electricity for the systems.
- Multiple routes to the servers, networks, and electrical reduce the single points of failure.
- The same is true within your organization. Single points of failure can include one person who knows it all; reliance on any one entity for the survival of the organization is normally doomed to fail. This is true even if the person is the CEO.
  - If an accident happening to one person or one piece of equipment or one wire can cause an irreparable issue, then you have a major problem that you need to resolve.
  - You need to focus on replicating that entity.
  - Equal partnerships, especially if the two partners add their innate skills in making the business successful, normally take out insurance on one another so that if they are no longer able to provide those skills to the organization, the other partner could buy out the family members and own the business outright so that inexperienced heirs could not be equal yet contributing less than the original partner.

Since cloud computing is in vogue and you may not have the authority to review the cloud vendor's environment, you should at least look at the cloud agreement.

Dealing with vendors can be an art of negotiating as well as building a win–win scenario for both organizations. When I worked in the IT environment for a manufacturing firm and set up their first WAN, I made it quite clear to the hardware and network providers that if they didn't want to think like any valued full-time employee in our organization, they need not pursue a relationship with our IT team.

We presented the point that when we establish the new WAN, we expect to see some unforeseen things pop up. We weren't interested in any finger-pointing as to who or why; we, as a group, will diagnose the issue and fix it so that the organization will be provided with the communication links that they expect. After the flames subside and the smoke clears, we will do a lesson learned so that any anomalies that occurred during this implementation won't happen in the future to any of our vendors or business partners.

If they think we are just a customer, then they are not a partner.

Whether your organization established or is establishing a cloud or a hybrid cloud, the business requirements and expectations should be outlined in the agreement. When you subscribe to a network, data, and/or application provider that has not proven to be a true business partner, you need to ensure that their protection of your data, message traffic, and availability is outlined in the agreement, including any liability for nonperformance.

This assurance of availability needs to include their ability to provide a feasible business continuity management program.

With any outsourcing, the operational responsibility is still within your organization, even though you have let some other organization manage your business responsibility. If there is a breach of confidential information, loss of data, loss of reputation, etc., your customers will blame you.

PART IV
PUTTING IT
ALL TOGETHER

6

ASSESSMENT REPORTING

The ultimate goal of any assessment is to provide the business unit with assurance that they are doing the right things the right way or to provide ideas and recommendations to do things even better.

If there are no concerns or recommendations found during the assessment, then the assessment and the testing provide assurance that the business unit is accomplishing the business process in an effective and efficient manner.

If, however, the testing and the assessment do result in one or more process improvement recommendations and the recommendations are not acted upon, then the time and the effort expended for the assessment may have been, in essence, useless.

If your assessment provides ideas, insights, and/or recommendations, then you would like to ensure that the business unit acts upon your recommendations. For someone to act on another person's recommendation, he or she must first believe that your concern is warranted and he or she must believe as you do, that something should be done about it.

Belief → Action → Change

Belief spurs action and action spurs change.

It is my belief that many of us would just rather let the business manager know of our findings, concerns, and recommendations, and then be on our merry way; however, in most organizations, it doesn't normally work that way.

In many organizations, other people who feel as if they are stakeholders in that and possibly all business units' success may want to review the assessment report. This is especially true if the assessment costs the organization money.

If you are a government organization in the free world, you may be required by law to make the report available to all citizens of the

241

country or the municipality since they are, in essence, the people who paid for the assessment through taxes, etc.

In most organizations that I have dealt with, many of the senior leaders want copies of any analysis or audit report whether it is for their business units or other business units within the organization.

When it comes to audit reports, it seems that everyone wants to be included and get a courtesy copy of each report. It is almost as if they want to know when other business units have issues. I am unsure of the total rationale for some report distributions. There are times when I believe that the other leaders want to be able to point fingers at the most recent audit report recipient so they can feel better when they receive their assessment report. Whether the rationale is to help make their team and their management style look better; to help them achieve higher budgets, promotions, and/or higher bonuses; or to provide ideas as to how they can improve their business process, I can't positively attest to any of those rationales. It may be a combination of various reasons.

The art of communication stems from one entity (the sender) speaking or conveying a message in a language or a form such that another entity (the receiver) can visualize and understand the picture that the sender is conveying. Sometimes people use acronyms that others may or may not understand and, therefore, the message being conveyed is not received as the same message.

In addition, if you want to change something and the other person has the ability to make that change, then the other person must first believe in that change and recognize that the change will make him or her happy and/or successful in his or her endeavors. The recommendation and the change must include a "what's in it for me?" question.

Share the Picture

When I retired from the military service, I went to work for a manufacturing company that was almost 150 years old. During their history, they started using product orders (instructions) when they were producing bogie springs for sale. The bogie spring is the coil spring between the truck or the tram chassis and the wheel to reduce the bounce for the passenger's comfort. Since the company started using product orders years before I joined their IT team as a systems programmer, everyone in the office knew what they meant when they said that the bogie was situated in the coiling area. Since I had just left the U.S. Air Force, the picture that I got was there was an unwanted enemy in the coiling area while they were conveying the fact that the production order (cookbook) was physically located near the coiling machines. Needless to say, I hadn't a clue as to what we could do about the enemy craft in the coiling area. Call the police or what?

For those gurus that work in the banking industry, you may think *ATM* only means *automated teller machine*; however, if you talk to your IT WAN folks, they may tell you that *ATM* stands for *asynchronous transfer mode*. The IT ATM allows about 45 Mbps transfer speed for WAN communication as opposed to the older T1 circuits that provided about 1.524 Mbps or a 1 Meg line as opposed to the 23–64 Kbps channels in an ATM line that could be mixed and matched any way the organization wants it. We used to split the channels of our communication lines in support of computer data and tie some together for a 256 Kbps circuit for dial-up videoconferencing. I once wrote a paper called "BCP–ATM," which stood for *Business Continuity Planning— According to Me*. Be careful when using acronyms and ensure that the meaning is the same for the sender and the receiver.

Report Distribution

Although many of you may not believe that the assessment report distribution is important, I disagree.

Whether you found detrimental issues for a business unit or merely some process improvement that you recommend, airing the business unit manager's items of concerns across the organization and in the government sector across the citizenry can be embarrassing to the business unit manager as well as the business team.

For those who do not work for the government, government auditors are normally required to make their audit reports a matter of public record; you have my sincere condolences. Airing the business unit's missteps, issues, and problems may publicly embarrass the manager and the team members in the eyes of the organization, and their friends, neighbors, and business associates, and, worst of all, their family.

Another reason to limit the audit report distribution is due to the fact that each person who sees the report will look at the report based on his or her perspective of life and the organization. The IT guru as well as the engineering department members will be looking for a report that includes detailed technical information; the chief financial officer will be looking for the costs, value, reportable tax loss, etc.; while the chief executive officer or president as well as the auditee partner will be searching for how to fix the problem fast and get on with the work. Some other managers and directors may be looking to see how the other department's audit issues can further their standing within the organization, their department's budget, and their personal promotion or salary increase. I know that you will find it hard to believe, but there are some organizational members who do not solely focus on the good of the organization. Some people actually believe that there is a shortage of opportunities and they need to constantly put down others so they may look better; whereas some of us believe that there is enough for everyone and we delight when others get promoted as we look forward to our promotion.

If you think that I am incorrect, look at the more recent elections and the negative campaigning. The political candidate's campaign is based on showing the opposition candidate's faux pas, missteps, and errors in judgment. Unfortunately, it works in many elections.

I am a firm believer that you need to keep the dirty laundry found during any assessment focused on the business unit and those organizational members who can fix the issue or mitigate the impact or the probability of failure. The idea is to focus on the concern and the risks or the inefficiency and don't let people, politics, promotions, or hidden agendas get in the way of dealing with reality. Nobody is perfect.

Please note that the author of the assessment report also faces a conundrum as to how to present the concern and the recommendation in such a way as to communicate the author's and the assessment team's perspective to a multitude of business professionals with different backgrounds and different agendas. The legal person is looking for this, the IT technologist is looking for that, the HR guru for that, the chief financial officer for that, etc., etc., etc.

Focus on the Issue/Concern

Throughout my time as an auditor, I have never met a manager who said, "I have been waiting with anticipation for this audit report.

Although I am pretty busy today, I will cancel my wife's plans for this evening so I can sit back and gain your perspective of my operation. Thanks so much for helping," or "Not tonight, honey. I really want to read this audit report."

It is my belief that many audit managers, corporate audit executives, directors, etc., want the board, senior leadership, and other directors, etc., to be aware of how hard they and their teams work to help the organization maintain their risks within the organizational risk appetite. As such, they provide a standard audit report format starting with the background where they go into detail about why they are doing this assessment and how they took these samples based on this populations, sampling, etc., etc., etc.

How many times have you read a report that reads similar to the following?

In consideration of that update transaction process with an approximate population of 140,000 transmissions per month, we chose a random sample of 73 transactions to provide us with a 95% confidence level plus or minus 5% and a possible sampling error of 5%. From the errors found when assessing those 73 transactions, it was determined that the average error rate for customer record updates is 6.33%. This exceeds the risk acceptance level for this business operation as derived from the organization's documented risk appetite and the impact that this business process has on the success of the organization.

The report statement took over 90 words to tell the reader that the business process had a 6.33% error rate.

The *we determined, we chose*, etc., statements are focused on the auditors and not on the business. It is as if the audit team is trying to show how hard they worked and is not focusing on the business or the concern. Please realize that I did hear one organization's board ask the general auditor, "Why do we pay so much for an audit team that doesn't find that many Severity One issues?" As many may realize, the definition of internal audit focuses the group on assurance and consulting.

The definition of assurance is as follows:

1. A positive declaration intended to give confidence; a promise
2. Confidence in one's own abilities
3. Providing a confident feeling that things are fine

Be happy—don't worry.

The consulting process is based on helping the business functions survive and prosper as well as advising about risks, controls, and risk mitigation or treatments.

Another report paragraph that really used to get to me is as follows:

Based on our sample, we found that 12% of the requests were not approved by the appropriate supervisor in accordance with a standard operating procedure.

Some immediate thoughts about that audit issue are the following:

- Why should the business unit manager care about the form being signed?
- Why do the forms need to be signed by the appropriate supervisor?
- Who is the appropriate supervisor and why should I care?

For my first assignment as a member of the KPMG risk assurance practice, I was asked to audit a regional bank using the Federal Financial Institutions Examination Council (FFIEC) examination standard. When I provided my manager with a matrix of the issues that I found, she reviewed it overnight and gave it back to me with red markings on many of the issues that I found. Most of the red markings said, "SO WHAT?" Although I did find a few significant risk issues along with a number of issues with their business continuity plan, I had not provided the impact the issues had on the business.

The issue was written to denote that the current condition did not pass the FFIEC-based test.

So what?

My manager reminded me that if the issue does not directly affect their business, why should they really care? Why should they do anything about it?

A weakness in a control, even a security control, does not guarantee that the weakness will be leveraged and used to commit a fraud, loss of asset, loss of customer, confidentiality issues, etc. The weakness may have the likelihood to occur that is so negligible that the risk is too low to even worry about.

The issue must adversely affect the business for the business to spend resources on a risk. Without risk, you have no business. Some folks truly believe that "the larger the risk, the larger the return." Of course, it could also be said that the larger the risk, the larger the possible loss or gain.

To start a business is easy; to continue the business is an art.

Old Chinese proverb

The Institute of Internal Auditors outline states that you need to present five items in your definition of a finding:

1. Criteria—What criteria do we use to base our concern on? Regulation? Fraud? Standards? Etc.?
2. Condition—What we found; our observations and/or results of our tests.
3. Cause—Root cause. What is the root cause? As we don't want to treat the symptom, we want to treat the root cause.
4. Effect—Explain the impact on the business unit, the process, and/or the organization (rationale to do something about the situation); *so what?*
5. Recommendation—What is our recommendation to alleviate the issue, the concern, and/or the impact?
   a. The recommendation should focus on the root cause, the corrective action, the risk removal/mitigation of impact or likelihood, the controls, or the recovery actions.

In lieu of following those five requirements in that order, what if we present the *issue* and the *effect* on the organization as the first statements of the finding? That way, we put the business unit or the process prior to presenting why we did the audit, the criteria that we used to base our testing, how we accomplished the testing, etc., etc., etc.

It is a shame to say it, but many business leaders that I have met are so busy trying to meet goals and especially stretch-goals that all they want to hear from the audit is what are the issues and how can we fix the issues quickly so their managers will let them do what they do best, produce results.

How does a lack of an authorized approval signature adversely affect your organization's business process, reputation, profitability, etc.?

The fact that there was a noncompliance finding that indicated a lack of following procedures by someone does not show any impact on the organization or the business unit. Whether someone did not adhere to a standard procedure or even an industry regulation may be a symptom; however, those statements do not show any impact on the organization or the root cause. Not following a procedure or even a law does not always constitute a failure. I do think that the business unit should determine the root cause and then decide about the action.

Does a missing signature constitute a real problem, a monetary loss, a symptom, a training need, a legal dispute, fraudulent transactions, an outdated procedure, etc.?

As I mentioned earlier when I brought up the New York statute concerning the railroad car crossing a city street, the statute was outdated; but no one rescinded it until they had to abide by it; and I will bet that some of the procedural documents that you come across will be outdated as well. The same is true for some of the steps used in a production process.

Why do we care that the form wasn't signed by some supervisor?

I will make the assumption that there is or was a reason for the signature step. If the step was developed to help ensure that one person could not order or assign some asset without a second person's approval in an effort to inhibit fraud or embezzlement from occurring, then I can see the rationale. The protection of organizational assets may then be the impact, but the cause (*root cause*) of the issue is *definitely not* included in the statement.

I would expect that the *root cause* could be a lack of training, a lack of caring, complacency, poor management, an attempt to defraud, or maybe some emergency requirement.

Focus on the issue and not the audit work.

For example,

- Five staff workers share their passwords; therefore, there is no accountability for general ledger adjustments and memos.
- Ten percent of the requisitions were not authorized by managers; therefore, based on average requisitions, the organization may have a possible loss of $237,000 in assets.

   (Do you think this will get the business manager's attention?)

   - Your recommendation may include a full review of those transactions by qualified fraud investigators to determine if legal action needs to be taken by the organization against any perpetrators.
     - If fraud is found, then a full review of all transactions may ensue (big dollars—reputation risk increases, etc.).

As I mentioned earlier, don't use industry or audit jargon to illustrate any pertinent information, especially if your assessment report goes to other leaders and stakeholders.

If you are an international firm, you need to be aware of who will need to understand the report and how that area's, sect's, or country's customs may affect the written or spoken word.

In the United States of America, we may keep our business card in a wallet situated in our pants' back pocket, in essence, next to our behind; while in the Orient, they keep their business cards in their vest or chest pocket near their heart. They have a tendency to value their name and contact information more dearly than many U.S. businesspersons.

Draft Report

In my opinion, the draft report should be shared with the business unit line managers prior to any escalations of issues, concerns, opinion, and recommendation to the upper-level managers, directors, etc.

This way, the manager has the opportunity to review your findings and guide you to the rationale or other items that reduce the impact or value of the findings, and to make sure that there are no surprises at the conclusion of the reporting and the presentation of your report to those leaders who requested the assessment.

If you ever surprise a manager in front of his or her supervisor or above, you may never get that manager's attention in the future.

If you are a lineman of a football team and blindside the quarterback on the other team while he has the ball, you may be applauded by your teammates and fans; however, if you ever want to have a continuing business relationship with a person, you don't want to blindside that person in front of his or her supervisor or management.

I am a big proponent of participatory assessments, where the business unit line management is invited to participate in each phase of the assessment and to review the tests and the findings as they occur.

When I was assessing business units as both an internal and an external auditor, I tried to share my findings as we determined that they were findings. Don't forget that if a process fails a test, it does not always constitute an issue. There may be other information that needs to be reviewed, some mitigating process that fixes my concern, etc.

CASE **6.1**

When I was assessing organizations, one of the tests was to obtain the employee termination list over the past 12 months and match those personnel with the current access lists for the employee areas, servers, network, and applications. During a Statement on Auditing Standards (SAS) 70 review of a regional bank, they had only five terminations over the past 12 months. One of those people was still listed as active on the network and application access lists. Mathematically, this was a 20% error rate.

Through further investigation and queries, I found that the person provided her notice of termination so she could spend more time with her family. Her manager accepted the notice of termination and completed the proper forms to remove her employee access to the building, servers, network, and applications. After submitting the proper paperwork for the employee termination to security, the manager realized that she really needed that person to stay on for another month until some of the other employees were back from vacation and training. The supervisor asked the employee to stay on for another month and the employee said okay. The supervisor then alerted the organizational security and they removed the employee from the automatic termination list for the previously scheduled date. The internal security expected that the supervisor would send new paperwork for the new termination date while the supervisor thought that her call to let security know that she was going to retain the employee for another month was enough to take care of the change. In other words, there was no process in place to take care of changing a termination date using the same termination paperwork.

Based on the circumstances, I searched the computer and network logs to determine if the employee did access the network, server, or application following her adjusted departure from the organization. I found that her user ID was not used since her last full day of work at the bank.

If you consider the initial finding of a 20% error rate, the issue could have caused an unsatisfactory rating; however, since the 20% was really only one occurrence and there was no impact on the organization, the issue became a recommendation that they include a new procedure to handle adjusted termination dates in the future.

Use your recommendation to share the ideas brought out by the assessment team and then listen to the business unit for they will surely come up with an even better, more efficient, or more effective way to satisfy the concern.

Prior to my retirement from auditing, my last organization had a practice in dealing with the recommendation and the audit reports. When we developed the draft report, we included our recommendation. As we reviewed the draft report with the business management, they developed their management action plan, which could have been our recommendation or a more detailed action plan to reduce risks, issues, or our concerns. We would then remove our recommendation and include the business unit's action plan, including suspense dates, in our report. That way, the issue and the business management's response were the key to the report that went forward to the senior leadership and the audit committee.

We saw no value in showing our recommendation along with their plan as they hopefully accomplished the same thing. The only time we left our recommendation in the final report was when the audit team did not agree that the management action plan did enough to alleviate our concern. We would have discussions with the business unit; but if there was no agreement about their action plan and our recommendation, we left both in the assessment report.

This way, senior leadership could review our concern and recommendation and the plan of action by the business owner. Admittedly, I don't recall this being done for any of my audits. If they came up with an action plan that I did not believe would reduce the concern to a reasonable level, we discussed it. Once we agreed to a plan that would reduce the issue to an acceptable level for both teams, that plan became their action plan.

A Picture Can Say Volumes

Earlier in the assessment planning stage, you developed two diagrams to denote the VSM of the process that you observed along with a spatial diagram of the same process (spaghetti [as-is]).

During the fieldwork and continuing on into the reporting stage, the assessment team, including business unit members, developed the to-be diagrams (VSM and spaghetti) as you analyzed the current process and the available technologies showing the results of the team's recommendations.

I believe that if you do make a difference to the process that can be shown in those diagrams, then you should include the diagrams in the report so that business management and senior leadership can see the current *as-is* and the recommended *to-be* process so they can compare the current and the possible future state of the process if they approve the recommended adjustments.

The VSM (Figure 6.1a and b) shows management the reduction in value stream and cycle time; while the spaghetti diagrams will show a side-by-side comparison of the number of steps required to complete the process.

As you can see by the comparisons (Figure 6.2a) between the *as-is* (Figure 6.2b) and *to-be* diagrams (Figure 6.2c), the management will have a visual of the more efficient and effective way to see the recommended adjustments to the process.

Use the diagrams and other matrices where they are needed to show your point of view and rationale for the recommended changes, but don't overpower the reader with too much nonessential information.

Many people are visual people; that is why many executive reports are presented as stoplight report showing red, yellow, and green.

If the report becomes too lengthy, then use an appendix to present the other corroborating diagrams or matrices, which helped you formulate your conclusions.

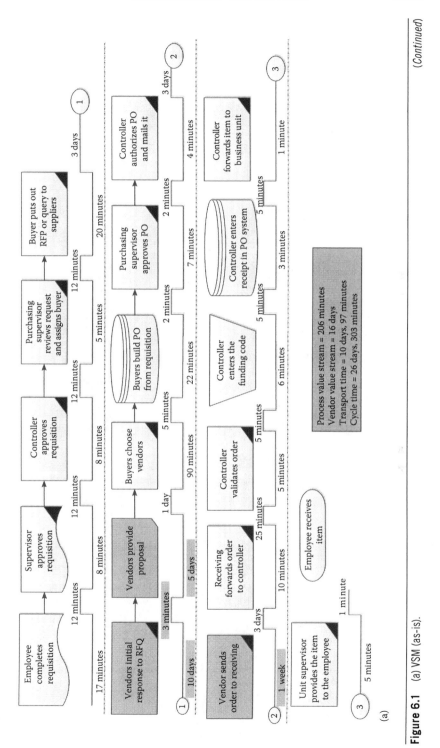

Figure 6.1 (a) VSM (as-is).

(Continued)

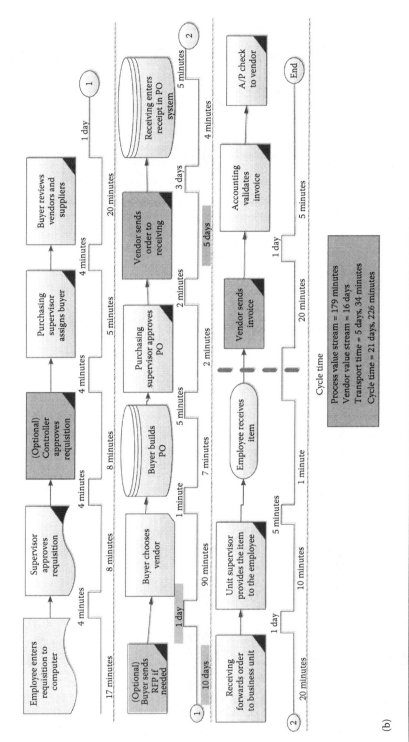

(b)

Figure 6.1 (Continued)   (b) VSM (to-be).

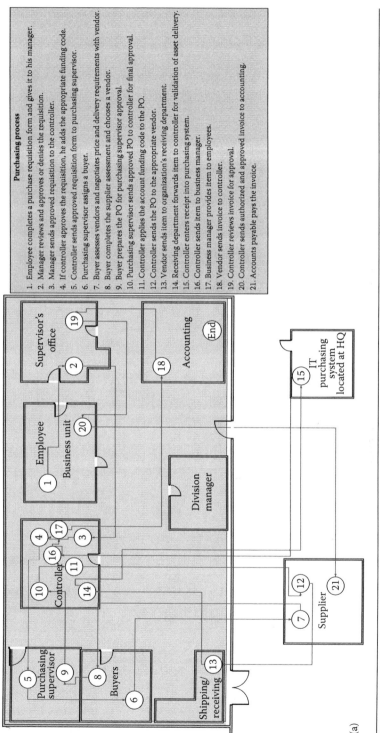

Purchasing process

1. Employee completes a purchase requisition form and gives it to his manager.
2. Manager reviews and approves or denies the requisition.
3. Manager sends approved requisition to the controller.
4. If controller approves the requisition, he adds the appropriate funding code.
5. Controller sends approved requisition form to purchasing supervisor.
6. Purchasing supervisor assigns a buyer.
7. Buyer assesses vendors and negotiates price and delivery requirements with vendor.
8. Buyer completes the supplier assessment and chooses a vendor.
9. Buyer prepares the PO for purchasing supervisor approval.
10. Purchasing supervisor sends approved PO to controller for final approval.
11. Controller applies the account funding code to the PO.
12. Controller sends the PO to the appropriate vendor.
13. Vendor sends item to organization's receiving department.
14. Receiving department forwards item to controller for validation of asset delivery.
15. Controller enters receipt into purchasing system.
16. Controller sends item to business manager.
17. Business manager provides item to employees.
18. Vendor sends invoice to controller.
19. Controller reviews invoice for approval.
20. Controller sends authorized and approved invoice to accounting.
21. Accounts payable pays the invoice.

Figure 6.2   (a) The process steps of the current environment (as-is) and the proposed process (to-be).   *(Continued)*

(a)

Current process (as-is)	Proposed process (to-be)
1. Employee completes a purchase requisition form and gives it to his or her manager.	1. Person places a purchase request into the system.
2. Manager reviews and approves or denies the requisition.	2. Supervisor approves request if in budget.
3. Manager sends approved requisition to the controller.	2a. If the funding is above manager's authority, the controller adds account funding code for approval.
4. If controller approves the requisition, he or she adds the appropriate funding code.	3. When approved, the request goes to the purchasing supervisor.
5. Controller sends approved requisition form to purchasing supervisor.	4. Purchasing supervisor assigns a buyer.
6. Purchasing supervisor assigns a buyer.	5. If similar items have been purchased, the buyer builds the PO from the requisition; if not, an RFP is built from the requisition.
7. Buyer assesses vendors and negotiates price and delivery requirements with vendor.	6. Purchasing supervisor approves and sends PO to the buyer.
8. Buyer completes the supplier assessment and chooses a vendor.	7. Vendor sends item to organization's receiving department.
9. Buyer prepares the PO for purchasing supervisor approval.	8. Receiving department enters receipt into purchasing system.
10. Purchasing supervisor sends approved PO to controller for final approval.	9. Receiving forwards item to requesting manager.
11. Controller applies the account funding code to the PO.	10. Vendor sends invoice.
12. Controller sends the PO to the appropriate vendor.	11. Accounts payable pays the invoice.
13. Vendor sends item to organization's receiving department.	
14. Receiving department forwards item to controller for validation of asset delivery.	
15. Controller enters receipt into purchasing system.	
16. Controller sends item to business manager.	
17. Business manager provides item to employees.	
18. Vendor sends invoice to controller.	
19. Controller reviews invoice for approval.	
20. Controller sends approved invoice to accounting.	
21. Accounts payable pays the invoice.	

(b)

Figure 6.2 (Continued) (b) Purchasing process—spaghetti (as-is). (*Continued*)

Mention the supporting documentation in the main report; but don't overpower the report with too much detail.

Since you may have so many different and diversely focused readers, keep it simple and to the point. For those technically oriented people who may require more detail to accept your findings, put that in the appendices so as not to bore the other readers.

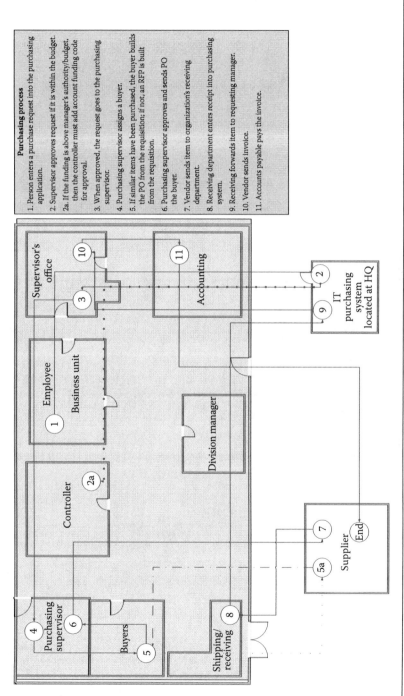

Purchasing process

1. Person enters a purchase request into the purchasing application.

2. Supervisor approves request if it is within the budget.

2a. If the funding is above manager's authority/budget, then the controller must add account funding code for approval.

3. When approved, the request goes to the purchasing supervisor.

4. Purchasing supervisor assigns a buyer.

5. If similar items have been purchased, the buyer builds the PO from the requisition; if not, an RFP is built from the requisition.

6. Purchasing supervisor approves and sends PO the buyer.

7. Vendor sends item to organization's receiving department.

8. Receiving department enters receipt into purchasing system.

9. Receiving forwards item to requesting manager.

10. Vendor sends invoice.

11. Accounts payable pays the invoice.

Figure 6.2 (Continued)   (c) Purchasing process—spaghetti (to-be).

Presenting the Report

In the past, internal audit had a bad reputation because it had no skin in the game. Internal auditors visited a business unit, announced to the organization the business process issues, and then went away until next year. As such, auditors were not viewed as business partners.

Internal audit is part of an organization. If the organization has problems then the internal audit teams have those problems as well. Following any assessment, if there are issues or concerns, the audit staff should never just point to the problem and say fix it.

Make sure that your business partner (the business manager) recognizes that the issue is not only his or hers, but *ours*. In today's audit environment, I like to stand next to the business unit manager, point out the issues that concern *us*, and then ask, "How can *we* fix that?"

I have seen many audit out-briefs where the auditors enter a meeting room and they all sit on one side of the table, while the business unit personnel (audit customer) sits on the other side of the table. The audit team and the business unit just choose sides for the contest and now they are ready to start the discussion and/or debate.

Personally, I like to show up early and take a chair in the middle of the other team. If we have multiple people, I love it when we intersperse ourselves within the business unit members. It is a small thing that hopefully reminds everyone that we are all one organization.

Let's face it; not all issues can be fixed and sometimes the fix costs more than the risk, the worry, or the rewards.

CASE 6.2: 2013 STATE AUDIT REPORT

A northwestern state audit team found that the Department of Transportation lacked appropriate vendor management techniques in place to keep the planned toll road construction on time. Due to the delays in building the toll road, the cost to the taxpayers in lost revenue may be in millions.

The head of the Department of Transportation profusely thanked the audit staff for their diligent approach and professionalism throughout the audit process. He wanted to thank them for sharing their knowledge and ideas and welcome them back when they would like to review other areas and business processes.

As he addressed the issues, he did state that due to the abnormal weather systems experienced this past year, transportation management did not want to start on time and prolong the traffic adjustments necessary for the construction while at a standstill due to the adverse weather conditions. Prolonging the construction time frame would disrupt the normal traffic flow for our citizens; yet the weather would not have allowed us to finish on the scheduled time. In addition, as the weather fronts started to dissipate and we could begin, we did receive a much more favorable construction loan interest rate, which was due to the downturn in the economy. The reduced interest rate will exceed the revenue of multiple years of toll collections.

I have included the audit report and the thank-you letter in Appendix B so you can review the report at your leisure or review it online at http:// portal.sao.wa.gov/ReportSearch/Home/ViewReportFile?arn=1010219 &isFinding=false&sp=false.

Vet the Draft Report with Management

It has been my practice and the practice of my last two organizations to share the findings with middle management prior to completing the formal report. This practice helps to ensure our data and findings based on our scope and objectives are true and accurate. I have had audits where I shared the issues with the business line managers and they enlightened me to other secondary and even tertiary controls that were developed to mitigate or remove the risks and my concerns for the organizational business process. This practice may immensely help those government organizations that provide their audit reports for public scrutiny.

I will admit that the practice almost backfired on one occasion. After reviewing our findings on two occasions with the line manager and his director, when we did an out-brief with the senior vice president, the manager refuted that the data that we used were incorrect and, therefore, the issues were not as we presented it to the senior vice president.

I was a little taken aback until I remembered who provided us with the data. I looked at the manager and asked, "Did you provide us with incorrect data on purpose? If so, I guess we could extend the audit. But please provide us with the correct data this time." He then refuted his prior statement. In fact, he just sat there for the rest of the presentation.

One of the other findings was that the monthly report on the business unit's data entry error percentages used an incorrect formula to measure the actual error rate. Based on the correct formula, the error rate was 10 times the error rate that they had been reporting for the past year or so.

When we arrived on site, the business unit's error rate for data entry was reported as less than 1%, which I thought was outstanding. Based on the last national survey that I had read, the national average was 5% for data entry errors across the nation. Then we noticed that their process was based on the errors found during a second site review by another employee in the same business unit. That would have been fine if they divided the number of errors by the sample size; however, they based their computation by dividing the number of errors found within the sample by the total population they used to pull the sample. Since they normally did a second sight on a sample size of 10%, the real error rate should have been 10 times the number that they were reporting each month.

The data tell the story. Provide these to the business unit in a language and a format that makes it easy for them to understand the concern, what you are trying to help the organization improve, and how you believe it can be improved.

7

IT AND COBIT

For this chapter, we will look at the management of the individual IT goal in support of the organization to provide the technologies to help the business units succeed.

Up until now, we have been looking at the business process and how IT helps the business become and remain successful. IT itself is a business process that has the day-to-day business issues and the support processes like HR, accounting, purchasing, and other back-office business units. They have sort of a circular relationship since IT supports each of the business processes as a provider of equipment and services; yet IT is a customer of each one of those business units as well.

The ITs are audited in the same manner that each business process is audited. In my mind, there are four types of audits:

1. Financial audits
2. Compliance audits
3. Operational audits
4. IT audits

The IT auditors rely on a framework developed by the Information Systems Audit and Control Association (ISACA) called *COBIT*. COBIT is an acronym that stands for *Control Objectives for Information Technologies*. I believe that the original COBIT framework was developed by the ISACA based on the U.S. Military Orange Book.

Previous versions of COBIT included the need for the establishment of an IT steering committee by enlisting various business units in an effort to ensure that the IT division's strategic and tactical direction and focus was on the organizational needs and not just focused on the technologies.

The organizational business concern about IT was that many of the technically oriented people may have a tendency to adopt new or unique technologies due to their personal desire to learn about the newer concepts and maybe to add information to their résumés. COBIT was concerned that the technologist might put more weight on the new or interesting technology and not enough weight on the business needs. This could result in purchasing and implementing more technical infrastructure than necessary to support and help the organization grow. This may cause an overspending condition, which would not align with the organizational desire to protect financial resources and assets.

COBIT 5 has a strong focus on the organization's strategy and goals. COBIT, like the International Professional Practices Framework that governs the internal auditor field, recognized that moving toward the organizational goals is productive; therefore, the goals and strategies must be the keystone for the organization, which includes audit, IT, HR, etc.

If the technology cannot support and enhance the strategy and goals, then it has no place in the IT inventory. There is a realization that the IT division of the organization is a business process that directly supports the business.

The focus of COBIT 5 is on the IT customer. The voice of the customer and the needs of the customer are a predominant focus area of COBIT 5.

The cascading process outlined in COBIT 5 starts off by reminding the IT guru that the enterprise exists to create value for their stakeholders. This is true for public, private, profit-oriented, and not-for-profit organizations as well as governments. We all have stakeholders and we are asked to provide value to those we serve.

The stakeholder's needs cascade down to develop the enterprise IT goals.

The enterprise goals cascade to the IT-related goals, which cascade to the enabler goals.

- Operational goals of management:
  - Legal and regulatory compliance
  - Contractual requirements
  - Service-level agreements
  - Inventory information
  - Quality management system information
  - Business/production process models
  - Customer demands or requirements

- Operations and execution:
  - Downtime reporting
  - Continuous improvement data → trending
  - Plan → do→ check → act → records → results
  - Transaction data
  - Inventory information
  - Quality management system
  - Business production process models

The most current version of COBIT is COBIT 5, which combines the Value of IT (Val IT) and Risk IT concepts along with a focus on governance and maturity levels. The design is similar to other cascading frameworks. *It is a business framework for the IT business.*

COBIT itself starts with the framework for governance and management of an enterprise IT. The basic principles of COBIT 5 are the following:

- *Principle 1*: Meeting the stakeholder's needs—Enterprises exist to create value for their stakeholders by maintaining a balance between the realization of benefits and the optimization of risk and use of resources.
- *Principle 2*: Covering the enterprise end to end—COBIT 5 integrates the governance of enterprise IT into the enterprise governance by covering all functions and processes within the enterprise as one, in lieu of governance by silos.
- *Principle 3*: Applying a single, integrated framework—Although there are many IT-related frameworks, standards, and best practices, COBIT 5 aligns a majority of the known frameworks into one integrated framework.
- *Principle 4*: Enabling a holistic approach—Efficient and effective governance and management of enterprise IT require a holistic approach.

  To accomplish a holistic approach while employing several interacting components, COBIT defined seven categories as *enablers* in support of a comprehensive governance and management system for the enterprise:
  - Principles, policies, and frameworks
  - Processes
  - Organizational structures

- Culture, ethics, and behavior
- Information
- Services, infrastructure, and applications
- People, skills, and competencies

  (Enablers are broadly defined as anything that can help to achieve the objectives of the enterprise.)
- *Principle 5*: Separating governance from management—The COBIT 5 framework makes a clear distinction between governance and management, i.e., because they employ different types of activities, require different organizational structures, and serve different purposes.
  - *Governance*—I have always viewed governance as dealing with the strategy, direction, and goals. Governance to me is synonymous with leadership.
  - *Management*—Management deals with efficiency and effectiveness.

As I see it, the governance of any organization or entity is the responsibility coupled with the authority of the leaders who oversee that entity of the organization or unit.

For organizational governance, senior leadership develops the strategic plans; whereas management uses the resources provided by the leadership to accomplish the strategy and achieve the organizational goals. The governance of the organization is in the hands of the senior leadership of the organization (CEO, CFO, chief information officer, etc.); whereas the governance of the production line is the responsibility of the line manager.

As I mentioned above, the organizational leadership not only creates the strategy and the goals; they fund the management to accomplish those goals. The management is responsible to build an efficient and effective process using the resources that are provided by governance.

Governance is truly at every level of the organization and at every level of life.

When you drive a vehicle, you govern the direction of the vehicle along with the goals (destination and schedule). You also govern the speed of travel. The outside regulatory environment may try to regulate your speed and even the side of the road that you travel for each direction or the fact that they provide some roads for one way only. You might exceed the speed or may even travel the wrong way on a one-way street. You govern your response to the regulatory environment and take the risks presented by not abiding by the regulations. I will admit that I have exceeded the speed limit on occasion, received tickets, and been fined for that action. On the flip side, I haven't knowingly traveled the wrong way on a one-way street.

We govern what we have controls of; we govern whenever we provide resources and direction; we govern when we raise children, build teams, businesses, and processes.

COBIT Management Environment

As you think about the processes of any business unit, they are focused on having the correct people accomplishing the correct processes at the correct time. IT, like any other business unit, relies on payroll, HR, etc., to accomplish their mission.

Over the years, COBIT has segregated the operational processes into plan, build, run, and monitor. Now the segments are known as the following:

- APO is an acronym in COBIT 5 that stands for align, plan, and organize areas. The management under the APO processes activities includes the following:
  01. Management of the IT management framework
  02. Management of strategy
  03. Management of enterprise architecture
  04. Management of innovation
  05. Management of portfolio (applications, services, etc.)
  06. Management of budget and costs
  07. Management of HR
  08. Management of relationships
  09. Management of service agreements
  10. Management of suppliers
  11. Management of quality
  12. Management of risk
  13. Management of security

- Business impact analysis (BIA), the *build, acquire,* and *implement* domain for management, is noted in the following BIA guidance:
  01. Management of programs and project
  02. Management of requirements definition
  03. Management of solutions identification and build
  04. Management of availability and capacity
  05. Management of organizational change enablement
  06. Management of changes
  07. Management of change acceptance and transitioning
  08. Management of knowledge
  09. Management of assets
  10. Management of configuration
- Delivery support systems (DSS) stands for the *delivery, service,* and *support* environment and includes the following management guidelines:
  01. Management of operations
  02. Management of service requests and incidents
  03. Management of problems
  04. Management of continuity
  05. Management of security services
  06. Management of business process controls
- MEA, the final domain covered in COBIT 5, stands for *monitor, evaluate,* and *assess*. It is denoted by the letters *M, E,* and *A* and that domain has three subsets:
  01. Monitor, evaluate, and assess performance and conformance
  02. Monitor, evaluate, and assess the system of internal control
  03. Monitor, evaluate, and assess compliance with external requirements

Similar to the capability maturity model (CMM) and the CMM Integrated (CMMI) developed by Carnegie Mellon depicted by five maturity levels to rate the application development process, COBIT provided a similar maturity model based on ISO/International Electrotehnical Commission (IEC) 15504 that defines the various levels within the five-step CMMI maturing model:

PA 5.2   Process optimization
PA 5.1   Process innovation

PA 4.2   Process control

PA 4.1   Process measurement

PA 3.2   Process deployment

PA 3.1   Process definition

PA 2.2   Performance management

PA 2.1   Work product management

PA 1.1   Process performance

CMM was developed by the software engineering group at Carnegie Mellon to depict the process maturity of a development process (Figure 7.1).

As we have mentioned earlier in this book, we need to ascertain how the assessment process works. As you may realize, the framework steps covered in COBIT 5 are a process; and as we stated earlier, all processes should be accomplished with the three Es in mind. We must help to ensure that the process is effective, efficient, and economical. To do so, we will apply some of the Lean Six Sigma tools in an effort to gain a new perspective of the process used for the COBIT 5 domain.

For our purpose, we will use the DSS domain.

As we consider DSS01, we realize that DSS01 coordinates and executes the activities and the operational procedures required to deliver internal or external IT services, including the execution of

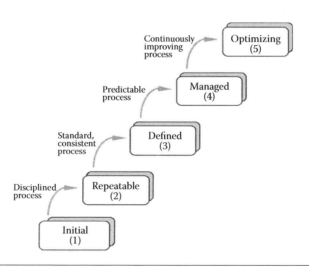

Figure 7.1 Maturity levels.

predefined standard operating procedures and the required monitoring activities.

The purpose of the process is to deliver the operational service outcome to the customer as planned and/or agreed to by the participants. To accomplish this task, we employ various business practices (BPs) as noted in the following:

- *BP1*: Perform the operational procedures—Maintain and perform operational procedures and operational tasks reliably and consistently.
- *BP2*: Manage outsourced IT services—Manage the operational (internal and external) IT services to maintain the protection of enterprise information and the reliability of service delivery.
- *BP3*: Monitor IT Infrastructure—Monitor the IT infrastructure and related events; capture and save sufficient chronological information within the operation logs in an effort to enable the reconstruction, review, and examination of the time sequences affecting the operations and/or other activities surrounding or supporting the operations.
- *BP4*: Manage the environment—Maintain measures for protection against environmental factors; install specialized equipment and devices to monitor and control the environment.
- *BP5*: Manage facilities—Manage facilities, including power and communication equipment, in line with laws and regulations, technical and business requirements, vendor specifications, and health and safety guidelines.

To illustrate how the SIPOC matrices can provide insight into the assessment process, I have provided matrices for your review (Table 7.1).

COBIT is the regulatory framework used by internal and external auditors to rate and assess the ITs within an organization.

COBIT APO01-BP7 covers the technology management's responsibility for continual improvement of processes.

- This includes building a continuous improvement program.
- This is to ensure that they are capable of delivering against enterprise, governance, management, and control objectives.

Table 7.1 SIPOC—DSS01

SOURCE	INPUT	BUSINESS PRACTICES (BP)	OUTPUT	CUSTOMER
		SIPOC—DSS01: MANAGE OPERATIONS		
Governance IT	Operation and use plan	BP1: Perform operational procedures	Operational schedule / Backup logs	Internal operations
External agency agreements of services	Service-level agreements (SLAs)	BP2: Manage outsourced IT services	Independent assurance plans (BCP SSAE16, etc.)	Internal and external business units
Internal business units	Operational-level agreement (OLA)			
Management procedures	Service definitions	BP3: Monitor IT infrastructure	Asset monitoring rules and event conditions / Event logs / Incident tickets and logs	DSS04.01 / DSS04.02 / Internal / DSS04.02 / IT operations / IT operations / IT operations
ABC Meter Company	Humidity control monitor / Temperature humidity alarm / Water censor alarm	BP4: Manage the environment	Daily humidity chart / Emergency call, if needed	Operations management
Armed Guard, Inc.	Security guard		Action to reduce environmental hazard	
Electric utility company	Electricity 110–120 V AC	BP5: Manage facilities	Application availability	Each business unit
Communication provider	Data and voice communication lines		IT support	Company personnel
ABC Power Company	Uninterruptable power supply		Data	All business units
Internet Service Provider	Internet access line		Printing capabilities	All business units

APO01-BP8 focuses on maintaining compliance with policies and procedures. The mandate

- Puts in place procedures to maintain compliance with and performance measurement of policies and other enablers of the control framework.
- Enforces the consequences of noncompliance or inadequate performance.
- Tracks trends and performances so that you can consider these in the future design and improvement of the controls.

Within COBIT 5, you are provided with the IT goals (ITGs) to use as a baseline or path to conformance with the COBIT 5 framework.

Each area is assigned specific process goals numbers, ITG*nn*, where the *nn* denotes a number (01, 02, etc.). There are metrics developed to ascertain the performance measures for the ITG items.

For DSS01, you have three ITG numbers, 04, 07, and 11. It sounds like two out of three are based on the gambling game of craps. I doubt that the COBIT writers thought of that, but why not? Table 7.2 depicts ITGs as presented in COBIT 5.

Table 7.2   COBIT 5 ITGs

DSS01: MANAGE OPERATIONS		PURPOSE: DELIVER IT OPERATIONAL SERVICE OUTCOME AS PLANNED		
ITG	GOAL	METRICS		
ITG04	Manage IT-related business risks	Number of significant IT-related incidents that were not identified in risk assessments	Frequency of updated risk profiles	Percentage of enterprise risk assessments including IT-related risks
ITG07	Delivery of IT services in line with business requirements	Number of business disruptions due to IT service incidents	Percentage of business stakeholders satisfied that the IT service delivery meets agreed upon service levels (OSA)	Percentage of users satisfied with the quality of the IT service delivery
ITG11	Optimization of IT assets, resources, and capabilities	Frequency of capability, maturity, and cost optimization assessments	Trend of assessment results	Satisfaction levels of business and IT executives with IT-related costs and capabilities

Some process goals that coincide with the IT goals and associated metrics are the following:

- Operational activities are performed as required and scheduled.
  - Number of nonstandard operational procedures executed
  - Number of incidents caused by operational problems
- Operations are monitored, measured, reported, and remediated.
  - Ratio of events compared to the number of incidents
    - Transactions processes versus incidents and trend direction
  - Percentage of critical operational event types covered by automatic detection systems

To enable us to use COBIT as a process, let's establish a table based on the ITGs as established by COBIT 5. Since this book is focused on optimization, we should start with the alignment of the ITGs with the organizational goals and strategies and then move into the Delivery, support, and security processes. The governance, budget, and other facets of the IT-related goals help to lead you toward the DSS areas. Even the governance process can have a positive or negative effect on the day-to-day business support process of the IT groups.

As you look at Table 7.3 for an operational assessment, you can bring to mind the steps necessary to establish the IT environment and to build or acquire the necessary tools, IT-related equipment, and the personnel to establish and maintain the IT environment in support of the organizational business processes.

As you review COBIT 5, you will find that they present a RACI matrix in an effort to convey their message to the reader (Table 7.4).

You will note that a couple of letters (A and R) are in boldface. These items are two areas that I disagree within the RACI diagram shown on page 173 of the *COBIT 5 Enabling Process* (2012).

Based on my definition of the C in RACI, it denotes that the person or the position is consulted prior to the operational step in a process and I see too many Cs in the COBIT 5 framework. I believe that the authors really meant for the C to be used as a contributor to help ensure that it is designed correctly rather than a micromanagement entity to be asked prior to each time the step is accomplished.

Table 7.3 SIPOC of ITGs for DSS01

SOURCE	INPUT	PROCESS	OUTPUT	CUSTOMER
Organizational leadership (C-suite)	Enterprise strategy	ITG01: Alignment of IT and business strategy	IT strategic plan	IT leadership
IT leadership	IT strategic plan		IT guidance and investment strategy	IT staff and procurement
Compliance team	IT compliance required registry	ITG02: IT compliance and support for business compliance with external laws and regulations	Number of IT-related compliance issues or number of compliance issues related to an IT vendor	Senior leadership
Business units	Clarified and agreed-on business expectation	ITG07: Delivery of IT services in line with the business requirements	Percentage of business cases for IT-enabled investments having clear and agreed-on business expectations/requirements	Business requirement documentation
IT reporting tracking team	Service-level performance reports		Percentage of business owners satisfied with IT service delivery meeting agreed-upon service levels	IT staff and leadership
Supported business units	Quality review survey results based on customer feedback		Number of business disruptions due to IT or IT vendor service incidents Percentage of users satisfied with the number of services the IT delivers	IT leadership and C-suite
Supported business units and inquiries	Identified gaps in IT services to the business		Percentage of users satisfied with the number of services the IT delivers	IT teams and C-suite
Business units	Results of processing effectiveness reviews		Percentage of business users convinced that recently updated IT services have considerably improved processing effectiveness	IT teams and C-suite periodically

(Continued)

Table 7.3 (Continued) SIPOC of ITGs for DSS01

SOURCE	INPUT	PROCESS	OUTPUT	CUSTOMER
IT and business management/leadership	Recognition and reward program	ITG08: Adequate use of applications, information, and technology solutions	Percentage of business users considering the IT services provided as enhancing and facilitating their work	IT teams
			Percentage of business process owners satisfied with the collaboration with the IT department	
	Assessments of the use of innovative approaches		Level of business user understanding of how technology solutions support their processes	
System reporting	Review of operational use		Percentage of unused features that were explicitly specified in the functional requirements	IT management and business managers
Technology architecture committee	Data architecture, especially master data management and process architecture model	ITG09: IT agility	Number of critical business processes supported by up-to-date infrastructure and applications	IT management and business leadership
System and application reporting	Service portfolio, including data ownership		Average time to turn strategic IT objectives into an agreed-on and approved initiative	IT management and configuration/change management
System reporting and business unit surveys	Service portfolio operational metrics		Satisfaction level of business executives with IT's responsiveness to new requirements	C-suite and IT members
Business owners with assistance from security teams	Data classification guidelines	ITG10: Security of information, processing, infrastructure, and applications	Percentage of business users having a thorough understanding of the data classification guidelines	Business and IT teams

(Continued)

Table 7.3 (Continued)   SIPOC of ITGs for DSS01

SOURCE	INPUT	PROCESS	OUTPUT	CUSTOMER
Business unit leaders (data owners)	Approved user access rights (in terms of roles and data sensitivities)		Time to grant, change, and remove access privileges compared to agreed-on service levels	IT security administration
	Classification of information sources (security taxonomy)		Percentage of information classifications according to the security taxonomy	
	Data security and control guidelines		Number of IT services with outstanding security requirements	
Internal security and help desk reporting	Security issues/incident counts		Number of security incidents causing financial loss, business disruption, or public embarrassment	
Technology architecture team	Enterprise architecture (data/information architecture model)	ITG11: Optimization of IT assets, resources, and capabilities	Frequency of capability, maturity, and asset optimization assessments	
			Satisfaction levels of business and IT executives with IT-related assets, resources, and capabilities	
Business user survey	Data integrity procedures		Percentage of business users satisfied with the integrity of the business data	
Internal IT assessment and IT audit	Portfolio alignment with information strategy (data redundancy; architecture gap analysis)		Number of audit findings on timely follow-up and resolution for data integrity issues	Internal audit and the board
			Satisfaction level of business and IT executives with the alignment of the IT strategies with the information strategies	

Table 7.4 RACI for DSS01

KEY PROCESS	BOARD	CEO	CFO	COO	BUSINESS PROCESS OWNER	CHIEF RISK OFFICER	COMPLIANCE OFFICER	AUDITOR	CIO/CTO	PROGRAM DEVELOPER	IT OPERATIONS MANAGER	INFORMATION SECURITY MANAGER	BC MANAGER
												RACI DELIVERY SERVICES AND SUPPORT	
DSS01.01 Perform operational procedures									A		AR	C	C
DSS01.02 Manage outsourced IT services						I			A		R		
DSS01.03 Monitor IT infrastructure				I	C	I		C	I	C	A	C	I
DSS01.04 Manage the environment					I	C	A	C	C	C	R	R	I
DSS01.05 Manage facilities					I	C	A	C	C	C	R	I	I

Note: BC: business continuity; CEO: chief executive officer; CFO: chief financial officer; CIO: chief information officer; CTO: chief technology officer.

I believe that COBIT uses the C as a consultative agent to help the process rather than a micromanager that needs to be involved and approve each step.

To continue on with the tools, let's look at the DSS01 and the VSM as shown in Figure 7.2.

In this VSM, I chose not to include the IT vendor area. The basic concept of turning over the management of an IT environment to an outside vendor, whether you rely on the vendor to provide the WAN, all networks, all programming, some oversight work, all IT work, etc., is that the focus must be on the vendor providing the same great service to the supported business units as if the vendor was part of the organization and has a vested interest in the organization.

Whether he or she realizes it or not, each vendor becomes a stakeholder in the success of the organization. If the organization fails to provide the external and the internal customers with the IT resources that they require to maintain and help the business or venture grow, then the vendor will lose their business as well. Similar to the relationship between the three Es (effective, efficient, and economic), vendors are independent and yet interdependent on the success of their customers. Without the customer, they have no business.

You will also notice that the steps shown in the diagram are those depicted in the DSS01.01, DSS01.02, and DSS01.04 activities listed in COBIT 5 process reference guide (*COBIT 5 Enabling Process*, 2012, Chapter 5).

I left the time that each step takes blank, so you can complete that information at your leisure based on your organization data. I do recommend about 90 days of data to obtain a reasonable average measurement.

Since I have retired, I no longer have access to on-site activities or the authorization to measure process information. Besides, the actual steps taken by your organization to fulfill the framework step will be more meaningful to your organization's risks and concerns, and not just some general metrics to measure the steps leading any ITG.

If you do want to outline your internal IT processes in an effort to find any unnecessary steps that your process takes in accomplishing the IT business, then I do recommend that you use the RACI, spaghetti, and VSM to really look at your workload. Based on your diagrams and measurements, try to help ensure that all steps provide business, regulatory, or customer value.

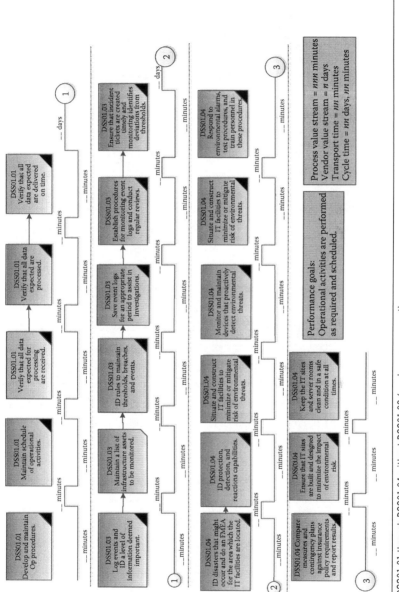

Figure 7.2 VSM DSS01.01 through DSS01.04 without DSS01.03 (vendor management).

What I have found in the past has been redundancies left over from previous regimes, one-time security issues, far past thoughts and ideas, or too many managers wanting to monitor the environmental issues or the productivity. I have also noted a number of goal-oriented metrics listed for the corporate scorecard that reflected the IT environment scorecards as they were listed in the 1980s.

During a corporate review, I noticed that they never missed a goal and their corporate balanced scorecard required an uptime goal of 98.7%.

When I worked in manufacturing back in the 1980s, we strived for 98.8% uptime and had to provide 4 hours per month for our field engineers so they could perform a scheduled preventive maintenance on our mainframe computers.

As soon as the organization started working with the WWW to communicate with our customers as well as our vendors (business associated partners), the uptime of 98.8% no longer suited the organizational needs.

As you look at the growth of applications for the smartphones that a large number of people use today, you must realize that the populace wants everything now. Waiting for the 5 o'clock news and the weather is a thing of the past (I will admit I do watch the news and the weather even though I finally broke down and use an iPhone).

The *now* generation expects to gain answers to their queries at all hours of the day or the night. They expect your web presence to be available almost 24 hours each and every day (24-7). They do put up with the fact that many sites become unavailable between 2:00 and 4:00 AM due to nightly backups or preventive maintenance; but they do want the answers and they want them now.

As such, and considering that your organization does business on the Internet, 98.8% is no longer something to strive for and use as a goal. Web and computer availability in today's global business economy needs to exceed 99%. Lean Six Sigma focuses on attaining a 99.9997% error-free environment. Therefore, as you look at real-time business, you are really looking to attain 99.45% availability or above. That should provide for an outage (preventive maintenance) of 4 hours each month ($4/720 = 0.0055 = 0.55\%$).

As we move along with the value stream, we can really put together the basic information in matrices to show the inputs, process steps, step timing, lead and lag timing, and possibly even the output (Table 7.5).

Table 7.5 SIPOC—VSM Worksheet—DSS01

DSS01: MANAGE OPERATIONS

PURPOSE: DELIVER IT OPERATIONAL SERVICE OUTCOMES AS PLANNED

INPUT	DSS STEP	STEP ACTIVITY	AVG. TIME	LEAD TIME	LAG TIME	OUTPUT
Standard operating procedures (SOPs) IT schedule SLA OLA	DSS01.01: Maintain and perform operational procedures and operational tasks reliably and consistently	1. Develop and maintain operational procedures and related activities to support all delivered services. 2. Maintain a schedule of operational activities, perform the activities, and manage the performance and throughput of the scheduled activities. 3. Verify that all data expected for processing are received and processed completely, accurately, and in a timely manner; deliver output in accordance with enterprise requirements; support restart and reprocessing needs; ensure that users are receiving the right outputs in a secure and timely manner. 4. Ensure that applicable security standards are met for the receipt, processing, storage, and output of data in a way that meets enterprise objectives, the enterprise's security policy, and regulatory requirements. 5. Schedule, take, and log backups in accordance with established policies and procedures.				Completed IT schedule Event log ITG07: Delivery of IT services in line with business requirement ITG13: Delivery of benefits on time, on budget, and meeting requirements and quality standards

(Continued)

Table 7.5 (Continued)   SIPOC—VSM Worksheet—DSS01

DSS01: MANAGE OPERATIONS

PURPOSE: DELIVER IT OPERATIONAL SERVICE OUTCOMES AS PLANNED

INPUT	DSS STEP	STEP ACTIVITY	AVG. TIME	LEAD TIME	LAG TIME	OUTPUT
Security requirements SOP SLA OLA	DSS01.02: Manage the operation of outsourced IT services to maintain the protection of enterprise information and reliability of service delivery	1. Ensure that the enterprise's requirements for security of information processes are adhered to in accordance with contracts and SLAs with third parties hosting or providing services. 2. Ensure that the enterprise's operational business and IT processing requirements and priorities for service delivery are adhered to in accordance with contracts and SLAs with third parties hosting or providing services. 3. Integrate critical internal IT management processes with those of outsourced service providers, covering, e.g., performance and capacity planning, change management, configuration management, service request and incident management, problem management, security management, business continuity, and the monitoring of process performance and reporting. 4. Plan for independent audit and assurance of the operational environments of outsourced providers to confirm that agreed-on requirements are being adequately addressed.				Event log Production log ITG02: IT compliance ITG07 ITG13 ITG10: Security of information protection IT compliance with internal policies

(Continued)

Table 7.5 (Continued) SIPOC—VSM Worksheet—DSS01

DSS01: MANAGE OPERATIONS

PURPOSE: DELIVER IT OPERATIONAL SERVICE OUTCOMES AS PLANNED

INPUT	DSS STEP	STEP ACTIVITY	AVG. TIME	LEAD TIME	LAG TIME	OUTPUT
	DSS01.03: Monitor IT infrastructure Monitor the IT infrastructure and related events; store sufficient chronological information in operations logs to enable the reconstruction, review, and examination of the time sequences of operations and the other activities surrounding or supporting operations.	1. Log events, identifying the level of information to be recorded based on a consideration of risk and performance. 2. Identify and maintain a list of infrastructure assets that need to be monitored based on the service criticality and the relationship between configuration items and services that depend on them. 3. Define and implement rules that identify and record threshold breaches and event conditions; find a balance between generating spurious minor events and significant events so event logs are not overloaded with unnecessary information. 4. Produce event logs and retain them for an appropriate period to assist in future investigations. 5. Establish procedures for monitoring event logs and conduct regular reviews. 6. Ensure that incident tickets are created in a timely manner when monitoring identifies deviations from defined thresholds.				ITG11: Optimization of IT assets, resources, and capabilities ITG10: Security ITG14: Availability of reliable and useful information Event and incident logs Procedure adjustment recommendations

(Continued)

Table 7.5 (Continued) SIPOC—VSM Worksheet—DSS01

DSS01: MANAGE OPERATIONS

PURPOSE: DELIVER IT OPERATIONAL SERVICE OUTCOMES AS PLANNED

INPUT	DSS STEP	STEP ACTIVITY	AVG. TIME	LEAD TIME	LAG TIME	OUTPUT
Event and incident log and analysis	DSS01.04: Manage the environment	1. Identify natural and human-made disasters that might occur in the area within which the IT facilities are located; assess the potential effect on the IT facilities.				BCM-suggested adjustments
Security-level designations and protection	Maintain measures for protection against environmental factors; install specialized equipment and devices to monitor and control the environment.	2. Identify how IT equipment, including mobile and off-site equipment, is protected against environmental threats; ensure that the policy limits or excludes eating, drinking, and smoking in sensitive areas, and prohibits storage of stationery and other supplies posing a fire hazard within computer rooms.				Business continuity scenario ideas
		3. Situate and construct IT facilities to minimize and mitigate susceptibility to environmental threats.				Equipment utilization metrics
		4. Regularly monitor and maintain devices that proactively detect environmental threats (e.g., fire, water, smoke, humidity).				Throughput metrics
						Alarm test results
						Self-test recovery

(Continued)

Table 7.5 (Continued) SIPOC—VSM Worksheet—DSS01

DSS01: MANAGE OPERATIONS
PURPOSE: DELIVER IT OPERATIONAL SERVICE OUTCOMES AS PLANNED

INPUT	DSS STEP	STEP ACTIVITY	AVG. TIME	LEAD TIME	LAG TIME	OUTPUT
		5. Respond to environmental alarms and other notifications; document and test procedures, which should include prioritization of alarms and contact with local emergency response authorities, and train personnel in these procedures.				
		6. Compare measures and contingency plans against insurance policy requirements and report results; address points of noncompliance in a timely manner.				
		7. Ensure that IT sites are built and designed to minimize the impact of environmental risk (e.g., theft, air, fire, smoke, water, vibration, terror, vandalism, chemicals, and explosives); consider specific security zones and/or fireproof cells (e.g., locating production and development environments/ servers away from each other).				
		8. Keep the IT sites and server rooms clean and in a safe condition at all times (i.e., no mess, no paper or cardboard boxes, no filled dustbins, no flammable chemicals or materials).				

(Continued)

Table 7.5 (Continued)   SIPOC—VSM Worksheet—DSS01

DSS01: MANAGE OPERATIONS

PURPOSE: DELIVER IT OPERATIONAL SERVICE OUTCOMES AS PLANNED

INPUT	DSS STEP	STEP ACTIVITY	AVG. TIME	LEAD TIME	LAG TIME	OUTPUT
	DSS01.05: Manage facilities Manage facilities, including power and communications equipment, in line with laws and regulations, technical and business requirements, vendor specifications, and health and safety guidelines.	1. Examine the IT facilities' requirement for protection against power fluctuations and outages, in conjunction with other business continuity planning requirements; procure suitable uninterruptible supply equipment (e.g., batteries, generators) to support business continuity planning. 2. Regularly test the uninterruptible power supply's mechanisms, and ensure that power can be switched to the supply without any significant effect on business operations. 3. Ensure that the facilities housing the IT systems have more than one source of dependent utilities (e.g., power, telecommunications, water, gas); separate the physical entrance of each utility.				BC management assurance Business unit assurance of system availability Investors and customer assurance of process availability Environmental policies Health & safety for employees and customers Insurance assurances

(Continued)

Table 7.5 (Continued) SIPOC—VSM Worksheet—DSS01

DSS01: MANAGE OPERATIONS

PURPOSE: DELIVER IT OPERATIONAL SERVICE OUTCOMES AS PLANNED

INPUT	DSS STEP	STEP ACTIVITY	AVG. TIME	LEAD TIME	LAG TIME	OUTPUT
		4. Confirm that the cabling external to the IT site is located underground or has suitable alternative protection; determine that the cabling within the IT site is contained within secured conduits, and wiring cabinets have access restricted to authorized personnel; properly protect cabling against damage caused by fire, smoke, water, interception, and interference.				
		5. Ensure that cabling and physical patching (data and phone) are structured and organized; cabling and conduit structures should be documented (e.g., blueprint building plan and wiring diagrams).				
		6. Analyze the facilities housing's high-availability systems for redundancy and fail-over cabling requirements (external and internal).				
		7. Ensure that IT sites and facilities are in ongoing compliance with relevant health and safety laws, regulations, guidelines, and vendor specifications.				

(Continued)

Table 7.5 (Continued) SIPOC—VSM Worksheet—DSS01

DSS01: MANAGE OPERATIONS

PURPOSE: DELIVER IT OPERATIONAL SERVICE OUTCOMES AS PLANNED

INPUT	DSS STEP	STEP ACTIVITY	AVG. TIME	LEAD TIME	LAG TIME	OUTPUT
		8. Educate personnel on a regular basis on health and safety laws, regulations, and relevant guidelines; educate personnel on fire and rescue drills to ensure knowledge and actions taken in case of fire or similar incidents.				
		9. Record, monitor, manage, and resolve facilities incidents in line with the IT incident management process; make available reports on facilities incidents where disclosure is required in terms of laws and regulations.				
		10. Ensure that IT sites and equipment are maintained according to the supplier's recommended service intervals and specifications; maintenance must be carried out only by authorized personnel.				
		11. Analyze physical alterations to IT sites or premises to reassess the environmental risk (e.g., fire or water damage); report results of this analysis to business continuity and facilities management.				

I do realize that some people who opened this book were looking for a checklist to use when they want to accomplish an IT operational assessment, a checklist so they could repeat the same assessment over and over again and not think about the differences of each organization, the people within that organization, the culture of that organization, or even the customers that might use that organization's product and services. To those who just want to use someone's one-size-fits-all checklist, I apologize.

I tried throughout this book and this chapter to present you with ideas, perspectives, concepts, and tools to help you improve your business and use of technologies.

I once showed up to do an SAS 70 (now updated to Statement on Standards for Attestation Engagements [SSAE] 16) for a regional bank and one of the business unit managers said that each year a different person comes in to do an SAS 70; and even though they assess different applications and environments, the exact same report with the same words are provided each year. One year, they forgot to change the program name in the SAS 70; so halfway through the document, they used last year's program name.

What I found through life is one size does not fit all.

Focus on your organization, their strategy, their goals, their business, their customers, and their processes.

Every process can be improved.

Have fun improving your organization's processes. If it isn't fun or self-fulfilling, then it is work.

8
EPILOGUE

Throughout this book, I have tried to provide you with information and tools to help you take a new look at your specific environment or the environment of your customer that you service. The effort should help you help them prosper.

Remember that operational assessment is a business management tool to help improve the operation, reduce the risks of failure and business disruption, and improve the process.

Employing the process steps to attain your organization's goals and support the organization's strategies is called productivity.

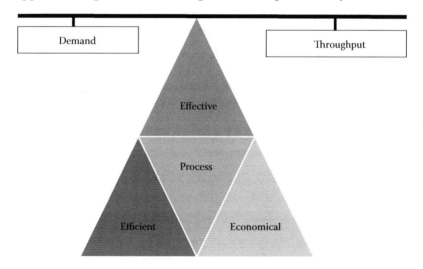

As Socrates once said, "I cannot teach anybody anything; I can only make them think."

Try to think about what I shared.

Stay well,

stay happy, and

stay productive.

Steve Katzman

Appendix A: Risk Assessment/ Management

Risk, as described by the Institute of Internal Auditors (IIA) and the Committee of Sponsoring Organizations of the Treadway Commission (COSO), is an event that could occur that will affect your process in a positive or a negative way.

The IIA defines risk as the possibility of an event occurring that will have an impact on the achievement of objectives. Risk is measured in terms of impact and likelihood.

Risk management is defined as a process to identify, assess, manage, and control potential risk events or situations to provide reasonable assurance regarding the achievement of the organization's objectives.

Most people need to be assured that the risk of doing business is kept to a level which the organization can accept. The organizational governance usually decides how much risk is acceptable and they refer to this as the organizational risk appetite. Based on whether the risk level is high, medium, or low, each business unit sets up their allowable risk.

When we consider the business unit risk, we normally put a value to that risk as we can accept a 4% error rate, etc., while the risk appetite is a more holistic view of risk. The appetite is a more general feeling about risk versus rewards, a gestalt or a psychological feeling about risk. A conservative organization may have a very low threshold for risk, while a gambling casino may have a much higher level of acceptable risks. Lawyers have a tendency to not accept risk, while a sales and marketing organization may have a high threshold for risk.

When we rate risk, we need to understand the value of the business process and the impact that it has on the organization. The value of the process risk may be quite different from that of the processes' impact on the organizational risk. A typo on a customer-facing process may have a greater impact on the organization's reputational risk than a typo on an employee's telephone number.

For each risk, we measure the impact and the likelihood that the event would occur. If you understand the business, the impact may be easy to measure; however, likelihood may be slightly different.

Don't forget that likelihood is based on probability, which is an estimate or best guess. We hear a lot about the 100-year floods; however, is it really every 100 years right on the dot or just that the flood rarely happens?

There was a major earthquake (magnitude 7 on the Richter scale) off the coast of Charleston, South Carolina, in 1896. Since an earthquake did not occur in 1996, will one occur every 120 (2016), 150, or 200 years? Are we overdue or are we just guessing as to when it will occur?

Because the probability of events that have not occurred or been tracked over time is not as reliable as the cost or impact of a loss, I have always placed more weight on impact if the impact is listed above low (normally shown as green). I call it the *9/11 risk measure*. After all, what is the probability that two airplanes would crash into two adjacent buildings? Although the probability would have been considered low, the aftermath, including two areas of wartime actions and loss of life, was a major impact not only to New Yorkers.

Many executives appear to like the traffic light approach to reporting, so many organizations use low, medium, and high approaches to rate risk. When I used that type of reporting, we tended to use four levels to denote low, medium, high, and "we need a business change" and then we rated each level 1, 2, 4, and 6, respectively.

To report the likelihood, we used *possible*, *likely*, *highly likely*, and *probable* with ratings of 1, 2, 3, and 4, respectively.

We did sit down and discuss the risk ratings for impact and likelihood with our counterparts in the compliance and the Sarbanes–Oxley Compliance Assessment teams so that we would define the level for impacts and likelihood. The impacts would be based on expected loss of dollars and the likelihood was based on a percentage to denote the likelihood. Once you can define the impact and the likelihood, you can get apples to rate against oranges, etc.

When we built the matrices, we built a heat map like that shown in Figure A.1.

Once we have our heat map set up, I multiply the likelihood by the impact.

As you can see, the impact multipliers for medium are twice the multiplier for low, and the levels of high, medium and low are denoted by various shades normally portrayed by red, yellow and green respectively are based on the multiplied number as follows:

- 0–4 for low-level risks
- > 4–8 denote medium-level risks that should be acted upon
- > 8–24 *must be acted upon*

You will note that anytime you have a critical impact, you must do something even when the probability is possible and not likely.

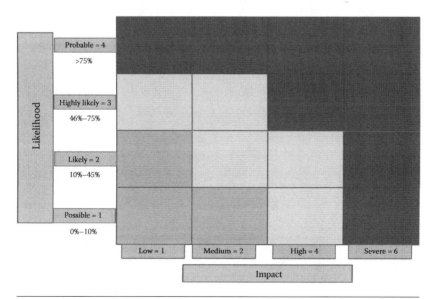

Figure A.1 Heat map.

Critical impact could be caused by severe natural or human-made disasters as well as systemic disasters. For example, a supplier can't or won't deliver necessary information or items to you in time for your customer deliveries. A hurricane adversely affects your ability or capability to complete your mission to build or deliver your customer obligations.

Each organization must determine the value that would define when the impact moves from low to medium, from medium to high, and from high to critical.

For a large organization such as Chase, Bank of America, and GE, the move from low to medium may occur at $1,500,000 or higher and $1 billion or $2 billion for a move from medium to high or to critical; whereas Joe's TV and Radio Repair Business (a factitiously named organization) may have $100 to move from low to medium and $2500 to move from high to critical.

STATE AUDITOR'S OFFICE
PERFORMANCE AUDIT

Washington's Tolling Program: Lessons Learned from Project Delays

August 2, 2013

Washington State Auditor
Troy Kelley

Report No. 1010219

Appendix B: Washington State Audit Report

August 2, 2013

Washington's Tolling Program

Washington State Auditor: Troy Kelly

State of Washington Audit Division—Executive Summary

Delays creating a statewide all-electronic tolling system

Washington is one of just a handful of states that have successfully established a statewide all-electronic tolling system. The system is fully operational, and through March 2013, has collected more than $67 million to help pay for the new SR 520 bridge. However, Washington began collecting tolls nine months behind schedule, a delay that represents a lost opportunity to collect an additional $40 million in tolls. Project delays and issues creating the new system caused public confusion.

We found the Washington State Department of Transportation (WSDOT) faced challenges managing a complicated project that involved collaboration across the department, where roles and responsibilities were unclear, including who made decisions, who was accountable, and how the vendor was to be managed. WSDOT has taken some steps to address these issues, and it is important it continues to take action to resolve these challenges because tolling is central to the department's ability to pay for large construction projects. The Legislature has authorized additional tolling projects on SR 99, I-405, and the I-5 Columbia River Crossing, and others will be considered in the future.

ISSUES CREATING A NEW STATEWIDE TOLLING SYSTEM

- Technology barriers
- Disagreement about needs
- Tight deadline
- Unclear & ineffective management

Pressure points magnified the project's challenges

Three factors created a high level of risk to the project's success.

Technology barriers—WSDOT wanted a statewide system that would be easy for customers to use on multiple highways and bridges. However, because Washington state law requires precise accounting to track tolls collected at each facility, the system needed more advanced accounting elements than those already used in other states. These elements went beyond what the tolling industry had previously delivered.

Disagreements about needs—WSDOT project stakeholders disagreed about whether they should treat project deliverables as if they were purchasing a service, or an IT product. WSDOT's vendor did not immediately realize, nor did WSDOT recognize the vendor's lack of understanding of the accounting system needs until several months into the project, which complicated project planning and vendor management.

Tight deadline pressure—The Federal Highway Administration paid for the new tolling system under a grant designed to support innovative methods to ease traffic congestion. These grants were intended for projects that could be completed quickly. The grant agreement included a specific SR 520 tolling start date. WSDOT feared that failing to meet that date would result in the loss of federal funding. Although the Federal Highway Administration extended the deadline several times to meet WSDOT's needs, the deadline pressure affected WSDOT's project management decisions.

CONSEQUENCES

- Project delays
- Lost opportunity to collect $40 million
- Public Confusion
- The Toll Division needs clear decision-making authority

RECOMMENDATIONS

- The Toll Division establishes policies and procedures for managing complex project
- Secretary ensures clear expectations for future tolling projects

Unclear management approach complicated an ambitious project

WSDOT did not fully follow the requirements outlined in the State Administrative and Accounting Manual including adequately planning for and managing project risk, proactively managing the project, and holding the vendor accountable throughout the project. WSDOT created the Toll Division while this project was under development in 2009 to manage its tolling program and collaborate across the department with multiple divisions and offices on tolling projects.

For this project, WSDOT's Toll Division lacked the executive support, decision-making authority, and the policies and procedures needed to develop the statewide all-electronic tolling system and start tolling the SR 520 Bridge on schedule. These management challenges were magnified by an ambitious project, uncertainty about its demands, and a tight deadline tied to a $154 million federal grant.

Incorporating risks—Although WSDOT identified numerous risks to the project's success, it did not fully integrate those risks into project development and management, and its vendor selection process. For example, all vendors received low overall scores and WSDOT selected a vendor that scored very low on it proposed technical accounting approach, a known high-risk area. When the vendor subsequently struggled to perform, WSDOT was not prepared with contingency plans.

Managing the project—WSDOT struggled to proactively manage both the project and the vendor. It developed a sound project management plan, but did not always follow the plan and did not update it to reflect changes. Some internal stakeholders disregarded the plan by communicating directly with the vendor. When the project management structure was changed, the plan was not updated and the vendor received conflicting direction, causing further delays.

Holding the vendor accountable—As the vendor struggled to understand project requirements and meet project deadlines, WSDOT conducted less project oversight as it became more involved in the vendor's work. Because WSDOT's primary goal was to have an operational system, it delayed assessing damages and did not apply all available financial penalties for poor performance. As the system neared completion, WSDOT reduced vendor payments to cover additional costs caused by the delay. Once it started collecting tolls on SR 520, WSDOT reached a financial settlement with the vendor.

Summary recommendations

To improve WSDOT's management of future tolling projects and to minimize the risk of project delays, we recommend:

1. The Secretary ensures roles, responsibilities, and decision-making authority is clear for projects managed by the Toll Division.
2. The Assistant Secretary for Tolling establishes policies and procedures to guide the development and implementation of tolling projects.
3. The Department of Transportation report on its progress implementing these recommendations to House and Senate Transportation Committees and the Office of Financial Management, as required in the 2013–2015 transportation budget.

Introduction

The Washington State Department of Transportation (WSDOT) developed a statewide all-electronic toll collection system to collect tolls on the State Route (SR) 520 Bridge, on other existing toll facilities, and future toll facilities. WSDOT hired a vendor to provide the information technology system needed to implement all-electronic tolling and to provide customer services.

WSDOT and its vendor experienced challenges in developing the new system that created significant delays in tolling the SR 520 Bridge resulting in a lost opportunity to collect an estimated $40 million in tolls. Washington now has a statewide all-electronic toll collection system that meets the contract's requirements, but the delays and other problems with the project frustrated customers, the public, and the Legislature. To help avoid similar issues with future tolling projects, our audit was designed to answer the following question:

What lessons can be learned from WSDOT's development and implementation of statewide all-electronic tolling?

Audit results
Every state contract is expected to meet state requirements

Developing the back-office functions and Customer Service Center for WSDOT's statewide all-electronic toll collection system depended heavily on information technology solutions. Industry experts estimate the failure rate for complex information technology projects to be as high as 50 percent. The state provides requirements to state agencies on how to procure, manage, and monitor contractors, and guidance on how to increase the probability of success for such projects. WSDOT was required to follow applicable state requirements and guidance for procurement and contractor managing and monitoring.

Washington State's Office of Financial Management requires state agencies to follow the *State Administrative and Accounting Manual* when selecting contractors, managing and monitoring contractor performance, and holding contractors accountable to fulfill the requirements of the contract.

WSDOT used an information technology purchased service contract for the Customer Service Center project. State guidance for these contracts advises purchasers to also include personal services contract provisions from Chapter 15 of the State Administrative and Accounting Manual as needed. Because the tolling project contract included elements of both purchased and personal services, WSDOT was expected to follow the requirements of Chapter 15.40 of the manual for this project, specifically:

- Take a risk assessment approach to contracting by identifying and planning for risks associated with the project and with the contractors
- Proactively manage and monitor the contractor
- Hold the contractor accountable to the requirements of the contract

The State Technology Manual provides guidance to help state agencies assess the value of their planned information technology investments, to identify and plan for risks, and to increase the success of their acquisitions. The manual outlines the critical indicators of success that agencies should ensure are present when developing and procuring information technology projects. These critical indicators include having strong executive management support, an experienced project manager, skilled staff, a formal project management process, effective contractor management, and a realistic project scope.

The Institute of Internal Audit's Global Technology Audit Guides provided specific guidance for auditing information technology project management. *Guide 7: Information Technology Outsourcing* provides guidance on how to recognize and balance the benefits and risks of outsourcing projects through vendor selection and contractor management by clarifying roles and responsibilities, defining key contract terms, and establishing a process to monitor progress. *Guide 12: Auditing IT Projects* includes information on project management methods, and states that success requires:

- Having documented milestones for project tasks
- Clear roles and responsibilities
- A process for consistently monitoring project performance against a consistent set of deliverables and performance metrics

- Performing project risk assessments
- Developing mitigation actions and contingency plans to pro-actively manage and resolve identified risks

Unclear roles and inadequate policies contributed to delays

WSDOT has successfully established a statewide all-electronic toll system that accommodates variable tolling on SR 520 as required by its federal grant. The system allows customers to use all state tolled facilities with a single pass and account. It is one of just a few state-wide all-electronic tolling systems in the nation, and the first one to demand the comprehensive accounting functionality needed to track toll transactions by facility.

Developing and activating this system, however, proved challenging for the department. Washington's system became fully operational nine months behind schedule, on December 29, 2011, when it began collecting tolls on the SR 520 Bridge. In determining what lessons could be learned from the SR 520 tolling delay, we found WSDOT did not adequately address risks, proactively manage the project, or hold the vendor accountable to the terms of the contract. WSDOT identified numerous risks, but did not fully incorporate those risks into the project. The department did not always follow its project management plan or update it to reflect changes, and delayed applying damages for the vendor's poor performance.

Identifying and incorporating project risks

When WSDOT was preparing its request for proposal, all-electronic tolling technology and implementation procedures were not well developed, and few all-electronic systems in the United States handled the volume of traffic—over 100,000 trips a day—WSDOT expected on the SR 520 Bridge. As a result, the project presented inherent risks because the industry did not have experience designing such complex systems. Exhibit 5 on the following page illustrates the complexity of WSDOT's requirements.

WSDOT used a Quality Assurance team, a workshop with other states that had developed all-electronic tolling systems, and a required investment plan to identify risks. Despite these efforts to identify risk, however, the knowledge gained was not fully incorporated into the request for proposals, the vendor selection, or project management.

The Quality Assurance team identified disagreements over nature of project

WSDOT hired a Quality Assurance team with expertise in information technology, tolling, and project management processes. The team started its work in March 2009, as WSDOT developed its request for proposals. The Quality Assurance team continually assessed the state of the project by comparing deliverables against established standards for quality, identifying project risks, recommending management strategies, and providing input. The Quality Assurance team identified some initial projects risks for WSDOT:

- The project lacks a clear project vision and objectives from the project sponsor.
- The request for proposals is being managed as an engineering services project—inappropriate because this is an information technology project.
- Project sponsorship is not inclusive of those that have a vested interest in project outcome as the project is perceived as compartmentalized within engineering even though it contains substantial information technology and business processes components.
- Requirements are not consistent in their level of detail as there seems to be a lack of agreement on what is needed for the finance and accounting component of the system.

The Quality Assurance team gave WSDOT monthly reports that noted when issues had been resolved. They also acknowledged the positive actions taken by WSDOT project managers to continue to move the project forward despite its many challenges.

Peer states highlighted the need for accounting expertise, clear communication

WSDOT held a workshop with peers from other states to learn from their experiences establishing and operating all-electronic tolling customer service centers. The workshop took place in May 2009 just before WSDOT issued the request for proposals. The group included representatives from the Florida Turnpike Authority, the Miami-Dade Expressway Authority, Colorado's E-470 Public Highway Authority, and the Texas Department of Transportation. Participants focused on accounting, reporting, and revenue recognition needs and pointed to many risks associated with all-electronic toll collection accounting systems. Workshop participants told WSDOT they needed to ensure:

- The system meets Generally Accepted Accounting Principles, which will be a challenge as the industry is more focused on operational processing rather than financial accountability
- The vendor has experience in governmental accounting
- There is clear communication between WSDOT departments, and between WSDOT and the vendor, to effectively establish business rules and implement processes
- WSDOT does not rely on the vendor's accounting expertise

WSDOT's Investment Plan identified the project's severity

WSDOT developed an Investment Plan outlining its project proposal and risks as required by the State Technology Manual and submitted it to the Information Services Board. The Board approved the plan before WSDOT issued its request for proposals in June 2009. The Investment Plan explained that WSDOT would be contracting with a vendor to provide services based on the vendor's existing systems, and that WSDOT would not own or design the system. WSDOT expected that vendors had all-electronic toll collection software that could be easily and quickly modified to meet their needs, which did not prove to be the case.

The board assessed the project against its criteria and gave it a 'Level 2' rating for high severity and medium risk. In its Investment Plan, WSDOT suggested the project was 'high severity' because the system would interact with citizens, process sensitive data, was of interest to the Legislature, and failure to complete the project would result in the loss of federal funding, and 'medium risk' because it was based on proven technology, had strong executive sponsorship, and agency and vendor staff had a strong ability to mitigate project development risks.

Despite clear indications of risk, WSDOT failed to fully address them

The results of these actions to identify risks to the project were not fully incorporated into the request for proposals or the process used to select a winning vendor. Disagreement among the project stakeholders over whether they were purchasing a toll collection service or developing a new technology system contributed to this omission. The belief that a system existed that would meet the department's unique needs proved to be a significant misjudgment with implications for the completion of the project.

Vendor selection process did not fully incorporate risks

WSDOT evaluated five vendor proposals. At the time, it was aware of many risks associated with the project, including the aggressive timeline and the need to hire a vendor with governmental accounting and information technology experience. Had WSDOT weighted high risk areas and better incorporated the advice of its risk area experts, the process could have resulted in the selection of a different vendor.

Expert Review Panel identifies concerns

The Legislature recognized the inherent risk of developing a new all-electronic tolling system and WSDOT's limited experience with all-electronic tolling. Therefore it hired an Expert Review Panel to review WSDOT's strategies and request for proposals. The Expert Review Panel began its work after WSDOT released its request for proposals in June 2009. The panel's preliminary recommendations in September 2009 said the request for proposals had incomplete business rules, an extremely aggressive schedule, and too much reliance on post-pay toll enforcement rather than pre-paid accounts. As a result, WSDOT delayed the SR 520 Bridge tolling start deadline by five months and made other changes to incorporate the panel's feedback.

A vendor with a very low score in a high-risk area won the contract, in part by having the lowest price, as shown in Exhibit 6.

Vendor scoring was not weighted according to risks

The proposal evaluation process split the points evenly among various technical components of the request for proposals. It was not weighted according to risks. As a result, the number of points assigned to high-risk areas was too low to significantly impact the overall score of any proposal. For example, while WSDOT identified the high risks associated with accounting, that area represented less than 10 percent of the total score.

Consensus scoring reduced the influence of subject area experts

WSDOT's five-person vendor evaluation team included three members of the Toll Division, and one representative from information technology and one from accounting, two high risk areas. However, the consensus scoring method used to evaluate each proposal minimized the influence of the subject area experts.

Using consensus scoring, each member evaluated all aspects of each proposal and provided a score for the six categories. The team then agreed on a consensus score for each category of each proposal. Team members said it was very difficult to reach consensus on vendor scores, in part because the reviewers had very different backgrounds. Team members also stated that using consensus scoring led to lower scores for all proposals.

The procurement chair stated that if she had it to do again, she would establish a group for each technical aspect—information technology, accounting, toll operations, and customer service—to evaluate and score those specific proposal segments. This approach may have also provided better consideration of the known high risk areas.

Low scores indicated high risks

All five proposals received low scores. The highest-scoring proposals received less than 350 (35 percent) out of 1000 points, which does not meet WSDOT's threshold for a 'very good' proposal.

The proposal that received the highest technical score came at a much higher price than all the other proposals. Because all vendors had low technical scores, the 200 points offered for price heavily influenced the overall scoring. The winning vendor received 18 percent of the possible points for its qualifications and technical approach, and 100 percent of the possible points for price. The final selection was based on the proposal scores and interviews with the vendors.

The winning vendor had its lowest score in the high risk area of accounting/financial approach: it received only 4.5 of the 87.5 possible points available. WSDOT engaged in additional discussions with the vendor to clarify these expectations. The vendor provided written confirmation that it understood the requirements and described how it would meet them.

At the time the winning vendor was selected, the Quality Assurance team noted that the low scores for all the proposals indicated a very high risk project no matter which vendor was selected, and suggested that additional schedule time would likely be needed due to the weaknesses in the proposals identified by the evaluators.

In its Lessons Learned report given to WSDOT near the end of the project, the Quality Assurance team said that low proposal scores indicate either the vendors are under-qualified, or the request for proposals is flawed. In such instances, the Quality Assurance team would recommend withdrawing the request for proposals and adjusting project expectations "... rather than moving forward with an ill-prepared and unqualified vendor." The Quality Assurance team also noted that the winning vendor drastically under-bid on its proposal, which should have indicated to WSDOT that the vendor did not fully understand the requirements, a fact that became apparent later.

The grant deadline did not allow enough time to start over

WSDOT knew the project deadline did not allow enough time to revise the request for proposals and conduct a new procurement. Rather than risk losing the federal grant funds, WSDOT signed a $23 million contract in December 2009 with the winning vendor which included a SR 520 Bridge toll start date of March 19, 2011.

WSDOT accepted the risks associated with the low proposal score and the potential for issues with the vendor's technical accounting and finance approach. WSDOT believed the vendor could develop a system to meet its needs within the project timeline because they had created all-electronic tolling systems for other states.

Given the risks, WSDOT should have developed contingency plans, but did not

WSDOT project staff said they did not have contingency plans early on in the project because the vendor agreed it would be able to meet the requirements of the contract. The project director agreed that they did not have contingency plans. The Quality Assurance team said that given the known risks, the project team should have spent more time creating contingency plans that provided specific mitigations and triggers for when to use them. WSDOT did include risks in its project management plan, but did not include fully-vetted alternatives to handle the most critical risks. While the project team continually tracked project risks, its efforts were not focused on contingencies. The mitigations were focused on monitoring the situation, reviewing work items, coordinating and meeting with vendor, and ensuring clear expectations.

WSDOT did not plan for the risks associated with the vendor developing a complex information technology system because it did not initially understand the gap between the vendor's existing system and what was specified in the contract. In addition, because WSDOT's Toll Division staff viewed the project as purchasing a service rather than developing an information technology system, which carries a higher level of risk, they were not as prepared as they could have been to address that level of project risk.

When the vendor began struggling to meet deadlines and showed signs it did not fully understand the accounting and finance requirements and the required level of integration with WSDOT's accounting system required by the contract, WSDOT responded to these risks on a case-by-case basis, and did not develop formal contingency plans or alternatives. The Quality Assurance team's Lessons Learned report said that WSDOT tried to mitigate risks and meet the deadline by becoming more involved in the contractor's work.

Managing the project

WSDOT did not consistently follow effective management practices

Successful project completion depends on effective and proactive project management. The State Administrative and Accounting Manual's

Chapter 15 specifically required state agencies to proactively manage and monitor its contractors, and to take corrective action to hold them accountable. The Global Technology Audit Guides say effective methods to manage and monitor projects require using a defined management process to monitor progress. The defined process should include clear roles and responsibilities, clear communication and decision-making protocols, defined milestones, and a process to consistently monitor performance against deliverables and performance metrics.

The management process WSDOT established for the project included many elements required to monitor its progress. Unfortunately, WSDOT dropped or modified many of those elements when faced with the vendor's inability to complete project tasks on time and under the tight deadline. The process also lacked the detail needed to effectively monitor the vendor's progress, because it was not designed to monitor development of a complex information technology system.

Although roles and responsibilities, as well as communication and decision-making protocols, were outlined in the Project Management Plan, some internal WSDOT stakeholders did not follow them and instead communicated directly with the vendor. This created conflict within the project and resulted in sometimes contradictory direction to the vendor. WSDOT's internal conflicts and the vendor's performance problems resulted in significant project delays.

WSDOT did not follow or update its project management plan

WSDOT developed a project management process to manage the project and monitor the vendor's progress in its project management plan. The plan defined WSDOT and vendor roles and responsibilities, communication and decision-making protocols, as well as the tools to monitor progress.

A project manager with tolling industry experience was responsible for leading the project. The plan established the project manager as the primary point of contact between WSDOT and the vendor. WSDOT hired a general toll consultant to support its staff. Exhibit 7 shows the five technical teams composed of WSDOT and consultant staff created to manage and review the vendor's work in their specific technical area.

Project stakeholders were kept informed about project status through a series of committees established to provide project oversight and input on project decisions. For example, the Toll Executive Committee was led by the Toll Division Director and included WSDOT executives tasked with making policy decisions related to the project.

The plan established the process for monitoring the vendor's work, including tools to track the schedule and monitor the deliverables. It also included holding weekly status meetings with the vendor to discuss the status of deliverables, potential project risks, and to develop a list of action items for WSDOT and the vendor. The results of these meetings were captured in weekly status reports.

Not following the plan created more project risks

As the project progressed and the vendor started missing deliverables dates, project staff did not always follow the plan. Project staff told us they viewed the plan as more of an outline than a strict plan. In summer 2010, as the vendor started missing deliverables dates, the vendor complained to WSDOT executives that the project team was requiring the vendor's staff to attend too many meetings and 'do too much.'

To avoid more delays, and to give the vendor more time to complete work, WSDOT started reducing its review of design documents. By September 2010, the Project Director notified the project team to stop all review of detailed design documents. Not reviewing all the critical detailed design documents can create problems by allowing the vendor to pursue software design before getting WSDOT's approval, potentially creating the need for more work later. The Quality Assurance team said in its Lessons Learned report that developing the plan "… was highly beneficial in setting expectations and getting alignment within the project team. Within a few months, the plan no longer reflected how the project was being carried out and the solid processes set forth in the document were not being routinely used by the team or enforced by project managers." The Quality Assurance team concluded that not continuing to follow the project management process established in the plan had a negative impact on the management of the project.

WSDOT changed the project's management structure

In March 2011, WSDOT changed the project's management structure in response to continuing issues with the vendor's performance and internal stakeholders' concerns. Exhibit 8 shows how the new structure elevated WSDOT's Information Technology and Accounting and Financial Services directors into decision-making, rather than advisory, roles. The Director of Toll Systems and Development, as UPA Project Director responsible for execution of the grant projects, remained in that role. WSDOT staff explained that under this new structure, if lower level project staff could not resolve an issue, it would be elevated to the five directors shown in blue. If the directors could not resolve the issue, it would be elevated to the Deputy Secretary for resolution.

Although the purpose of this change was to help clarify expectations through more direct control of the project by internal stakeholders, WSDOT staff we talked to said the change actually caused further project delays as the vendor struggled to understand how to work within this new structure.

According to Quality Assurance team reports at the time, WSDOT staff and its consultants were actively engaged with the vendor's staff to complete its work, and doing all they could to move the project forward. But the change in the project management structure brought new challenges as it became more difficult to get clear direction without a coordinated approach from the directors.

Decision-making authority and vendor requirements not clearly established in the new process

The project plan documented the agreed-upon project management processes, but similar project management processes were not established under the new structure. For example, the plan was not updated to clarify roles and responsibilities and decision-making authority. As a result, it was unclear what decisions could be made by the new project leads. One project team leader told us that the four directors had to meet to discuss new issues that arose, and if they could not agree, they escalated them to the Toll Division Director to make the decision, which took time.

Along with this change in the project's management structure, and as system testing intensified, WSDOT stopped holding weekly status meetings with the vendor as prescribed in the plan; the vendor stopped keeping its schedule up to date as required. The lack of status meetings and schedule updates made it difficult for WSDOT to monitor the vendor's progress effectively.

The contract and project management plan limited vendor oversight

Several project team members said it was difficult to understand if the vendor was making progress. The plan was based on the high-level milestones and deliverables included in the contract, and did not have more detailed deliverables needed to monitor the development of the system's components. If the contract had been designed to develop an information technology system, it would have included more detailed deliverables.

The Project Director told us that, looking back, it would have been easier to monitor the vendor's progress had the contract been broken into more detailed deliverables with more checkpoints. WSDOT's Information Technology Director said the structure of the contract made it difficult to monitor progress because the vendor would not provide more detail on its progress when asked and would only report on progress of the milestones in the signed contract. That prevented WSDOT from seeing pieces of the system as the vendor was developing them.

Because WSDOT did not receive detailed work products, it took several months to learn that the vendor's plan to use its existing accounting technology would not work. When the vendor began to understand what was really required of the system's accounting and financial functionality, it started searching for an off-the-shelf software package it could use. When that was unsuccessful, the vendor decided it would have to develop one. This decision by the vendor was made more than six months into the contract.

Holding the vendor accountable

WSDOT did not use contract penalties effectively

The purpose of a performance-based contract is to compel the vendor to meet the requirements through effective management and monitoring of the vendor's work. WSDOT developed a performance-based contract for the project that included penalties tied to unsatisfactory or late completion of major milestones.

For example, the contract included financial damages of $300,000 a week for each week the start of SR 520 tolling was delayed and $10,000 a day for each day the start of Customer Service Center Operations was delayed. Had these damages been enforced, penalties could have exceeded $12 million.

However, when the vendor started slipping on its deliverables and missing its milestones, WSDOT chose not to require them to pay the amounts stated in the contract. According to project team leaders, WSDOT's primary goal was to have an operational system to meet the grant deadline. WSDOT weighed the risks associated with applying full damages and feared that doing so would create further delay to the project's completion. WSDOT was also concerned about the vendor's financial stability because it was struggling to provide services for clients in other states. WSDOT believed the risk of not completing the project and starting tolling on SR 520 was too great for it to apply full damages.

WSDOT reduced its vendor payments to cover delay-related expenses

WSDOT reduced payments to the vendor by $1.5 million between February 2011 and December 2011 to cover the department's expenses related to the system delays, in a contract change order agreed to by the vendor. These delay-related expenses included paying for toll enforcement, paying the previous system's vendor to extend its operation of their system for an additional period of time, and doing the vendor's work.

After the change order was signed, WSDOT delayed requiring the vendor to pay additional damages while it worked with them to complete the project. WSDOT project staff told us that they wanted to seek a reasonable settlement once the tolling system was fully operational.

In the summer of 2011, the Secretary of Transportation reconvened the Expert Review Panel to review the situation as the vendor was not meeting the contract's required schedule and deliverables. The panel recommended that WSDOT should consider options that supported its focus on completing the project and while also having a financial impact on the vendor. The panel's report said, "WSDOT should focus on getting the best possible system in the shortest time when determining damages."

WSDOT and the vendor reached a settlement

In June 2012, WSDOT signed an agreement with the vendor to settle claims associated with the project delays. WSDOT reported the value of the settlement as $6.4 million. It included:

- Granting WSDOT the license to the system source code, software, and the background documents needed to operate the system, valued at $4 million
- Reducing payments to the contractor by $400,000 a year for the remaining two years of the contract, for a total of $800,000 in reduced payments
- Reducing payments to the contractor by $400,000 a year for four additional years if WSDOT agreed to extend the contract, for an additional $1.6 million in reduced payments

The vendor was under pressure nationwide

After signing the contract with WSDOT to develop the system, the vendor won contracts in four other states. During this time, the vendor was also involved in lawsuits with one of its clients and subject to liquidated damages from another for failure to meet schedule and contract requirements. These pressures on the vendor resulted in reduced staff and resources for WSDOT's project and impacted the vendor's financial condition.

WSDOT lacked clear executive direction on toll project management

In establishing a statewide all-electronic toll collection system, WSDOT engaged in a complex and ambitious project that was very different from its typical construction projects. WSDOT lacked experience with this type of project, which increased the associated project risks.

WSDOT recognized it must evolve as an organization to manage such complex types of tolling projects. But it struggled with establishing clear roles and responsibilities, and determining who is responsible for making decisions about the projects. The policies and procedures needed to guide management of tolling projects, including the new division's interaction with other department divisions, had not yet been determined or established.

WSDOT establishes the toll division, but not clear roles, responsibilities, and decision-making authority for it

WSDOT established the Toll Division in 2009 to manage its tolling program. The new division evolved from the department's Urban Corridors Office, which had the responsibility of managing WSDOT's mega-projects. The Toll Division was tasked with toll system development and procurement, toll operations, and strategic financial planning for all toll facilities. This required it to interact with other department offices and divisions to accomplish its work.

Cross-functional collaboration in an organization requires executive leadership to provide clear expectations about desired outcomes and promote effective communication among partners. Project staff we talked to stated it was unclear what the roles and responsibilities of the Toll Division were, or how other WSDOT divisions and offices were to interact with the new division. Staff involved in the project had different views on the degree to which they were to be involved in the project, and did not know who was responsible for making decisions.

From the beginning, there was conflict among internal WSDOT project stakeholders. In October 2009, after the department established the Toll Division, the Quality Assurance team reported "… that some project team infrastructure issues remain unresolved as WSDOT shifts to the new tolling organization structure … including the need to clarify roles and shift from reactive decision-making processes to more deliberate, process-based decision-making processes, and a more strategic perspective for tolling."

Although WSDOT executives and the project sponsor were aware of these conflicts from early on in the project, they never effectively dealt with them, and conflicts persisted throughout the project. In July 2010, when it first became clear that the vendor was experiencing performance problems, the Quality Assurance team reported that communication between the project team and other functional groups within WSDOT remained a challenge, despite efforts by the project sponsor and project manager to include stakeholder input in their plans and deliberations.

WSDOT changes the project's management structure to no avail

In response to the concerns of WSDOT's internal stakeholders regarding the vendor's poor performance and its impact on project timelines, WSDOT executives changed the structure of the project's management team in March 2011. The new structure placed some internal stakeholders in decision-making roles instead of advisory roles.

While the intent of this change was to ensure greater stakeholder involvement in the project, the Toll Division's ownership of the project and its authority to make final decisions were not clear or supported by WSDOT's executive management. As the vendor continued to provide inadequate resources and staff to the project, its performance was not improved by receiving sometimes conflicting direction from multiple project leaders. WSDOT project staff we talked to stated they believed the change in the project's management structure did not improve the situation with the vendor and resulted in further project delays.

In April 2011, the Quality Assurance team recommended ending the use of four directors, as it seemed to be impeding progress on the project. The team recommended a single project manager again be placed in charge of the project. They also stated that "… little progress has been made towards resolving the conflict between Toll Division and its key stakeholders."

The Quality Assurance team suggested that the frustration of WSDOT internal stakeholders was based on their view that the Toll Division did not understand what they did or their needs. These issues were partly resolved when the Deputy Secretary became more involved by acting as the primary project manager and making decisions about how to proceed.

In August 2011, the reconvened Expert Review Panel had similar things to say about WSDOT's internal management issues on the project. In its view, "The authority for full decision-making has never been given to the Toll Division." The lack of authority provided to the Director and lack of clear ownership of the project by the Toll Division contributed to internal conflicts and project delays.

Intervention from the Deputy Secretary helped, but it was a not a long-term solution, according to the Expert Review Panel. It suggested the position of Toll Division Director needed to be strengthened to allow for the level of decision-making needed, and the possibility of incorporating the information technology and accounting and finance elements into the Toll Division in the long term.

Although the role of Toll Division Director was elevated to Assistant Secretary in November 2012, Toll Division staff told us that roles and responsibilities, and the decision-making authority of the Toll Division, are still unclear. The appointment of a new Secretary of Transportation in February 2013 provides an opportunity to improve clarity.

Toll Division lacked executive support in managing the vendor

The Toll Division's lack of experience and lack of executive support had a significant impact on its ability to manage its work and complete the project on time.

For example, we found that although WSDOT did have a project management process that defined project roles, responsibilities, communication and decision-making for the project, it was not followed or supported by department executives. This made it difficult for the Toll Division to incorporate internal stakeholders into the project, and hold others to the project management process established in its project management plan.

WSDOT executives also did not always provide the support the project team needed to be successful in managing the vendor. For example, project managers stated that they saw early on the vendor was struggling with the project schedule due to a lack of resources and they raised their concerns to department executives. The executive response was that it was too early in the project to be worried, according to project managers we interviewed.

In addition, when project team leaders put pressure on the vendor to follow the deliverables schedule and meet protocols established in the project management plan, the vendor complained to WSDOT executives, who asked the project team 'to back off,' resulting in fewer meetings and less frequent review of deliverables.

In its discussions with department management, the vendor also denied that there were issues with the project as the Tolling Division project team was suggesting. One of the members of the Quality Assurance team we talked to stated that the project management team made good decisions in its interactions with the vendor, but that those decisions were repeatedly superseded by poor decisions made by WSDOT executives.

Incorporating a new entity into a mature organization like WSDOT is difficult. This was particularly true for the Toll Division, which touched so many existing administrative functions within the department. In these situations, executives need to ensure that the new division has the support it needs to effectively build partnerships early on, and the new division needs to include its internal stakeholders early and incorporate their input.

While the Toll Division deliberately established a process to inform and seek input from internal stakeholders, it struggled to build effective partnerships throughout the project. Toll Division staff we talked to also stated that this was complicated by the fact that the authority of the Division was not clear within the department. The uniqueness and complexity of the project and the lack of executive support in the Toll Division's ownership of the project resulted in internal conflicts and delay.

Audit conclusions

Delays in completing the project resulted in tolls starting on SR 520 nine months later than originally planned. Based on the original contracted date of March 19, 2011, and the actual start date of December 29, 2011, the state lost the opportunity to collect an estimated $40 million in tolls.

In addition to lost toll collections, delays and missteps related to the transfer of operations on the Tacoma Narrows Bridge to the new vendor led to a loss of public and legislative trust in the department's ability to manage its tolling program.

Because tolling is now central to the WSDOT's ability to pay for large infrastructure projects, such as SR 99 and I-405, it is important that the department continues its efforts to resolve these issues.

Our audit was designed to determine what lessons could be learned from WSDOT's experience with the project and how they might apply to future projects managed by the Toll Division.

We determined WSDOT did not fully follow the requirements of the State Administrative and Accounting Manual, including adequately planning for and managing project risk, proactively managing the project, and holding the vendor accountable throughout the project.

WSDOT's Toll Division lacked the executive support, the decision-making authority, and the policies and procedures needed to develop the statewide all-electronic tolling system and start tolling the SR 520 Bridge on schedule in March 2011. These management challenges were magnified by an ambitious project, uncertainty about its demands, and a tight deadline.

Audit recommendations

To improve WSDOT's management of future tolling projects and to minimize the risk of project delays, we recommend:

The Secretary ensure roles, responsibilities, and decision-making authority are clear for projects managed by the Toll Division.

Specifically, the Secretary needs to address the issues caused by the cross-functional nature of tolling projects which requires input and support from multiple divisions and offices. Clarifications should be documented in writing, and communicated to and followed by WSDOT executives, managers, and staff. Further, the Secretary and the executive team need to follow and support these clarified roles and responsibilities and hold staff accountable to them. If changes are needed, those changes need to be documented, communicated, and followed.

The Assistant Secretary for Tolling establish policies and procedures to guide the development and implementation of tolling projects.

These policies and procedures need to ensure state requirements and guidance are followed, including identifying and planning for risks throughout the project, proactively managing the project and monitoring the work of the contractor, and holding the contractor accountable to the contract requirements. In addition, the Assistant Secretary needs to

ensure these policies and procedures are followed by holding all parties working on Toll Division projects accountable
to them. They should be in writing, agreed to by executive
management, communicated to applicable WSDOT managers and staff.

**The Department of Transportation report on its progress
implementing these recommendations to House and
Senate Transportation Committees and the Office of
Financial Management, as required in the 2013–2015
transportation budget.**

Agency Response

STATE OF WASHINGTON

August 1, 2013

The Honorable Troy Kelley
Washington State Auditor
P.O. Box 40021
Olympia, WA 98504-0021

Dear Auditor Kelley:

Thank you for the opportunity to respond to the State Auditor's Office
(SAO) Performance Audit on *Washington's Tolling Program: Lessons
Learned from Project Delays,* which we received on July 18, 2013. We
reviewed the report and provide our formal response below.

The Washington State Department of Transportation (WSDOT)
places high importance on performance audits to help ensure that we
make the best use of taxpayer dollars. Ongoing improvements are a
key to our success, and we appreciate this audit report's contributions
to our efforts.

Since its inception, WSDOT's Toll Division has transitioned from
a start-up operation to a much more stable toll operation program.
WSDOT is now viewed as a leader in all-electronic tolling, with
other states seeking the financial functionality and reporting levels
now in use at WSDOT.

While the audit report contains valuable information, it speaks broadly about the tolling program. The audit only reviewed one portion of the tolling program: contracting for back-office functions and customer service center operations. Other portions of the program—such as the roadway toll systems, the financial plan, and the migration of nearly 150,000 existing customer accounts from the old back-office system to the new system—were implemented in a much smoother fashion.

Launching an all-electronic tolling program for the SR 520 bridge and a new statewide back-office system would have been challenging for any agency. WSDOT had an aggressive implementation schedule that was required for the $154 million federal grant. We worked through these challenges by holding the tolling vendor accountable and by being steadfast in our commitment to the citizens of Washington in achieving an all-electronic tolling program.

WSDOT appreciates the SAO's recommendations to further enhance the tolling program. The Toll Division is developing policies and procedures to streamline and improve future toll project implementations. These improvements are especially important as toll revenue augments gas tax revenue in financing major project construction, maintenance, and preservation.

Since tolling began on the SR 520 bridge in December 2011, $67.4 million in toll revenues have been collected. Revenue and traffic continue to be on track to providing $1 billion in funding to replace the vulnerable SR 520 Bridge.

The audit report states that WSDOT lost the opportunity to collect $40 million in tolls. WSDOT's evaluation concluded that the delayed start date for SR 520 tolling is not expected to affect planned toll charges, which are used to pay off 30- and 40-year bonds for construction of the new bridge. With a delayed start, bond repayments will shift out the same number of months that the start was delayed. In fact, the delay had a favorable effect on the terms of the bonds issued. Had tolling started earlier, the state would not have received the lower interest rates that will result in savings over the life of the bonds.

We appreciate your work on this report and the collaborative nature in which it was conducted. We will address your recommendations to make improvements to the tolling program and to ensure WSDOT continues its mission to keep people and business moving.

Sincerely,

Lynn Peterson
Secretary
WA State Department of Transportation

David Schumacher
Director
Office of Financial Management

Attachment
cc: Cast of many directors and government officials.

Appendix C: Typical Swim Lane Diagram

Figure C.1 is an example of a swim-lane flow chart denoting the change in venue during a process. Whenever the process crosses to a different swim lane, the risk normally increases. This may be due to the lack of communication between the business units, incorrect data entry information, or a delay due to bottlenecks or business unit schedules.

Figure C.2 is a reminder of what this book is about. I don't believe for a minute that any business unit or organization can create a sustained balance between throughput and demand. The attempts using just-in-time processing as well as supply chain management and Lean Six Sigma techniques come close and even hit the mark for a period of time; however, the business and customer environments change almost continuously. Therefore, we must adjust the process to fit our need as we learn about the change. I guess that is why we focus on continuous improvements.

Seek first to understand and then to be understood.

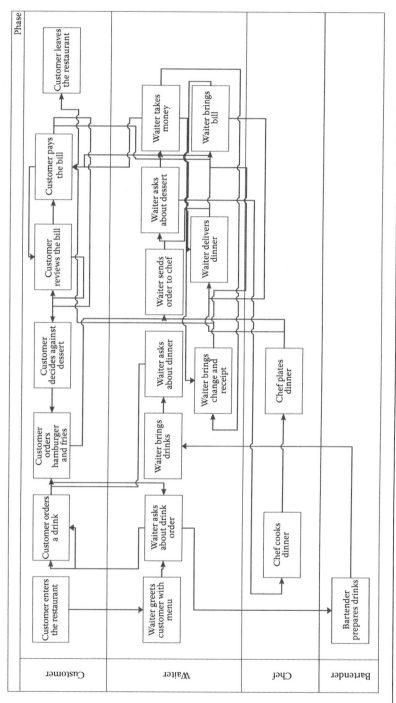

Figure C.1 Restaurant customer order and delivery.

Bibliography

Covey, S. R., *The 7 Habits of Highly Effective People*, 1990.

Goldratt, E. M., and J. Cox, *The Goal*, 1986.

ISACA, *COBIT 5 Enabling Process*, 2012.

ISACA, *COBIT 5: Enabling Information*.

ISACA, *COBIT Process Assessment Model (PAM): Using COBIT 5*.

ISACA, *COBIT Self-Assessment Guide*.

Rath & Strong Management Consultants, *Rath & Strong's Six Sigma Pocket Guide*, 2002.

Thompson, C., *IIA All-Star Conference*, 2014.

Wikipedia, "Luca Pavioli," http://en.wikipedia.org/wiki/Luca_Pacioli.

The Institute of Internal Auditors (theIIA.org) magazine, Knowledge Base

The IIA Research Foundation

International Professional Practices Framework—IIA 2013

The IIA local chapter meetings and continuing professional education (CPE) presentations

The IIA public and e-learning seminars

The IIA Common Body of Knowledge Resource Exchange

The IIA All Star Conference—An IIA conference presented each year

The IIA local and regional chapters

ISACA local and regional meetings and CPE events

North American Computer Audit, Control, and Security (NACACS) Conference—Presented each year by ISACA

The ISACA IT Professional Networking and Knowledge Center

SAN Security Training courses, including "Auditing Networks"

MIS Training including but not limited to "Intermediate IT Auditing" and "Trouble-shooting Networks"

Subscriptions to:
> Computer World
> Information Week
> Network World
> InfoWorld
> IT Digest
> IT Whitepapers
> Tech Digest
> CIO Security
> Tech Target
> Many others

COBIT Information can be found at www.isaca.org/Knowledge-Center /cobit/Pages/COBIT-Assessment-Programme.aspx.

Various vendor white papers, web training, and periodicals, such as the following:

- Cisco Press articles, including "Design Best Practices for Latency Optimization"
- "Fluke Network Tech Briefs" and other white papers such as those provided by CDW, KPMG, Deloitte, and Pricewater-houseCoopers, just to name a few of the organizations that share concepts and ideas to help you understand and improve your technical environment

Global knowledge training for IT professionals (vendor focused, IT focused, and IT business focused), great Microsoft server, networks, Cisco, net appliance, databases, disk management, agile development, customer relationship management (CRM), enterprise resource planning (ERP), Information Technology Infrastructure Library (ITIL), VOIP, etc. I have taken a few Cisco and Microsoft training that I found useful.

Index

A

ACH network, *see* Automated Clearing House network

As-is diagrams, 6, 79, 256

Auditing, 31–47

  background, 31

  checklists, 35

  enterprise risk management, 34

  inspector general, 33

  operational assessment, 35–38

    COSO enterprise risk management, 36–37

    Criteria of Control Board, 37

    critical to quality, 35

    definition of operational auditing, 38

    IIA operational auditing definition, 36

    return on investment, 37

    Sarbanes–Oxley Act, 37–38

    voice of the customer, 35

  operational assessment drivers/impetus, 38–39

    application problems, 39

    high-value operation or process bottlenecks, 39

    industry metrics, 39

    internal controls, 39

  operational factors, 40–42

    cause and effect, 42

    economy, 40

    effectiveness, 40

    efficiencies, 40

    process triangle, 41

  operational objectives, 40

  process, 42–47

    collaboration, 47

    common core, 47

    keeping the end in mind, 44–47

    management by objective, 47

    operational performance goals, 42–43

perspectives, 44
value add, 43–44
Audit out-briefs, 258
Automated Clearing House (ACH)
  network, 75

B

Barron's Accounting Dictionary, 38
Bell chart, 187–188
Brainstorming, 134–135
Business continuity management,
  218–223
  business impact analysis, 221
  business interruption event,
    phases of, 219–221
  contingency planning, 219
  factors, 218
  required point objective, 218
  required time objective, 218
Business continuity planning (BCP),
  117–120
Business impact analysis (BIA), 118,
  221, 266
Business process, IT and, 152–199
  application request, 153
  backup routines, 180
  baseline metrics, 180
  bell chart, 187–188
  business support VSM, 163–167
  COBOL, 155
  control chart analysis, 179, 183,
    184
  database management systems,
    155
  data collection, 179–182
  data entry screens, 167–170
  digital wave form, 164
  Ethernet, 153, 165
  IT security, 191–199
    application layer, 194–195
    corporate network, 196
    data, description of, 192

database management systems,
  195
data layer, 195
demilitarized zone, 195
firewall, 196
network layer, 193–194
physical layer, 193
security architectures, 193
systems network architecture
  protocol, 194
transmission control protocol/
  IP packet, 195
typical organizational
  network, 197
universal serial bus plug-in,
  196
Wi-Fi, 198
organizational network
  transmissions, 170–172
processing delay, 152
propagation delay, 152
queuing, 156–163
  arrival of requests (Poisson
    arrival), 156
  available data, 158
  CPU utilization, 157
  delay, 152
  failure modes, 159–160
  graph, 156
  living document, 160
  questions, 162
  VSM, 158
retransmission delay, 152
scatter control chart, 188–190
simple network management
  protocol, 190–191
transmission delay, 152
typical user network, 154
utilization assessment, 172–174
WAN environment, 174–179
  appliances used, 174
  data file batch transmission,
    178

maximum Ethernet message
size, 178
OSI model, 175
serialization delay, 176, 177

C

Capability maturity model (CMM),
266
Carrier sense multiple access/
collision detect (CSMA/
CD), 153
Certified Information Systems
Auditor (CISA), 8
Chief executive officer (CEO), 34
Chief financial officer (CFO), 37
Cloud computing, 236
COBIT (Control Objectives for
Information Technologies),
see IT and COBIT
CoCo, *see* Criteria of Control Board
Committee of Sponsoring
Organizations of the
Treadway Commission
(COSO), 34, 36–37, 291
Common business-oriented
language (COBOL), 155
Control charts, 142–151
assessment rules, 146
graphical metric capture, 143
IT control charts, 151
levels, 143
process states, 145
special causes, 144
variations, 143
Western Electric rules, 147–151
Corporate network, 196
COSO, *see* Committee of
Sponsoring Organizations
of the Treadway
Commission
Cost centers, 17
Credibility gap, 6

Criteria of Control Board (CoCo),
37
Critical impact, 293–294
Critical to quality (CTQ), 17, 35
CSMA/CD, *see* Carrier sense
multiple access/collision
detect
C-suite executives, 50
Customer value stream, steps of, 19

D

Database management systems
(DBMSs), 155, 195
Delivery support systems (DSS), 266
Demilitarized zone (DMZ), 195
Detection rating score scale,
124–125
Dial-up network, 117
Digital wave form, 164

E

80–20 rule, *see* Pareto principle
Electronic Funds Transfer Act
(EFTA), 75
Enterprise risk management
(ERM), 34, 36
Ethernet, 153, 165

F

Failure mode and effect analysis
(FMEA), 7, 123–125
detection rating score scale,
124–125
key process input variables, 123
occurrence rating scale, 124
severity rating scale, 124
Father of Accounting and
Bookkeeping, 32
Fieldwork, 123–237
anomalies, 141

business continuity management, 218–223
  business impact analysis, 221
  business interruption event, phases of, 219–221
  contingency planning, 219
  factors, 218
  required point objective, 218
  required time objective, 218
control charts, 142–151
  assessment rules, 146
  graphical metric capture, 143
  IT control charts, 151
  levels, 143
  process states, 145
  special causes, 144
  variations, 143
  Western Electric rules, 147–151
failure mode and effect analysis, 123–125
  detection rating score scale, 124–125
  key process input variables, 123
  occurrence rating scale, 124
  severity rating scale, 124
fieldwork analysis, 223–224
fishbone diagram, 128–131
  categories, 130
  cause-and-effect diagram, 131
  five-whys diagram, 130
five whys, 127–128
fraud red flag, 199
IT and the business process, 152–199
  application request, 153
  backup routines, 180
  baseline metrics, 180
  bell chart, 187–188
  business support VSM, 163–167
  COBOL, 155
  control chart analysis, 179, 183, 184

database management systems, 155
  data collection, 179–182
  data entry screens, 167–170
  digital wave form, 164
  Ethernet, 153, 165
  IT security, 191–199
  organizational network transmissions, 170–172
  processing delay, 152
  propagation delay, 152
  queuing, 156–163
  queuing delay, 152
  retransmission delay, 152
  scatter control chart, 188–190
  simple network management protocol, 190–191
  transmission delay, 152
  typical user network, 154
  utilization assessment, 172–174
  WAN environment, 174–179
IT security, 191–199
  application layer, 194–195
  corporate network, 196
  data, description of, 192
  database management systems, 195
  data layer, 195
  demilitarized zone, 195
  firewall, 196
  network layer, 193–194
  physical layer, 193
  security architectures, 193
  systems network architecture protocol, 194
  transmission control protocol/IP packet, 195
  typical organizational network, 197
  universal serial bus plug-in, 196
  Wi-Fi, 198

metrics, 135–140
  common problems, 140
  continuous, 136–137
  cycle time, 136
  discrete, 137–140
  network management, 138
  process adjustment, 136
  segmented analysis, 139
Pareto principle (80–20 rule),
    131–135
  brainstorming, 134–135
  cause-and-effect diagram, 133
  jumping to conclusions, 133–135
  typical chart, 132
process, 199–217
  analysis, 201–205
  bottlenecks, 206–207
  considerations, 213–216
  fraud red flag resting, 207–208
  observation, 208–211
  opportunities, 211–213
  OSI model, 216
  procurement process analysis,
    208
  request for proposal, 208, 212
  resource reallocation, 205–206
  segregation of duties
    environment, 212
  SIPOC matrix, 211
  spaghetti diagram, 210
  VSM, 208, 209
purchasing process, 224–237
  application norms, 230
  cloud computing, 236
  database load sharing, 234
  hybrid cloud, 237
  interconnection exchange cost,
    231
  IT bottlenecks and
    slowdowns, 233–237
  IT considerations, 228–233
  load sharing, 233
  page loading time, 231

  recommendations, 227
  round-trip time and distance,
    232
  spaghetti diagram, 226
  VSM, 224, 225
queuing, 156–163
  arrival of requests (Poisson
    arrival), 156
  available data, 158
  CPU utilization, 157
  failure modes, 159–160
  graph, 156
  living document, 160
  questions, 162
  VSM, 158
root cause analysis, 125
standardization or anarchy, 141–142
WAN environment, 174–179
  appliances used, 174
  data file batch transmission, 178
  maximum Ethernet message
    size, 178
  OSI model, 175
  serialization delay, 176, 177
Financial audit trilogy, 40
Firewall, 196
Fishbone diagram, 128–131
  categories, 130
  cause-and-effect diagram, 131
  five-whys diagram, 130
Five whys, 127–128
FMEA, *see* Failure mode and effect
    analysis
Fraud
  probability of, 188
  red flag, 199, 207–208

G

Gantt chart, 58
General Accounting Office (GAO), 33
"Gotcha Guys," 33
Government organizations, 14

H

Heat map, 293
Hybrid cloud, 237

I

Inspector general (IG), 33
Institute of Internal Auditors (IIA),
    5, 291
Interconnection exchange cost
    (IXC), 231
Internal Revenue Service (IRS) tax
    auditor, 33
International Electrotechnical
    Commission (IEC), 266
International Professional Practices
    Framework (IPPF), 188
Internet control message protocol
    (ICMP), 162
IT and COBIT, 261–287
    COBIT 5, 262
    COBIT management
        environment, 265–287
    align, plan, and organize, 265
    business impact analysis, 266
    business practices, 268
    checklist, 287
    CMM Integrated model, 266
    delivery support systems, 266
    IT goals, 270
    Lean Six Sigma, focus of, 278
    monitor, evaluate, and assess,
        266
    now generation, 278
    operational assessment, 271,
        272–274
    process goals, 271
    RACI matrix, 275
    SIPOC matrices, 268, 269
    VSM, 276, 277, 279–286
    WWW, 278
    enabler goals, 262

enterprise goals, 262
organizational governance, 264
principles, 263–264
Risk IT, 263
Value of IT, 263
IT goals (ITGs), 270
IT security, 191–199
    application layer, 194–195
    corporate network, 196
    data, description of, 192
    database management systems, 195
    data layer, 195
    demilitarized zone, 195
    firewall, 196
    network layer, 193–194
    physical layer, 193
    security architectures, 193
    systems network architecture
        protocol, 194
    transmission control protocol/IP
        packet, 195
    typical organizational network, 197
    universal serial bus plug-in, 196
    Wi-Fi, 198
IXC, see Interconnection exchange
    cost

K

Kano model, 18, 19
Key performance indicators (KPIs),
    50, 63–66
    availability, 65
    confidentiality, 65
    example, 64
    integrity, 65
    IT, 64
    service-level agreements, 64
Key process input variables (KPIVs),
    123
Key process output variable
    (KPOV), 179, 201
Key success factors (KSFs), 60

L

LAN, *see* Local area network
Latency delays, 108, 109–117
    cases, 113, 114, 116
    packetizing, 113–115
    routing across a WAN, 117
    serialization, 111–112
    transmission lines, 115–117
Lean framework, waste listed by,
    20, 72
Lean Six Sigma, 17
    certification, 3
    critical to quality, 35
    focus of, 278
    insights, 53
    variances in, 138
Local area network (LAN), 153
    Ethernet speeds, 165
    signal, 72

M

Management by objective, 47
Management information block
    (MIB), 151
Maximum Ethernet message size, 178
Media access control (MAC)
    address, 153
Metrics (fieldwork), 135–140
    common problems, 140
    continuous, 136–137
    cycle time, 136
    discrete, 137–140
    network management, 138
    process adjustment, 136
    segmented analysis, 139

N

National Credit Union
    Administration (NCUA), 50
9/11 risk measure, 292

Not-for-profit organizations, 14, 15,
    38
Now generation, 278

O

Occupational Safety and Health
    Administration (OSHA), 14
Occurrence rating scale, 124
Off-the-shelf (OTS) application
    software, 101
Open Systems Integration (OSI)
    model, 7, 107–109
    application level, 108
    data link level, 107
    Ethernet hub of, 170
    fieldwork, 216
    network level, 107
    physical level, 107
    presentation level, 107–108
    session level, 107
    transport level, 107
    WAN environment, 175
Operational assessment of IT,
    introduction to, 3–10
    assessment recommendations, 4
    Credibility gap, 6
    leadership, 4
    overview, 5–8
    planning, 6
    rationale, 8–10
    to-be diagrams, 7
Operational assessment planning,
    see Planning
Organization, 13–27
    goals, 13–14
        government organizations, 14
        not-for-profit organizations, 14
        profit-oriented organizations, 13
    measuring the success of an
        organization, 14–17
    cost centers, 17
    focus areas, 16

increasing cash flow, 14, 15
increasing donations, 15
increasing net profit, 14
increasing return on
    investment, 15
profit centers, 17
quality, description of, 17
tiers, 15–16
measuring the success of the
    process, 25–27
baseline, 25
input, 25
supporting processes, 25
throughput, 25
process, 21–22
description, 21
example, 21–22
goal of, 25
value stream, 22
productivity, 22–24
process flow, 24
ROI, 25
success of a process, 23
voice of the customer, 17, 18–21
categories, 18
customer value stream, steps
    of, 19
example, 19
Kano model, 18, 19
transportation cost, 20
OSHA, *see* Occupational Safety and
    Health Administration
OSI model, *see* Open Systems
    Integration model
OTS application software, *see* Off-the-
    shelf application software

P

Page loading time (PLT), 231
Pareto principle (80–20 rule),
    131–135
brainstorming, 134–135

cause-and-effect diagram, 133
jumping to conclusions,
    133–135
typical chart, 132
Planning, 49–121
activity (procurement audit
    planning), 87–99
customer, 89–90
planning data, 95–96
RACI matrix, 96–97
requisition form, 97
SIPOC chart, 91–95
spaghetti diagram, 97–98
VSM, 98–99
adding value, 63
background, 101–109
CIA and IT, 103–105
IT support goal, 103
latency delay, 104, 108
metrics (business dependency
    on IT), 105–107
network speed, 109
off-the-shelf application
    software, 101
OSI model, 107–109
proverb, 102
business acumen, 52–54
improvement of business
    processes, 52
providing assurance, 52
questions, 53
responsible, accountable,
    consulted, informed matrix,
    54
subject matter expert, 54
to-be environment, 53
business continuity planning,
    117–120
business impact analysis
    documentation, 118
questions, 119–120
risk assessment, 118
C-suite executives, 50

customer relationships, 51
IT support of the business unit,
   99–101
  COBIT, 100
  IT's business, 100–101
  user perception, 99–100
key performance indicator, 50,
   63–66
  availability, 65
  confidentiality, 65
  example, 64
  integrity, 65
  service-level agreements, 64
latency delays, 109–117
  cases, 113, 114, 116
  packetizing, 113–115
  routing across a WAN, 117
  serialization, 111–112
  transmission lines, 115–117
operational process, 66–67
  economy, 66
  effectiveness, 66
  efficiency, 66
  profit centers, 67
  work-in-progress inventory, 67
planning memo, 58–59
  development, 58
  Gantt chart, 58
  items included in, 59
planning phase, 49
process review (as is), 67–87
  baseline speed test (customer
   home network), 71
  diagnose before you prescribe, 68
  local area network signal, 72
  procurement process narrative,
   81–87
  SIPOC table, 68–72
  spaghetti diagram, 80–81
  value stream map, 72–80
project charter, 59–63
  authorization, 62
  business unit leader, 62

concerns of the organization, 60
critical success factors, 60
engagement plan, 61
key stakeholders, 62
metrics, 63
problem statement, 61
process improvements, 62
project goals, 61
project leader, 62
project priorities, 62
scope statement, 62
time frame, 62
RACI matrix, 54–58
  meaning of acronym, 55
  purpose, 54
  subject matter expert, 55
  workload analysis, 56–58
reconnaissance, 49
risk assessment, 52
Statement on Auditing Standards
  No. 70, 50
summation, 120–121
value stream map, 72–80
  defects, 75
  inventory, 73
  motion, 73
  overprocessing, 75
  overproduction, 74–75
  transportation, 72
  waiting, 74
PLT, *see* Page loading time
PO, *see* Purchase order
Poisson arrival (requests), 156
Process review (as is), 67–87
  baseline speed test (customer
   home network), 71
  diagnose before you prescribe, 68
  local area network signal, 72
  procurement process narrative,
   81–87
  SIPOC table, 68–72
  spaghetti diagram, 80–81
  value stream map, 72–80

Profit centers, 17
Profit-oriented organizations, 13
Project charter, 59–63
  authorization, 62
  business unit leader, 62
  concerns of the organization, 60
  critical success factors, 60
  engagement plan, 61
  key stakeholders, 62
  metrics, 63
  problem statement, 61
  process improvements, 62
  project goals, 61
  project leader, 62
  project priorities, 62
  scope statement, 62
  time frame, 62
Purchase order (PO), 199, 212
Purchasing process, 224–237
  application norms, 230
  cloud computing, 236
  database load sharing, 234
  hybrid cloud, 237
  interconnection exchange cost,
    231
  IT bottlenecks and slowdowns,
    233–237
  IT considerations, 228–233
  load sharing, 233
  page loading time, 231
  recommendations, 227
  round-trip time and distance, 232
  spaghetti diagram, 226
  VSM, 224, 225

Q

Quality, description of, 17
Quality Assurance team, 303
Queuing, 156–163
  arrival of requests (Poisson
    arrival), 156
  available data, 158
  CPU utilization, 157
  failure modes, 159–160
  graph, 156
  living document, 160
  questions, 162
  VSM, 158

R

RACI matrix, *see* Responsible,
  accountable, consulted,
  informed matrix
RCA, *see* Root cause analysis
Reconnaissance, 49
Reduced instruction set computing
  (RISC), 110
Reporting, 241–260
  art of communication, 242
  belief, 241
  diagrams, 252–257
    as-is diagram, 253, 256
    comparisons, 252
    to-be diagrams, 252, 254, 257
  focus on the issue/concern,
    244–252
    assurance, 246
    definition of finding, items in,
      247
    draft report, 249–252
    example, 249
    organizational risk appetite,
      245
    weakness, 247
  presenting the report, 258–260
    case, 258
    internal audit, 258
    vetting the draft report with
      management, 259–260
  report distribution, 243–244
    conundrum, 244
    government auditors, 243
    importance of, 243
    perspectives, 244

sharing the picture, 242–243
    communication, 243
    product orders, 242
Request for proposal (RFP), 208, 212
Required point objective (RPO), 218
Required time objective (RTO), 218
Responsible, accountable, consulted, informed (RACI) matrix, 54–58, 275
    meaning of acronym, 55
    procurement audit planning, 96–97
    purpose, 54
    subject matter expert, 55
    workload analysis, 56–58
Return on investment (ROI), 15, 25, 213
RFP, *see* Request for proposal
RISC, *see* Reduced instruction set computing
Risk assessment/management, 291–294
    critical impact, 293–294
    heat map, 293
    9/11 risk measure, 292
    organizational governance, 291
    risk appetite, 291
    value of business process, 292
Risk IT, 263
Risk priority number (RPN), 124
ROI, *see* Return on investment
Root cause analysis (RCA), 125
RPN, *see* Risk priority number
RPO, *see* Required point objective
RTO, *see* Required time objective

S

Sarbanes–Oxley Act (SOX), 37–38
SAS 70, *see* Statement on Auditing Standards No. 70
Scatter control chart, 188–190

Security, *see* IT security
Segregation of duties (SOD) environment, 212
Service-level agreements (SLAs), 64
Severity rating scale, 124
Simple network management protocol (SNMP), 7, 151, 190
SIPOC (source, inputs, process, outputs, customers) matrix, 68–72, 211
    COBIT management environment, 268, 269
    procurement process, 91–95
SOX, *see* Sarbanes–Oxley Act
Spaghetti diagram, 80–81, 210
    procurement audit planning, 97–98
    purchasing process, 226
Statement on Auditing Standards No. 70 (SAS 70), 50
Structured query language (SQL), 160
Subject matter expert (SME), 54, 55
Swim lane diagram (typical), 323–325
Systems network architecture (SNA), 194

T

Throughput, 25
To-be diagrams, 7, 252, 255
Transmission control protocol (TCP), 195, 217
Transmission delay, 152
Transportation cost, 20
Treadway Commission, 36

U

Universal serial bus (USB) plug-in, 196
User datagram protocol (UDP), 217

V

Value of IT (Val IT), 263
Value stream map (VSM), 72–80,
      208, 209
   business support, 163–167
   COBIT management
         environment, 276, 277,
         279–286
   planning, 72–80
      defects, 75
      inventory, 73
      motion, 73
      overprocessing, 75
      overproduction, 74–75
      transportation, 72
      waiting, 74
   procurement audit planning, 98–99
   purchasing process, 224, 225
   queuing and, 158
Voice of the customer (VOC), 17,
      18–21
   categories, 18
   critical to quality based on, 35
   customer value stream, steps of, 19
   example, 19
   Kano model, 18, 19
   transportation cost, 20
VSM, *see* Value stream map

W

WAN, *see* Wide area network
Washington state audit report,
      295–322
   agency response, 320–322
   audit recommendations, 319–320
   audit results, 300–319
   delays creating a statewide all-
         electronic tolling system, 296
   introduction, 300
   pressure points magnified the
         project's challenges, 297
      disagreements about needs,
         297
      technology barriers, 297
      tight deadline pressure, 297
   summary recommendations,
         299
   unclear management approach
         complicated an ambitious
         project, 298–299
      holding the vendor
         accountable, 299
      incorporating risks, 298–299
      managing the project, 299
Western Electric rules, 147–151
Wide area network (WAN), 152
   environment, 174–179
      appliances used, 174
      data file batch transmission,
         178
      maximum Ethernet message
         size, 178
      OSI model, 175
      serialization delay, 176, 177
   latency, database load sharing
         and, 234
   routing across, 117
   transmission delay, 152
   typical, 171
Wi-Fi, 198
Work-in-progress (WIP) inventory,
      67, 71
WWW (worldwide network), 196
   browsers, 176
   communication with customers
         through, 278
   ISP, 71
   propagation delay, 109–110